B.M. LUSTOL

Until My Dying Day

DORRANCE
PUBLISHING CO
EST. 1920
PITTSBURGH, PENNSYLVANIA 15238

Credit is given to the author--- 10,000 Dreams Explained, Pamela J. Ball
        AND
Credit photo of Kaieteur Falls
www:guyanatourism.com
National Exhibition Centre,
Sophia, Georgetown,
Guyana, South America

Dorrance Publishing Co
585 Alpha Drive
Pittsburgh, PA 15238
Visit our website at *www.dorrancebookstore.com*

ISBN: 978-1-6853-7140-1
eISBN: 978-1-6853-7983-4

Until My Dying Day

Acknowledgement

EXPRESSING MUCH THANKS to all whom through association has made this book possible. "For we wrestle not against blood and flesh, but against principalities, against the powers, against the rulers of darkness of this world, and against spiritual wickedness in high places," wrote Paul. -The King James Bible, Ephesian 6:12.

Until My Dying Day is one woman's struggle against man's rule that causes separation, if not strong to fight against their domination to keep alive, and that of friends and family, one can lose everything including their life. Her struggle against the wicked spirit forces to manipulate thoughts that could harm her and others she battles to protect and serve. Her story is one that touches the life of many.

TO MY READERS...
This novel has been the most difficult I have had to write, not because I did not construct my ideas ahead of time, but because everything written were reviewed before the chance to perfect it. Through my experiences I came to this fact, that awareness is an endless area of exploration for man in general, only in soundness of mind can awareness be enhanced. Written from physical and spiritual encounter with... experience from...reading and study of other peoples' works produce all that is in this novel, that give me joy in its production and hope that I have been able to leave behind for those going through similar experiences, will find educational.

Part One

CONTENTS

Prelude

I AM A GUYANESE, born in 1957 amid a pandemic of the Asian flu that almost killed me had my brother, Michael, who, with the ingenuity of a physician, did not pull the mucus out from my nose, would have killed me. The official name of my country is the Cooperative Republic of Guyana. The capital is Georgetown. It is a country on the North Coast of South America, formerly a British Colony known as British Guiana. In 1966, after 150 years of Colonial rule, we achieved independence and took the name Guyana. The Atlantic Ocean, east by Suriname, south by Brazil, west by Brazil, and Venezuela bound it on the north. It is home to one of four of the world's most extensive rain forests and has the world's highest free-fall waterfall called Kaieteur Falls, seen below.

The year was 1964, to my recollection, and then it could have been in the year of 1968. However, as I recalled specific incidents during some research from A Short History of Guyana, and A Political and Social History of Guyana, 1945-1983, the year seemed more to be 1964. I was about seven years old. The day was likened to a day that one could tell a storm was about to begin. The only difference is this was not a weather storm. The atmosphere, filled with the aftermath of ammunition used in the fighting between the Indians and blacks, had left the clouds to darken. The statistic shows 176 persons killed, 920 injured, 1,400 homes destroyed, and fifteen thousand of people forced to move. At 2:30 PM, troops arrived to end the rioting and establish order; five soldiers were killed, and fifty were injured.

As my mother and I walked to the store, sometime during the late morning, a thunderous voice said, "YOU PEOPLE DOWN THERE!"

Looking up at my mother, I asked, "Did you hear that?" I recalled she looked at me with that look she would give me when she needed my attention to acting wisely. Did Mother hear what I heard? I cannot say, however, her action indicated perhaps she did. As to whether we got to the store, that part of my memory has been erased. Was this part of my memory erased due to the tremulous chaos that occurred at the time?

On the other hand, did I choose not to recall? I have asked myself repeatedly. In doing some personal research, I noted amnesia is the partial or complete loss of memory caused by physical or psychological factors. A traumatic event can trigger physical-based amnesia; memory usually returns after a few days. However, the latter is not the case. This then calls attention to the fragility of our minds and incidents that can cause us to lose or gain memories. Would walking that road again bring back my memories of that past day? A road I would like to walk, this time without the violence. However, curious minds out to see the result of what had happened, there's difficulty in stopping their efforts to cause division. The question then left to ask, when the voice heard, "YOU PEOPLE DOWN THERE!" which sounded as a warning to me, was I born as the Devil's bride or had Jehovah chosen me at the age of seven? Whether this was God's voice, the Devil's, or the astronauts experimenting with us on earth, I do not know. I know that each one needs to search for answers to our purpose here on earth. Does man's destiny lie in his hands? Does God exist? Will there be everlasting life for lovers of Jehovah as promised in the Bible? Finding these answers may change your outlook altogether for those whose lives are without purpose. Dreams that filled my childhood were just mere incidents I shoved aside, unable to make head from the tail as to what I saw— some things unmentionable and something that was never discussed with my sisters, brother, or relatives until today, as knowledge has expounded beyond closed doors. Now all or most of my dreams of the past and present, springs reality of my life and others.

Five Years Earlier...

THE YEAR WAS 2016, Sunday, June 5. While doing chores around the house, the wind smelt like the corpse plant had just bloomed. It surprised me as I had not eaten anything that would cause such a stink in a few days. However, I know by now when my body is sending a message, and my thoughts immediately were on Veronica; knowledge from experience with her, I wonder if something is wrong. When the phone started to ring on Monday morning and her number was seen, fear entered as I picked up the receiver. "Hello."

"Hi Paula, Petal passed away today," she says.

"Oh, no! I knew something was wrong from yesterday. She left us yesterday but expired today." I knew what I was saying whether others believed or not, for I have and listens to my six senses. During my last visit, I did not see Petal but was informed of her illness, as was Veronica. We were surprised by her death, thinking that the therapy she was taking may have been okay. The incident caused me to make a return visit to the States.

The last month of the year 2012. Twice that month, I almost lost my life. The traffic light was on my right to cross. The intersection was dimly lit; many accidents had occurred at the intersection throughout the years with nothing done to fix the situation. Three steps from the front of the bus I was, and as I raised my eyes from the road towards the oncoming bus, the driver swung his head in my direction from making the turn out of the subway station pushing on the breaks and coming to a stop. As mentioned and repeated, angels are watching over us. Had I not looked up at the bus at that moment I did, I would not be here to tell the story of my life.

It was the last work week of the year. The night was dark, windy, cold, and raining. Instead of walking to the subway station, I crossed the street to the bus shed—the right of way was mine, as it was in the first incident. A wise decision on my part to walk a bit slow because everyone knows me to be a fast walker—when comments are made about slowing down with this comment, I laugh, "I'm trying not to let the Devil catch my feet." Almost to the walkway, a woman driver saw my umbrella and pulled to a stop. Once again, I would have been hit a few more steps. Yes, experiences gained through my actions in life and close calls of incidents that could have led to death, one can conclude the saying of this proverb to be the truth in Jehovah's judgment in a matter. "If thou sayest, Behold, we knew it not; doth not he that pondereth the heart consider it? And he that keepeth thy soul, doth not he knows it? And shall not he render to every man according to his works?" -King James Bible, Proverbs 24:12. Yes, He will eventually cause you to understand. That the preserving of life is his to hold.

It was in the early afternoon when a thunderbolt suddenly clapped, making the sound like a huge rock thrown onto the floor above my head and then rolling away. During a conversation with my sister about the incident, she asks, "So, what happened?" For reasons she, like others, would laugh and not take me seriously, the details were never told to Monica, and I declined to discuss them. A few days after that event, I felt an indent in the middle of my head while combing my hair. For a time, I began to wonder, what is this am I experiencing? My hair was getting thinner and began falling. One night, after a peaceful rest, I became enlightened about how our conscience, like that of our heart, plays an important role in the outcome of our lives. As our consciousness through sensation penetrates the mind causing one's heart desires to be motivated to find the truth of a matter; once found, a person then acts in fear of Jehovah or within his own will to whatever the outcome. At last, one can get the meaning of this proverb: "Evil men understand not judgment: But they that seek the LORD understand all things." - Proverbs 28:5. Yes, the preserving of our souls is Jehovah's mercy and loving-kindness towards one's understanding of past deeds dealt, and the revelation of the wicked one's action, reproving one to adherence of God's righteous principles. Eventually, I was enlightened by viewing a television show aired, an interview with Chris Hadfield, the astronaut who wrote a book on the body's reaction to gravity. I can confirm the comment made by my own body's reaction after the incident; I am not quite sure if it was within the year or over a year, but the dent within the middle of my head returned to normalcy.

The end of another year was fast approaching, and it was about to bring many changes within the company. I had received the news that my hospitalized aunt Ismay had passed away. Oh, how I wanted so much to visit her, as I knew that time was not on my side; she had outlived most of her brothers and sisters but suffered from many illnesses and felt if I did not get a chance to see her then, I was not sure of another time. So, I thought, and so it happened. My aunt died in January 2011, a few days after the New Year. When Lilly announced that she was leaving the company, my thoughts overpowered me; I broke down in tears. Feelings felt tears held back, all came to the surface that day, that the card written I was unable to read was just handed to Lilly with a goodbye embrace.

Some people make a life for others unbearable because they can and feels no accountability to a higher power or because they see life as a game and people as toys. They can because of being mentally sick (knowing the law is on their side to some degree) and have lost all hope in God and humanity. Alternatively, due to the competitiveness injected into society, many think, "Every man for himself" or "It's a dog-eat-dog world." However, whatever the root cause of their vindictiveness, my goal is to finish my book and not allow them to push me further into the ground so I cannot breathe. There is a generation whose teeth are swords, and jawbones are slaughtering knives to eat up the afflicted ones of the earth and the poor ones from among mankind, seen within this generation. The good that most tries to do by making life a bit easier and enjoyable, the more life becomes unbearable, especially for those who are not on guard by becoming aware of their surroundings and associates. Selfishness and greed have taken over the hearts of many. Finding out that the person claimed to have committed the act of disfellowshipping, I had never sat with before my meeting on August 21, 2012. This caused me to look back at my life to question: Who is my brother and sister in the congregation? Their actions were beginning to make some sense. Someone wanted to label me as forgetful or with a mental problem, and I had no idea who or why? There is one incident in life I cannot recall, but that is a revelation that only my God, Jehovah, will reveal to me in due time. As for now, I fight daily everyone who tries or attempts to tamper with my mind's memory.

It is written and often repeated: The truth will set you free! It certainly has in my case because all that "ONE" attempted so far to cause a mental breakdown has been killed by the strength furnished to me through my God, Jehovah. The wicked ones are clever, and the good ones must always think ahead to the possibilities; what if... They can cause things to occur frequently in one's life that the individual eventually thinks and believes something is what it is. Forgetfulness— not in my case—experiencing a temporary loss of memory (transient global amnesia, which each suffers at times in one's life) due to wicked actions, yes. With given time, I can recall my memories, thus killing the intended goal of the wicked ones. Throughout the years, I have had to fight with all my energy. It was a struggle most days with constant password forgetfulness. However, I am no one's fool. Within any company, when someone wants you out or wishes to acquire one's knowledge of a thing, making life a living hell— they will. Having access to the function of a network, computer information is gotten, can be tampered with, and manipulated. Therefore, I was not giving up without letting them know that I had some knowledge of the working world.

How can one fight a thing they cannot see? I tell you this, live by your truths, speak truthfully, walk with faith, and in confidence knowing your abilities; by doing this, one will distinguish the wicked one's burning missals

Chapter 1

THE BEGINNING

IT WAS A HABITUAL RITE of hers. For hours after her chores, she would sit by the window and watch me play; I dare not go past the distance of her eye's sight. We lived in a house at the very back of the yard, and in front of our home stood a huge concrete building that faced the main street called Alexander Street. Past memory of the girl who lived in the brick home intrigued my curiosity as to why she never walked, much older than me; she would always creep just as a baby would. Across the road was the cinema, where Mother and I spent many days when a good movie was playing, or we were just bored at home. For as long as I knew her, it was her routine to sit by the window to watch me off to school, and when I would get back, she would welcome me home. A very sickly child growing up, most of my time was spent in the hospital, and every day my mother would be there with my favourite snack: custard egg, and every time she had to leave, I would cry. A few times, I even ran away from the hospital, only to be taken back by her. "You need a doctor's care," she will say. "I have to take you back." Although I did run away a few times, life in the hospital was not all bad. The other patients and I would stay up late at night talking, playing games, or checking out what the nurses were up to; doctors were seldom seen. One morning as the nurse was doing her morning rounds, one patient requested the nurse not to give him his shot, he really pleaded, but she would not listen. "Come on," she replied, "turn on your side." As he did in his buttocks, she injected him. He died moments after of jaundice, a disease found in Guyana called yellow fever carried by infectious mosquitoes, when not treated, turns to jaundice. That incident caused me to run away.

A parent's love is very precious, and losing such love is a pain you carry for the rest of your life until you are made aware of the Creator's plan. We would sometimes sit and talk about my day at school or what was bothering me. One thing I disliked about her is when I would be looking for a concluded answer to my problems, she would ask questions allowing me to come to my own conclusions. Now that I have grown, I realize what she was trying to teach me: to rely on myself and do what my inner feeling tells me. In short, let your best friend be yourself; in this teaching, she was right. Some people, and sad to say, even some in your family, cannot be trusted. Your best friend can turn out to be your worst enemy. Inculcated thoughts entertained from our outer world; mental altering of information—from illegal entry into our homes and personal computers; this altered information taken in, that lack verbal communication with others, will move some to draw conclusions way beyond logic and practical knowledge of the other's action. Relationships today are degraded, thanks to the manipulation of information passing through the media, our social networks and phone devices.

§

It was a quiet mid-afternoon as we sat at the bedroom window; if she were in pain, this hidden from me as always would, and only reveal when things were most painful—was due to an innocent act of cutting corn from the side of her hand, which later became infected. She kept tending to it for months and into years it got before she eventually had the hand amputated. I watched my mother—Edna, is her name, went from being disabled to being efficient in the use of one hand; and often said to myself I will learn to use every part of my being, and this is how I became—ambidextrous, able to write with both hands. One day, long after my dad Reginald died, we moved from the city to a new development on the other side of town known as South Rumvelt Gardens, in the second house to your right as you enter the street. The house was fenced off from the other houses at its sides; my mother's flower garden lay to the right and left of the entrance. Because many hours are spent when she tends to it, Edna's garden was a flower garden, one the envy of the street except for a neighbor at the circler end of the street. At the back was a vegetable garden of string beans, okra, tomatoes, peppers, and spinach; to the left was a chicken coup with a few cocks and hens; it was a paradox of living in the country, although in the city. As we sat in her bedroom at the window talking, a glass of drinking water that rested on the ledge by accident fell as she was about to put her arm around me. I watched it fall as I said, "Oh, my!" It fell to the concrete and did not break—something you would expect to happen. I looked at her, my eyes opened wide in amazement. She looked back at me, and I saw a combination of sadness, joy, and pain in my mother's eyes. Many nights I thought of that incident, but finally grown, I have concluded that as human beings, we would often fall, but we can rise above our weaknesses or disabilities, repairing ourselves to a new; in the way we look at life and ourselves.

A once great writer Confucius wrote: "Our greatest glory is not in ever falling, but in rising every time we fall." In my case, looking back at all my trials and temptations, I have fallen, yes, but never to the point of breaking my will to survive. In the sense of the person, I am within and the things I stand for, such as mutual respect, kindness, justice, love, belief in a higher power and giving myself and others second chances.

§

I immigrated to Canada in January 1975, years after my mother died. As much as the day's excitement filled my heart, it was also filled with sadness about leaving my dogs behind. Leaving a world, I knew much of to one I know nothing of. Out of the airport and into a cold wintry night, the atmosphere was breathtaking as from the sky snow fell onto the ground; it paved white. Thoughts of what to expect crowded my mind. Picked up by my sister Monica we were driven to her home in Victoria Park—I must say, it is nothing compared with what it is today. Time changes people as it changes things—the city lights, the clothing stores, the restaurants, the people; things that were all new and different from where I was coming from touched me with emotions difficult to express.

We finally got to the apartment building, and I was surprised to see that animals lived in the apartments; however, after a moment's thought, it was logical they do as I was in a country with different climates. My nieces, nephew, and the children's sitter, Naz, greeted me. It was not a big apartment to hold us all, but we were happy. A few days later, we were at Honest Ed's World Famous Bargin Centre. known by many who immigrated to the country; it sold all affordable items to those on a financial budget. We purchased some winter clothing and later enrolled me in Victoria Park Secondary School. Life was enjoyable, but I was homesick and, most of all, missing my mother, but I had to learn to live with the loneliness I felt. After a few years with my sister, I moved out independently. The experience was good for me, but I would have to return every so often due to financial circumstances. Situations had me back and forth; I lived in many places, getting a feel of the areas and what I have found is this: in every place, there is beauty, but some people's actions bring down an area like they would the character of a person.

A new kid on the block, I moved onto The Esplanade in 1995. The Esplanade, meaning "open level space for public use," was unknown to me at the time. This is what I became to those highly educated than me. Yes, like a public space, people will use to get to where they want to go by walking or driving; I became like to correct thoughts, implement ideas and change circumstances. Now, they are aware of my knowledge of their actions. To try anything to destroy me is their last effort.

This is my story...

Chapter 2

THE ESPLANADE is a neighborhood where one can find anything their heart desires. You will find great restaurants like the Old Spaghetti Factory in the neighborhood, which serves great pasta. St. Lawrence Market has been a famous continuous market since 1796 and was formally proclaimed the market block in 1803. There is talk about future privatization. The South Market was home to Toronto First City Hall and Police Station, Number One, from 1845-99. The original council chamber now houses the Market Gallery. The market has become world-renowned selling fresh produce, seafood, meat, and cheeses, and continuing the tradition of the Farmers Market on Saturdays. Open on Sundays is a flea market, which is no longer as the site is under construction for another project.

Small and rising businesses: the Lilly Kimsa Theatre for Young People...the Berkeley Street Theatre...Canstage...the Hummingbird Theatre...Sony Theatre, and many more. People of all cultures and backgrounds; upcoming artists, pimps, prostitutes, homemakers, the homeless and the neighborhood gangs (a few of the members known by an acquaintance of a friend), run the street scene, have since then tried to improve the quality of their lives by making a CD, Still Smoking. A historical neighborhood was never quite destroyed by the great fire of 1849. Still standing are the buildings' years old, some telling a story of their past.

Yes, life in the area is quite interesting. If you were unaware of your neighbors' business, it was because you were either busy trying to make it or kept to yourself. Most knew the other's business, and even without factual truths, they made up stories of your life. Stories delighted by family gatherings. One that was told to me by my girl-friend Chelsi, who claimed she lived in one that housed a ghost you could hear in the middle of the night or early morning, was a bit laughable, as there is no such thing as a ghost. People call things they cannot see by all sorts of names, and it depends on the country you are from. However, the familiar one is ghosts. Laughable because, when buildings are old, the earth's movement will cause noise in the home. Laughable because we are living in a spiritual world with wicked spirit creatures that create noises around us, causing fear to the point of wanting to move from where we abide. But also in-fluences our minds from actions of those they have been able to se-duce to conduct wrongful acts, which causes a person to want to move from their home; some even act in cruel and destructive ways toward themselves and others.

My first impression of the building shown by Mac, the super at the time, was an inviting one. After a few years, things started to change, like the saying, "Come see me and come live with me are two different things." With all the cleaners did to maintain the building, some tenants saw that their work would never end. I occupied a unit on the second floor of the seven-story building, made up of bachelor's units, lofts, townhouses and one to three-bedroom units. Some of the tenants' vendettas escalated from the housing staff to my unit. Some days on exiting the unit, I will be greeted with bags of garbage and baby diapers. This evidence, pushed against my mental inculcated thoughts—thoughts of me trying to be someone I am not—in their opinion; me wanting a child I'll never have, and like garbage, I will be tossed out, are daily thoughts I battled. Daily I went about my ac-tivities, trying to maintain a job by being on time and performing to the best of my abilities, despite the "insomnia" I suffered. And I was good at what I did. It is said self-praise is no recommendation, but I would not say what I did if it weren't true. However, this was not good for some, as they saw that my efforts would not prevail, working under the circumstances subjected to. My ability to foresee my enemies' goals, office positions that came available, fear was not the only factor that stopped me from applying. Knowing that I would be giving all of myself in my performance, only to be told that I am no longer needed due to some dissatisfaction on their part, was the reason I neglected to apply and was satisfied just doing what I did as my sanity is maintained.

Chapter 3

PAST TIMES AND A REASON

MOVING AROUND A LOT has caused loss of touch with some friends. The only things left are photographs and memories of our shared good times. Throughout the years, I have made new friends. However, as time and experience have shown me, genuine friendships last a lifetime, no matter how near or far apart you are. To some, I am a devoted friend, but life has taken a toll on my efforts; I got tired of being the one to call, but I pray that those my thoughts are with are okay.

One day, on my way to work, while reading one of the local newspapers, I saw an article about Leon's son; letting me know that his family was doing well put a smile on my face. Leon is someone I met at a house gathering. When our eyes met, I knew we were destined to be together. Something in his smile told me he was unhappy and a person who does not like seeing others unhappy; after a brief conversation, I was going to change that. A week after our encounter, we got together. From that day on, our friendship grew from months into years until, one day, his wife happens to find out where I lived. The door opened to a knock, causing a scene so embarrassing as I lived in the basement of a home, so the tenants above heard all during the commotion. Leon intercepts her, throwing anything her hands could get to, taking her out of the home and leaving. People say that once in a lifetime, one finds their soulmate. This is not quite true. This was true at that time in my life, Leon was. But as we move a stage further in life, we encounter another. We never argued. Moments together always was appreciated, and sex was like having a delicious meal you have not had for a while. Yes, life with Leon was fun and will forever be cherished.

In the nineties, I joined a company called Bissell Vacuums,* an American company with many franchises in Canada. The one I worked for was owned and operated by Samson.* The name takes you back to biblical and medieval times. Yes, the company was strong, having many great sales producers, and seductive and cunning individuals, like Gilad Communication. It was during a teacher's strike when I joined the company. I started working in the telephone room, making cold calls, filling in for the receptionist, and was soon out in the field selling after much encouragement. In addition, becoming the top sales representative for Canada and the United States. My career with Bissell was interesting, in the way of meeting all types of people and enjoyable, as I was doing what I loved—helping others, traveling, and having fun. One day, on my way home (at the time working in the sales room), a conversation developed that had me laughing my heart out, when suddenly a strange feeling came over me, and since being close to a bus shed, I told the girls I'll take the bus home. "Are you sure?" one of them asks as I nod my head. "Yes!" We both spoke, "Then we'll see you tomorrow." I stood in the bus shed and watched as they walked away, and that was the last thing I saw before opening my eyes in the ambulance on its way to the hospital. A few days later back at work I was told that when they looked back about a block or two away, they saw a crowd gather at the bus shed and run back to see what it was since they had left there minutes ago. They got there to find out I was unconscious. They waited until the ambulance arrived, and lifted me into it before leaving.

Money was plentiful from my sales; returning to school was the last thing on my mind. Many years later, I did return to school, graduating with my Ontario Secondary School Diploma, and has attended other schools earning a Legal Assistance Certificate.

---

* Company names changed for protection
* Personal names changed for protection

§

MONEY—the most powerful thing that will intentionally corrupt one's mindset goals; see to it that it never changes you. I was temporarily happy and having lots of fun. However, having a good and meaningful life is not all about money; first, it is never losing sight of your goals with God's principles in your life. Secondly, having a solid academic education, and being creative with ideas or dreams are like seeds; when planted, you never know how they will grow. And lastly, when to make sacrifices. Money at any level of one's life is gained by having these three attributes. These are things one never thinks of when inexperience and having fun.

I lived and worked with people of my culture and other immigrants to Canada to make a better life for themselves and their families. Life then, though difficult, was nothing compared to now. It was easy to work hard and be recognized for one's effort. Today, working hard is not the only criterion for being recognized; performance is not all the judges want, but rather one's soul. In addition, many have lost their innocence. Today, challenging work could go unnoticed, especially if you lack knowledge on how to play their game or the sex appeal that grabs the mind. And showing yourself to be more knowledgeable and a take charge type of individual than your superior and your peers will jeopardize your position and friendship with your colleagues, especially if that one's appearance and/or abilities to be creative are lacking. Nevertheless, when the Devil and his workers— the wicked- are after you, none of the above matters, except most important, is one's mental strength to recognize when to hold, when to fold and when to walk away.

I was in a battle fighting for my sanity of self. No one I knew understood what I was going through. One day, I met Westley, who, by his invitation to travel, allowed me to meet others like myself, an opportunity I found clearer in understanding my dreams. However, before Westley, I had my eyes on someone at Bissell—Earl, who was being of a challenge. I knew he liked me, but for some reason, he lacked boldness or was cautious in exhibiting his advances. Therefore, I decided to break him. One day as he was in the basement getting a few boxes of equipment together for his day's work, the basement lighting dimly lit to my flirtatious edge. I stood next to him, chit-chatting about the day ahead as he looked through the boxes to be sure everything was in order. When he stood up, my movement slow, with my intended goal, I softly kissed him on his lips, and he responded. When I pulled away, it was as though he wanted me to do what I just did once again. This was the start of our relationship, which lasted for many years to the point of being engaged, to separating on different journeys.

The lesson taught is whatever you want in life and the desire to have it is strong; you do what it is to achieve it. However, show respect and be mindful of the place, the time and the other's life, as some things are not meant to be.

Almost everyone who worked at Bissell was having an affair. When my boss then decided to fall into temptation with the cunning Ms. Packet, that is when he lost my respect. I felt uncomfortable during office parties due to my knowledge of his involvement with some of the women present. Mrs. Samson, however, sure knew how to maintain balance. I guess when a woman has all she needs and wants and is as independent as she was, apart from the material things she knows, should a battle of wits ensue, should the marital relationship fail—is hers, there is no need to worry and make life miserable. It is like a poem I have mounted on the wall, the author unknown: Where there is Faith, there is Love; where there is Love there is Peace, where there is Peace there is God, where there is God there is no need. With the way he played around, at times having all the other women he was humping right in the same room, Mrs. Samson's action gained my deepest respect. He was like Donald Trump, having the money that brought the women's attention. On the other hand, perhaps he was truthful with her, so she had no reason to act ignorant. Yes, life at Bissell was likened to a soap opera filled with romance, passion, and drama.

My life was gradually changing. Bianca got me more involved with the church—Jehovah's Witness. Like a flower growing wild among all other beautiful ones, with the weeds I was amongst. Within the Bible, it is written: "Train up a child in the way he should go, and when he is old, he will not depart from it." -Proverbs 22:6. Growing among the people of all types sure did not make me forget my teachings; only utilize my God-given conscience. I watched Bianca's cunning actions with Andrew and often wondered if he was getting any sugar—maybe, and perhaps he was not, but the first time he took me out, he found his intention to see how strong I was out. My difference is I push and put myself into situations that others would not. I was willing to put my strengths or weaknesses to the test. I sure did put my weakness to the test and failed. For I could not handle both the weed—marijuana, which at the time I never smoked or knew anything of, but with the alcohol consumption and the second-hand smoke, Andrew got a piece of the pie for an unfair fight.

After the abortion of Earl's child, a foolish action occurred due to my being told that I wanted to trap him; the regret and pain I felt afterward caused me to leave Bissell to work for Sears Photography Studio. We were engaged to be married, but due to circumstances in our lives, years later, we both parted, going in different directions, to be seen many years later under different circumstances. I was thrilled at the studio. Working with the babies, young ones, and families filled the void of what I did not have that I wanted—a family of my own. I gave of myself working at Sears. And later showed management I was no fool, a person who learns fast and adapts quickly. My skills, time, and effort in keeping my employees—from being abused, to retaining them, with each month's delegated hours not used, this I took and added to their timesheets. Sacrificed my own bond and stole from the company this due to their unfair treatment. A future lesson that is teachable to all employers, when you take advantage of a good nature employee, one day, that employee will become wise to take advantage of you.

§

HONESTY—freedom from deceit; fairness is that quality of man that shows him to be truthful in speech, above cheating, stealing, misrepresentation or any fraudulent action. When found in oneself, a quality is outwardly displayed with one's affiliates. However, this quality is today as within all cultures; honesty among family members, friends, co-workers, and business partners is becoming an everyday attribute only used when it suits one's purpose. This is a fact we each must face and learn to deal with.

During my period of working at Sears Photography Studio, I met Jeff. He had dialed the wrong number. Still in bed when the phone rang, and in one of my flirtatious moods, the conversation was prolonged; by the end of the call, I had gotten his number and had made a date. We met a few days after our conversation, and about a month later, I moved in with him. He was what I was looking for. He was a clean person, could cook, was independent in carrying his weight, smoked a bit and did not mind leaving the house to party occasionally. However, the saying goes, "Not all that shines is gold." He had a weakness; he was jealous and allowed jealousy to control his actions. One can conclude that I was the type of woman he sought, as I was independent and carried my own weight. I am a good cook and conversationalist, encouraging regards his interest, and did things he could swear he was dreaming of at times.

It was a winter day. The streets were covered with snow; Jeff came home early for us to go shopping. I was in one of my mischievous moods and decided not to wear any other clothing other than my bra and underwear under my coat. I must admit, my body is not stunning but pleasant to look at; I know how to use and display my assets...lol. I met him in his car, and we drove to the grocery store. All the while shopping, I wanted to take his hand and put it into my coat, but afraid of his reaction, I waited until we got home. Upon removing my coat, he could not believe his eyes. We both laughed as he grabbed me by the hand. "You little devil; you really need a spanking." He pulled me into the bedroom, and we made passionate love. Jeff thought I was his possession. I knew my position and respected him in leaving notes about where I would be; if not done, this would cause disruption in the home. One day, I made the mistake of trying to further his photography career by speaking to his friend, and this was the first stage of failure of our relationship. He had beaten me so bad that my face was swollen black and blue, and my stomach hurt from the kicks he had given me. The excuse I had given for not being able to go to work was that I had sustained some injuries from a mugging. When my supervisor, Suzie, came over to visit, I hid in the room while he made the excuse that she was out. It was now just a matter of time before I left. Embarrassment prolonged my stay, as I had built up his image in my family's eyes. Moreover, to have them think of him any less at the time, I was willing to hide this. Not having enough funds and not knowing where to go for help, I stayed for just a bit longer, as I vowed this would never happen again, Until My Dying Day. Yes, until one day after a few days from another beating, while making lunch for us, I poured a bit of liquid he had brought home that was in the kitchen I knew was not for cooking and into the pot I poured it. I lost it, yes, to the point of almost destroying our lives, but fate had other intentions. I bled for a few days, and he was admitted to the hospital a week after. No one knows whether this was due to my action, as he was told he had gallstones.

Earl was called during the crisis, as I needed someone to talk with. Unknowingly, Jeff's aunt was keeping an eye on me. So, that evening, while Earl and I was having a shower from being out in the heat all day, Jeff's aunt came in and caught us in the shower. At last, my vengeance maturely meeting the derogatory remarks that undermined the relationship and thoughts of his aunt's and his actions towards me could be applauded. Things I overheard and put a deaf ear to, were now at the forefront. A few days after the incident, he came home from the hospital, and I knew it was time to leave. A day later, I called my sister to help me move.

Moving on with life after a breakup can be difficult for some people. Some will be vindictive and always be around to cause problems, especially if one party seems to be doing well. In Jeff's case, he accepted the invitation to meet at my home—at the time living on Ontario Street. After a good talk and a last roll in the sack, it was the last I saw of him.

After a few years of working at Sears Photography Studio and a few months after leaving Jeff, the company fired me. This really broke my heart, but I knew I was fortunate—not lucky, as I often say, "Luck I don't believe in. I believe what is for me will be mine." This is true in my case, for being caught was not in my life's destiny, as who knows what may have happened? Was it Jeff, instead of his aunt, who had entered the home, or what reason for termination? Perhaps today, living with a criminal or fraudulent record, but instead, a letter I once held that states the reason for termination is due to production; is no longer in my possession, and this is due to the illegal entry into my home and personal files—disappeared.

Since leaving Sears Photography Studio, I have held many other positions working for many companies. Holding two or three jobs at once to make ends meet. My next love was working with the Canadian Imperial Bank of Commerce in the reissuing department. This position taught me a lot about the world of banking, bankers, the importance of Credit Cards, and building one's credit. Neglecting the opportunity taught that of building my own credit, the bankers took advantage of my presence in doing their own banking.

§

SALES—a job that opens one's door of being timid and fearful, out into a world of being aggressive, fearless, and far from being silent, where one takes rejections with a grain of salt. It is an occupation that prepares you for the world and requires the ability to sell and sell well, whether it is goods, services, or yourself.

§

On the upper floors of the Lawrence Mall is located Gelid Communication LP. I joined Gelid in the year 2002, around the time of juggling three jobs. After the interview and the comment quietly made only for my ears, receiving a call to return for orientation was the last thing I had expected. However, innocent of the mistake on my résumé, I boldly met with the recruiting officer and a group of new recruits—some of whom soon left, having failed the test of stamina. Those that stayed had what it took and loved what they did. The bankers, though, will see that the employees were not going elsewhere until their profits were gained.

It was a day in August 2005, around four or five o'clock in the afternoon, that suddenly nature changed the atmosphere paradoxically from day to night. There is an old saying as there are many stories told of storms. I always recall the one who told me about the "gods" being at war. However, science has shown that a storm or massive storm takes warm air from the surface of the water, pushes it up until it cools, and comes back down. This cycle repeated several times, causing wind pressure to change and create a vertical system over the ocean with wind speeds of 38 mph. When winds are at this speed or higher, the tropical depression becomes a tropical storm. When storms reach 74 mph or higher, a tropical storm takes a cyclonic form and becomes a hurricane, with its strongest winds in the right front quadrant (northwest for storms going east to west, northeast for those going south to north).

Hilda's voice is heard, out from among the sounds of the flash of lightning and the thunder. "I'm not the one who got screwed in the ass!" I was sitting in the corner next to the post and the supervisor's desk that separated us wondered to whom she was speaking; as I looked at her, Hilda's stare was towards me. So, I turned to my left to see if she was speaking to someone behind, no one was there, and as I raised my eyes, I looked right into the (eye) mouth of an angry storm. And this is not kidding, the image's face with the mouth wide open. Within a few hours, the storm had torn down trees, cut power lines, damaged houses, and barns, and caused the cave-in of a few roads. Yes, who is there among humankind who can foretell the true eventuality of man or beast or even the elements of nature when at work? Curious as most are, no one can truly tell your future, as time and unforeseen circumstances can change lives and things within seconds. Did those four words "YOU PEOPLE DOWN THERE!" put fear or comfort into my mind? From the reading of our history, evidence seen with my own eyes, and words heard with my own ears, I sure live in fear but with comfort in God. This is the reason for my patience with self and most people I deals with; some neglect that they are dealing with humans whose ability is to change (destroy), create and decide for themselves. I believes in second chances as we all go through a learning phase and are taught from experience or mistakes.

After I got home from work that evening, I showered, had a snack, and went off to bed after watching Eliminate, a T.V. show of singles getting together to see if they will find the "one" they are looking for. The show is fun to watch; it allows you to see the creativity of some, taking a dire situation and making the best of it. It shows an opportunity taken is an opportunity to gain. To watch the catfights among the sexes to gain control and the shallow nitpicking that shows the stupidity of some and the integrity of others.

Chapter 4

STUFF DREAMS ARE MADE OF

DREAMS ARE EXPRESSIONS of the spiritual realm and a bridge between the tangible. They are the beginning of realities and are expressions of our past truths, illusions, wild fantasies, anticipations, irrational thoughts, experiences, and even telepathic visions. Dreams can help and encourage us or indicate a particular route we are going that may not be worthwhile.

DREAMS are thoughts or images occurring during sleep, seen in the imagination. The Bible states, "For a dream cometh through the multitude of business, and a fool's voice is known by multitude of words." - Ecclesiastes 5:3.

VISIONS are defined as the act or faculty (any one power of the mind, as the memory or imagination) of seeing—imaginative foresight. From the Dictionary of Psychology, it is a mystical or religious experience or divine revelation involving supernatural or paranormal perception.

§

Please, note that throughout this book, other authors are mentioned because their work validates my life experiences, and I greatly recommend reading. A few points I would like to state going forward, are from two books read, one by Joni E. Johnston, PsyD entitled *Complete Idiot's Guide to Psychology*. Freudian psychologists think that dreams serve two purposes. One, they guard sleep by disguising disruptive thoughts with symbols. Two, they provide harmless ways for people to fulfill their darkest desires, without suffering the social consequences.

Most, if not all of us, have sexual fantasies of the opposite sex, especially if it is someone we deeply care for, and those fantasies are strong enough you can penetrate your emotional thoughts to the other. This can cause a meeting of the minds that leads to a meeting of the souls/bodies, and eventually, this can cause suffering of a social nature. In the case that one may be overcome by the other's fantasy in giving into their desire or mental manipulation. Further in this book is such a situation given. Ms. Johnston went on to say that hard-core scientists suggest that a dream's major job is to provide regular group exercise for the brain's neurons. This is true as the brain's neurons try to paste together symbols or words heard to find the meaning, and the best way to accomplish this is by group sessions, whereby from each one's analysis of... can be drawn logical conclusion. The other book by Pamela J. Ball is entitled 10,000 Dreams Explained. States that we could accept dreams as an expression of the unconscious creative self. Which can contain messages either in an easy-to-understand form or in the language of symbolism, where initially, the meanings are not easily discernible. Thus, a reason why group sessions would be recommended. The Good Book states that wisdom is shown by its children.

Yes, there is no end to the making of books, and much devotion (to them) is wearisome to the flesh. One can do as I have; search to find their meaning; however, both authors mention, and I fully agree with them—we need to know ourselves—to understand our lives through our dreams or visions. Some people, including my own family, thought something was wrong with me when I tried to inform them of my dreams. Visions and dreams, since childhood, have been a part of my personality. Even before reading the Bible, life's experiences taught me some things about our past.

My first vision since coming to Canada occurred when I lived with my sister, Monica, and family on Gilder Drive and Eglington Avenue East. Seen was an elderly man sitting on a rock surrounded by people young and old. He was reading from a book, which I later realized was the Bible from what I heard. As I slowly observed what was going on, he had the book open as he read. "Stop storing up for yourselves treasures upon the earth where moth and rust consume and where thieves break in and steal...." The next day after getting home from school, I went into the room I shared with my nephew and nieces, got the Bible, and searched. I did not find the scripture. I recall the book's position in his hand; where he was reading from seemed closer to the end. I made an estimate in my mind, and the next day after school, I again searched, and Walla found it. I have since then never forgotten Matthew 6:19-21.

My second vision occurred when I lived on Gamble and Pape Avenues. The figure of a black man lay on the bed and standing over him was a fair-skinned man, the hair on his head white. He stood looking at the body before him, "Watch this!" I assumed this, he said, as I saw his mouth move and physically move the woman to come closer. The woman, also fair-skinned with her hair colour as his, is seen standing with him, and suddenly a voice is heard, "Danny!" At which point I heard and was now awake from my vision, once again, the voice called for Danny. At this point, I rose from my bed, stepped towards the window a few footsteps away, and inconspicuously hid behind the curtains looking to see whom the voice belonged to; I could see it was the superintendent's wife as she once again called, "Danny." She stood at the entrance of the driveway waiting, but no one was seen going toward her. She then walked off after a few minutes. I assume she went back into the building. After a few more minutes of standing at the window, I removed and went back to bed, having not seen the person she had called.

That is the beginning of my ability to hear voices, most times at rest, of the images seen. At this point, though I suffered bruises on my body, I was not quite strong to get myself out of my dreams. I lived in confusion for many years as I tried to understand my life's purpose. Gradually distanced me from people, some believing that there was

25

something wrong with me, but only I knew what I was afraid to say, for fear they may just as well conclude that I was sick or demonized.

Dreams can be confusing, like many books that are wearisome to the soul. Dreams can cause the mind to go astray or mad (furious or frenzied as with rage or terror; delirious, violent acting with great physical force; sane or reasonable); the conclusion of all this is to fear the true God. Fear of his disapproval is the beginning of wisdom, which is the safeguard and guidance of our souls to a better life. And to tell of his Kingdom's purpose for humankind.

§

Still asleep one Sunday morning, I could consciously hear the birds below the windowpane as they whistled and chirped at each other as sounds of male voices conversing heard. Between my state of sleep and being awake, I overheard someone saying, "And she threw mace at her." Immediately I woke up and stepped to the window as the boys across the street entered the building. A building at the completion of this book has since demolish, rebuild with a high-rise. I had put the comment heard out of my mind until one day, during a conversation with an employee who no longer works for the company, brought back to memory the comment I heard as he told me of Hilda's record. Nevertheless, like a few others, Hilda was not about to leave Gelid Communication of her own cognizance. The bankers were set on making profits from her and the other performances. To whom was Hilda speaking? Alternatively, were the words uttered meant for my ears. I lay in bed, replaying Hilda's words in my head and recalling conversations with Rudolf.

Hilda is a girl with short-tapered hair cut to her scalp. She is about 5'4" and dresses with the latest fashions; a slightly straight nose, thin lips with tattoos on her legs and arms, having a trunk on her that turns the head of both males and females. She is a genuinely nice person to speak with; she tells it as she sees it, but much too defensive and boisterous if you should ever get her angry. Informed of her criminal record way before she brought it to my attention one day as we were in the lunchroom; I said nothing but listened to what she said about her past. Now I am not condoning the action of Hilda that caused her to have a criminal record or those who "claim" to have a neurosis weakness, which can be a problem. With the help available to date, many can avoid the actions they take toward each other.

People, STOP being defensive about things said and actions that are done. Live your truths and start to take offensive actions by forcing your minds onto other matters. All will agree that we live physically to the point that we will do almost anything to keep our physical body (soul) in good health. However, the thing unconscious of—our spirituality—we neglect to learn how to control and use it as we do our physical bodies. Avoid looking at the actions of others that will stimulate violent/or improper reactions and pray for power beyond what seems unnatural. Of course, people know your life and will do anything and everything in their power that pushes your reaction. Let it be in ways that show your limitation of tolerance, as your action shows what you are made of, and hope this is of patience, love, kindness, and justice. Individuals should consider this before taking revenge, picking up a gun, or running to a shrink. Take time to get a chance to know yourself and understand the force that pushes (you). The force that causes some of us to go through life thinking it was just a dream or the world is against us. By patience with self the opportunity is gained by God's grace in recognizing the nefarious one. Then here is where one's faith and love of fellow man is tested; I speak from experience. The things that cannot be seen are the things that sap our energy and have us thinking that we are sick or living with a ghost in a hunted place. All because we neglect to take time to get to know ourselves, our weaknesses, and strengths. Call it what you may, force, power, vigor—the Bible calls it our spirit: "And the LORD God formed man of the dust of the ground, and breathed into his nostrils the breath of life; and man became a living soul." -Genesis 2:7.

Awake, before it becomes too late; man has used and then killed your bodies by their clever manipulation that leads to the loss of one's innocence. However, it may not be too late for some if you take to heart this scriptural advice, "Be not afraid of them that kill the body and after that have no more that they can do. But I will forewarn you whom ye shall fear: Fear him, which after he hath killed hath power to cast into hell; yea, I say unto you, Fear him." –Luke12:4-5.

Yes, I tell you, fear Jehovah for his adversary, the ruler of this world, Satan, keeps transferring himself—like a ventriloquist into lives. Without awareness, one can destroy self or, by presumptive action—get killed. Friends, with your spirit (force), you can rewrite the wrongs done by yourself or others.

§

Normally I will lay in bed a bit longer to clear my head of my night's dreams. At times I would read a chapter or three of the Bible before getting off the bed. Understanding the Bible and the religion of others is important. To clarify, understanding helps to see how facts relate to one another. Each day we look past the persons in front of us as only appearances we observed. Just listening, stopping to say a kind word or few can lead to learning much about the person, or life's lessons from their past. And, when conflicts arise, the true self of that individual is seen; their arrogance or actions confirm wisdom. Most, if not all, that is taught in the Bible about being "Kind to each other; Adhering to the authorities and your elders; Vengeance is mine, said the Lord; and He that lives by the sword will also die by the sword" is forgotten by so many today. The increase in violence is proof of some having a form of godly devotion but proving false to its power. Others use the Bible to justify their hatred—misleading a group blinded by their manipulation—a people, always learning and never coming to an accurate knowledge of the truth. It's better to love yourself as your enemy.

Life to date, with increased knowledge and better technology, one would think would be easier—however, life has become increasingly difficult. Office politics, political unrest, religious sects, economic pressures, and parents being unable to deal with their child's bully at school or to give proper supervision due to pressures trying to make ends meet; are more than enough to cause depression in our lives. Both young and old now experience this. The conflicts behind closed doors are no longer the factors that push people into their ritualistic practices; some practices that harm others affect the reactions of many, which causes physical and mental illnesses. Recent reports show one out of five people will experience a diagnosable mental illness, which would extend to the taking of innocent lives. To get to the heart of how mental illness starts, one must take them self out of a situation or look at one's situation as an investigator to see how others push our mental tolerance to the point of becoming like them—with a mental illness. A short story will give insight... In July 2019 my organization—Jehovah's Witness convention held at Exhibition Place in Toronto. After the conclusion of the meeting that day towards the exist stood two sisters dressed in brown clothing looked like mannequins pose for photo ops as you leave. That day when I got home a person who normally inspects my home before and on return notice that my electrical toothbrush was covered all over with brown stuff. Knowing my issue with illegal access into my unit, the building security was called in to report my finding. After explanation and some note taking, he left. I had no idea who came into the unit to do such mischief; an incident that could have moved me to be vindictive towards my brothers and sisters when I did visit the Hall. As the inculcated message infuriated my mind as to whether my sister's attitude sent me the message of my past conduct or whether, she was being controlled by the wicked one. However, my silent prayer to Jehovah was on behalf of my sister that she will be awaken and, is to give me the mental strength to endure that which lacks insight on the others' part. The topic of the convention was Love Never Fails proved my actions toward my family and those in control of the wicked one's intrusive actions used to discredit, embarrassed and manipulate circumstances that genuine love covers a multitude of sins, to the destruction of the presumptuous ones. We can also look at some of our famous entertainers' lives; like Michael Jackson, Amy Winehouse, Letitia Wright, Jade Smith, and Robert Williams, to mention a few; some who have overcome their depression, others died.

Statistics of young criminals at the age of twelve show how much the population suffers from a diagnosable mental health problem. In addition, lack of tolerance shows that mental health illnesses can affect people at any stage of life, culture, and income. Given these facts, only 10 percent of people who are depressed seek help. Further separation of families and friends due to religion, the rise of social sites, and the media's manipulation, tampering of information, and each one's lack of communication, coupled with haste to judge others from a lack of understanding, are all contributing factors.

Why did the Bible say that with all the knowledge we acquire, we acquire understanding? I will tell you why… because to understand is to be informed of…to comprehend, if not by our own experience, to imagine oneself in the position of others to help or assist. We are advised to love our enemies as ourselves. If we did, most would still be alive today. Watching the news of innocent people being killed or wounded because of political unrest pains me. Where are the leaders? "For the kingdom of God is not in word, but in power." - First Corinthians 4:20. Yes, constant words of debating instead of using their power for the good of humans. "He that is slow to anger is better than the mighty; and he that ruleth his spirit than he that taketh a city." – Proverbs 16:32 Our impatience is what causes foolish acts, as does the hurrying of our mouth or feet in taking defence to words others throw at us. Making the above sayings a part of our daily living would avoid many conflicts between families and friends. Listen to a song by Adel with the lyrics: "People say some crazy things, but it doesn't mean she is hurting.…" Yes, people do say some crazy things without thinking; I have been there. In time, knowledge is what corrects our actions and words thrown toward others; given an apology.

Chapter 5

SEASONS CHANGE, PEOPLE CHANGE

FINALLY, I decided to get out of bed to get something to eat and prepare for the day ahead. I heard the ringing tone of the phone. "Hello!"

"Hi babe, it's Rudolf. How you do?" he asked.

I met Rudolf one day on my way home from job hunting. As I was about to cross Church and King Streets, he rode up on a cycle next to me. "Girlfriend, you are looking fine. Where are you off to?" he asks. I looked to my side and up at him. His smile told me he was mischievous, and if he was looking for mischief, he came to the right place as I was in a mood to play and play nasty.

"I'm going into the park for a while."

The park is behind the church at the corner of Church and King Streets. It is called St. James Cathedral Church, opened in 1853 a historical landmark dating back to the year 1797 and has since been rebuilt a few times. It is even said that the Little Drummer Boy was buried beneath the grounds.

"Then I'll join you shortly," he said. He turned his cycle and rode back to his friend, a short, stocky black fella.

Shortly after I took a seat on the bench with my back towards the church, he rode up. He got off his cycle and sat next to me. A conversation began, as he informed that he was in the middle of a breakup with someone called Mari-June, and the person he was with was his best friend—Roy (many years since meeting and getting to know him passed away one day on his job). In addition to his breaking up with his woman friend, he was struggling with a personal problem he would like to talk about but not now. I not only wanted to hear what his problem was, but I wanted to release a problem of my own, that of built-up anger. So, I told him to come over to my place the next morning around 5:00 A.M. for breakfast and to continue the conversation; he agreed. I smiled as we parted. Is this a time I should shout for help? Why me? *I thought to myself.*

The next day, I waited for him, but he did not show. I felt he would not, him seen childishly scared of the dark. Later that day, when the door was open to the knock, he was standing with the cycle. An apologetic smile on his face was just not cutting it, as at this point, the built-up emotions I wanted so badly to release had gone. Perhaps the force was protecting us. All I felt as I looked at him was a feeling of sadness and pity. My intuition warned me of the disappointment I would expect in this relationship, but I was not listening to my sixth sense. However, putting aside my intuition after listening to his story of how his addiction started and his reluctance to go into a rehab center—unaware of the depth of his addiction, he is told it is okay to stay for a time. Rudolf saw fit the opportunity to be in my life for a long time after two months had passed. Charmed by his smooth talk; a smile with cute little dimples that caused me to smile whether I wanted to or not; his conning attitude he thought I could not see; and lovemaking, the relationship lasted for quite a few years until he started slipping. I would come home to find items in my home, not of mine, and cannot get an explanation that satisfies me; I will kick him out only to have him back after hearing another of his sad stories. Addicts are one of the best storytellers, as they are liars. (If the hat fits, wear it.) So good, they fail to make an honest living off their talent.

§

COCAINE, a bitter crystalline addictive alkaloid, is extracted from coca leaves and used in an analgesic. Today, coke or stone— the street name used, is made from many household items making this drug not only addictive but also poisonous to one's system. Therefore, after a while, addicts only feel "normal" when using. They go through a withdrawal process when they try to cut back or quit. Unpleasant symptoms that are both physical and mental, they experience.

In Rudolf's case, he would sleep for days if allowed to, not even bothering to take a bath or brush his teeth, agitated, and disoriented at times. He had a way about him that made me smile even when I was hurting or wanted to cry. I smiled at his question. "I'm doing fine. What about you?"

"Well, what can I say? Same old, same old."

"What does that mean?" I did not wait for an answer. "Don't tell me you are not working. Rudolf, I don't know what to say other than if you want to work, you'll find work."

"I don't know why you ask questions if you already know the answer," he said with laughter in his voice.

"You see, this is my point. Life is cavalier where you are a concern."

"Babe, you are much too serious; you must get with the program. I'm serious; I must talk to you."

"What about? Unlike you, I'm busy."

"I'm busy, too. It's not an easy job hustling drugs and chicks." He spoke with laughter as he continued, trying to sound a bit serious. "Seriously, I need to see you this evening."

I was curious to know what it was this time; already, at the back of my mind knew that he would be asking to stay for a few days. Moreover, after a few days, he will still be lying around, not wanting to leave with the same old excuse he is recuperating. Again, I am forced to take action that will nag at my heart. I know that the heart can be treacherous, and who really knows it. Nevertheless, to think of myself in his shoes and wanting someone to be there for me, I will inhale, exhale, and do what I must for his sake. "Okay, I'll see you on Tuesday, but I will not be home until after midnight."

"Okay, babe, I'll see you then." He hangs up.

He said he loved me, and he will have to prove it. I have given him much of my love, time, and sympathy, things money cannot buy. He has two persons entwined into one being. His actions, and at times his thoughts, were like a magnet that affected my state of mind, resulting in mental stress, producing physical pain and damage.

The Prophet Muhammad wrote, "Evil as an example are people who reject Our Signs and wrong their own souls" -The Quran, The Heights, Surah 7:177.

In time, I did experience the wrong I have done to my soul. Rudolf is known to be in a carefree mood most time. He was in a celebratory mood two days before the New Year. As usual I will do a complete cleaning of the home, a tradition continued from my mother's teaching—not to let a New Year catch you with a dirty home and without food. Her point is to clean up the past as you look to the future with new hopes of it being better than the last. Rudolf being in a celebrated mood was not an issue; what was, was his need to be smoking both weeds mixed with cocaine. The smell of the cocaine affected me. This is when I am forced to fight him mentally. His transferred thoughts confused me, bringing back memories of my dreams, things I had heard and seen that I would rather not deal with. Our conversation is deeper than usual, and I then battle with him for understanding.

I suffered with a nagging back pain from the start of the week due to stressful situations at work and home. My battle at work was not getting involved with those who smoked and spoke out of terms, some who never seemed to think or put themselves in the shoes of another before speaking. The knowledge that some were being used beyond their control, not being able to do much about situations, coupled with my tiring effort at home, was even more stressful. So, I was most pleased to have him leave when he told me he would be going over to his child's mother for a few days. Whenever he is on coke, his mouth would be likened to a faucet or water tap that, once turned on, would never stop running—he would talk nonstop for hours. He left, letting me know he would be back; if not, he would call. That evening I was unable to sleep. I got up a few times to use the toilet and drink water.

The morning had arrived, and as I tried to remove from the bed, it was impossible to do so. For over an hour, I shouted for help. My neighbor's voice—a door from mine, with someone is heard passing, but to no avail did my call for help given an answer. Finally, I dragged myself off the bed onto the floor and into the bathroom to urinate, but I could not get to the toilet seat. Fearful, I shouted and banged on the floor for help, still with no assistance from anyone, I lay there helplessly. I then dragged myself to the door and gave myself a lift with one arm while reaching the doorknob with the other, opened the door. I lay there and waited for the sound of anyone coming onto the floor. I could not use the phone because when the superintendent had the entrance door to the building fixed, my landline got damaged. I called Bell Canada to fix the problem and was told the cost of $500 would have to be deposited to have the phone line fixed. I refused to pay this amount, so my service was never connected. I was without a phone for over a year, then registered with Fido, one of the new tele-communication companies in rivalry with Bell Canada. My cell phone was in my handbag, out of reach. After approximately twenty minutes from the neighbor's passing—which seemed longer— the elevator was heard opening; at this point, a few hours had passed. Anxious at the elevator door opening, I immediately shouted for help. It was my neighbor, Ronda, who lived at the other end of the second floor. She came to my assistance by calling for an ambulance and getting my handbag. I was rushed to St. Michael's Hospital, and half an hour after getting there, I got the chance to urinate. My diagnosis is of having had a mild stroke—not the doctor's.

Stress is something that can disable or kill us if not investigated. Awareness of one's circumstances will assist in how well one handles oneself. I have lived and seen the outcome of stressful situations in my own and the life of others, to quote Dr. Bevan Morris, President of Maharishi International University, who explained Maharishi's viewpoint. Every day in every nation, people violate the law of nature by performing actions which injure themselves, their neighbors, and their environment. These wrong actions cause stress in the individual and within society. End of quote. Indeed, stress builds up to a certain point before the explosion into calamity brings about change.

Black Lives Matter, a case and point.

"Mindfulness," states Dr. Jane Riley on stress, "takes into consideration cognitive evaluation of events. When something distasteful or unfortunate occurs, we can choose to get bent out of shape and stressed out or let it ride." Turning to booze or pills will not help chronic stress. Instead, it alters our minds and adds to stressful feelings. A better way is to look to natural methods to lower anxiety, such as breathing exercises that lower heart rate and assist in relaxing. Another way to increase relaxation is physical exercises that help to take the mind off worries, and another is to find a group to release the mental anxieties being felt.

Life sure is for a moment. We must give to the Lord each day that we are awake to see the sun, thanks, and praise. Some take life for granted, and each day they get up with a mission to hurt others without remorse. Take whatever is given without thanks, steal from others without regret, cause disruption wherever they go, and in the process, have total disregard for their very lives and the lives of others. From this incident and another within initiated this poem written by me entitled, "I Am a Princess Dog."

§

Over the years, I grew to understand myself and the spiritual force upon me, enabling me to fight back without much damage to my soul. Unfortunately, used in a psychosis manner affected me and Rudolf's relationship, as it did others. My ability to love others strongly caused the effect of self-injury, in addition to those whose clandestine actions further manipulated both our thoughts. I was not about to fall victim, as he did to their intended goal.

I am a black woman, with a verbal fact that I will make known. Whether the words heard, **"You people down there!"** was uttered by God or Satan (the ruler of this system of things), or man (Astronaut experimenting with us on earth). The warning is going to be revealed if not by me by someone else a witness who is not afraid to speak out. It is written, "For nothing is secret, that shall not be made manifest; neither *anything* hid, that shall not be known and come abroad." – Luke 8:17. This is my obligation. However, how can a fact be known when one is made to be silent? The Bible gives an answer: "Even the one silent is proved to be wise." I felt alone in a world I did not make. Fear suppressed my anger in wanting to show and tell some people what they really are: thieves, manipulated by their own riches or hunger to have, seeking love, affection, and acceptance they never really did receive as youths or adults, and are left mentally disturbed. Admirers of outward appearances instead of being kind, fair and exercising justice. Their actions against my personal items and listening to my conversations were done with the hope of causing an off-balance of my emotions and mental capacity; to manipulate others into thinking that I am sick or forgetful. I was not about to let them win; this was a war of the spiritual kind, and I, its soldier. I was innocent of evil and had no idea of the devil's associated plans for me.

Nevertheless, as always, this was a new year, and I looked forward to it with all the changes it would bring. What I did not expect was the revelation of so many who had lost their sense of self. Mentally manipulated, partly due to a lack of spiritual strength and the ability to think beyond present circumstances in having patience toward others in a constructive way, which would produce positive results, they lacked. In the end, by hurting others, they hurt themselves. In what way? Depends on the action; caught they are put behind bars. Love, as much as it is a hurting emotion, does not hurt the other by hurtful words or actions—that pushes beyond the other's mental state. When that is done, you truly hurt yourself because their reaction may hurt you. My patience is not in any way being stupid. As is often repeated, "Patience is a virtue." This is so true. In having patience, one can see how easily a manipulated situation can become out of control. Doing so by one individual can affect another and soon into actions that benefit the rich's wicked intentions. I use the word rich not in financial wealth but in people's knowledge. It is time that the poor and the weak take back their self-esteem, and I am not about to sit ideally around without actions of my own. One is getting this book in the hands of suffers. I am aware of the Devil's designs and trained by the best—my teacher, not of this world, that most neglected in time. For me, time has always been my greatest reward of souls.

§

On a day in January, I was about to discover that all things happen for a reason. A headache for over two weeks caused a visit to my family doctor much sooner than I had planned. Living with a condition that seemed strange to some because of their lack of knowledge or experience of spiritual matters, it can be concluded that I was talented in handling my circumstances and others but still required assistance.

For Gelid Communication, I needed a letter regarding "insomnia," which was to advise my supervisor at the time of my inability to start my shift earlier than the time agreed on when I started the job. On this day, I would discover one of evil's designs to discredit my mental stability. This day, I would also discover that appearances do not always tell the truth. While I sat waiting for my name to call in a self-contained office on the ground floor of a high-rise building located at the corner of Danforth and Main streets, surrounded by offices and shops below. My thoughts wandered to the unfairness, insight lacks on the part of men who make the laws, and unto a quote from the Bible, which states, "For my thoughts *are* not your thoughts, neither *are* your way my ways, saith the LORD. For *as* the heavens are higher than the earth, so are my ways higher than your ways and my thoughts than your thoughts, saith the LORD." -Isiah. 55:8-9. On contemplating the words and how unfair life is, due to my condition that only a few understand, I recall the well-known author Sylvia Brown seen on the Montel Williams talk show where some understanding of mine came. I wonders about whom or where I can get the help I need. Sylvia Brown is a psychic and a firm believer in the spiritual realm. Although she is a great author, I disagree with some things she has said, such as being able to communicate with the dead.

To relate a few examples, two experiences occurred in my homeland. My sister Veronica and I were going to a friend's house one evening when suddenly we heard what sounded like a tin can thrown our way. The area was dark; we both looked back to see no one. We knew someone had to have thrown the tin can, but who remains the question. I did not know how my sister felt. On the other hand, I was not afraid, as I knew my sister was with me (her thoughts were probably the same); we kept on our way to the friend's house. This is another incident that played around in my memory, trying to recall if we did get to the friends' home, and I cannot recall—my memory is stuck in that time and that space.

The other experience refers to a call in the night. I was asleep with my mother and my sister Veronica in another room. Suddenly, a voice clearly heard, as if the person were in the house, called, "Veronica, Veronica!" My mother, sister, and I all got out of bed and met at the doorway simultaneously. The house still dark as no one thought of turning on the lights. As our eyes adjusted to the dark and each other, we looked around to see the other person whose voice we all heard, but no one other than us was standing. I recall we all went back to bed only to find out the next day that my sister's girlfriend had committed suicide from an overdose of morphine while on a boat over problems she was having with her boyfriend. Some may conclude her spirit came before she passed, words I am sure some of you may recall said by your grandparents or parents, while others would say it was a wicked angel's voice disguised as her. The fact is, we live in a world ruled by the spiritual realm, and the angels can disguise themselves as good and bad in our lives.

The point of this story is to recognize the reality of what I am about to say. As humans, we are made up of forty-two elements of this ground we live on. Medical history shows that at death, some of our vital organs remain alive for a few seconds after the heart stops. Depending on the person's mental state, their life force or spirit, within that window of time, can travel to a loved one or an individual in mind. Such as our thoughts do as we are living, revealing a situation—thus the saying, your spirit walked before you—some of you might recall hearing your grandparent or mother have repeated. This is because before the person arrives, their voice or a knock at the door is heard. The ability of some dogs to sense the arrival of strangers way ahead of their arrival. Now, this simple but powerful truth is manipulated by Satan into having people believe that the dead can communicate with the living, which is a lie that millions have come to believe. And that lie is further confirmed by psychics people confer to hearing what messages their dead ones must tell or how they are doing. Truth is, some of us are born with an ability like no others—we can tell a stranger some things about themselves; with this knowledge and manipulated guidance, psychics can and will mislead vulnerable minds. The Bible teaches that the dead are conscious of nothing... therefore, all our hands find to do, do with our sheer power. -Ecclesiastes 9:5, 6, 10. And here is where the ruler of this system has manipulated the thoughts of many. Another is man's invented technology in homes, capable of sending voice speech that confuses individuals into thinking they are receiving messages from God or a ghost.

A knock was heard at the door. It was Dr. Noah requesting entry. "Come on in!"

He looked at me as he asked, "What brings you here today?"

I give a brief explanation for my visit. Dr. Noah began to flip through my medical file to locate a letter from the psychologist he had recommended. The date and name on the letter seen were brought to his attention. He insisted that I had seen a psychiatrist prior to his recommendation. I was puzzled. I recalled being hesitant to go to a psychiatrist, thinking how this might affect my job search. Unable to locate the letter from the psychiatrist he recommended, he again began to flip through the file. He would wet his thumb and middle finger with saliva as he flipped page after page. I sat silent as the only sound heard was flipping pages from my file; his hands blotched with little brown spots since I last saw him. A bit older, his facial features remained the same, still having a full head of hair now turning whiter as the years went on, thick eyelashes on a full round face. He is tall with a pale complexion. As I observed him, a feeling of empathy came over me. He was still very polite and listened to my explanation of my facts. His disposition puzzled me. He seemed to want me out of the office as soon as possible. My feelings were confirmed by his rejection to see me later that day for a yearly physical. The letter was soon discovered by Dr. John. I recalled who he was, an Indian fellow of average height, a bit on the stout side, without a distinctive accent.

"Here!" he said as he handed me the letter. "All you need to do is give the company a copy. It is difficult for me to write on behalf of your condition. You could be up for more than forty-eight hours and not be affected mentally, and then you might; it's difficult to say."

His statement was a fact. Although asleep, I was still mentally awake throughout the night because with the state of insomnia, known as astral travel, so named for a person who is in one place or another, and conscious during sleep, on awaking, can tell where and what I had done. He then wrote out a form for an x-ray of my head and told me he would call if there was a problem. No follow-up call came, concluding all was safe. After leaving the office where I had the x-ray done, I recalled the day in question—the day I was recommended to the psychiatrist by Dr. Noah. After my visit, on my way out of the office I stopped at the reception desk to pick up the letter. A letter of recommendation was told to the psychiatrist.

His secretary—a blonde-haired nurse about 5'3" with a petite build and attractive features, said to me, "When you get to the doctor, give him this." I was handed an envelope with the doctor's name, address, phone number, date, and appointment time written on the front. Curious to see what was in the envelope, as it seemed awfully heavy just for a letter of recommendation, but it was never opened. As it was received, it was so given. The nurse was not only working for Dr. Noah but also seemed to be working for the quack who gave her a letter from some psychiatrist I had only a brief encounter with. This was just the beginning of the many clever designs that evil would play in my life to discredit my integrity.

Times had certainly changed. Everywhere you turn, lies are being told as the truth, accepted by some in authority, whose laziness to investigate matters leaves society believing that the only way to accomplish what you need is to lie. And, in some cases, be your own judge and executioner. And, in a bizarre paradoxical way, very insightful. For if one listens to their conscience, it would either accuses them of wrong that pushes their intellect to react in kind or excuses them from guilt from the actions of others. My personal circumstances were difficult, and my dreams confused me even more. It even became so that, at times, listening to the radio caused mental confusion. Situations around me affected my thoughts, as did messages from around the unit mentally entertained me. However, I was not about to let the Devil's workers win. It is written, "For the ear, trieth words, as the mouth tasteth meat." - Job 34:3. This scripture needs to be incredibly careful not to adhere to in wakefulness. The spirit realm and some humans capable of mental manipulation will lead anyone astray following the things heard during sleep. Some talk about following our dreams, and I must warn you that a dream towards one's inner mind goal set is different from a dream at night. Unknowingly guided by the wiser, vulnerable ones fall trapped to mental manipulation that will see them with a windfall or harm themselves by actions they took towards another, with the claim they were told by God. A reminder, God speaks to us through His word—the Bible, and we are awarded good gifts from him as he sees our needs.

A story related references my point. It was about a day or two before the occurrence of this incident. During the night, I heard a voice whisper, "You see what they are doing with my body!" When I woke in the morning, the words lingered on my mind all day. I was at my desk in the office when the news was given to me that Michael Jackson had died. I recall, and I do not know if my subconscious memory of the words I had heard, or some force caused me to echo that he was just asleep. I left work that day with a dreadful feeling and guilt for not working with my intuition before his death to call his family and ask to see him, but I felt they and those that take care of his affairs would deny me access to him, after all who am I, to their thinking another freak. But Michael's situation was like mine. And so, I put off the feeling to act on my intuition. We are living in a world being given spiritual experiences. We need to become awake to our surroundings, people, and family members we associate with and learn to listen more than we speak, for some dreams and images will lead to our personal growth.

Curiosity was the motive of many who touched my life. They wanted the truth, and even though I stood faithful to words heard and of past actions I took, this was not enough for the curious minds. I was not all knowledgeable when it came to spiritual matters, but I was aware of all I had heard and read, and I faithfully believed in a higher power and man's inherent nature to destroy and challenge each other. In my quest for justice, this is all the ammunition I need to stand firm.

A visit to my sister's home did not go very well. An argument developed over my determination to reveal what I had dreamt. She was at the time living on Benfrisco Dr in Scarborough. We were both angry at each other, so when Monica yelled, "I could hit you." In anger, I picked up a figurine from the ledge by the exit door I stood next to. I had not long passed Kienna standing in her crib and did not want to scare her by backing away into the hallway. This was the first time that I had felt such resentment and anger in not being able to express myself, having tried so many times in the past to do. Making them aware of the things that were diplomatically happening to me affected them too. Therefore, in fierce anger, I yelled, "Don't you dare hit me!" With that said, the figurine in my hands shattered to pieces. "Get out, get out of here!" Monica yelled. I left, walked to the side of the house, picked up a bottle and threw it at the house, and in an undertone, said, "You'll be sorry!" I left in tears that afternoon, all alone in a world I did not make.

I loves my family, even with all their little irritating faults, realizing not all families are perfect. It hurts me to think I have lost them like so many friends along the way. When asked about my family, most times, my comment will be with a smile. "I've lost them to society." I have since then forgiven my sister for her lack of understanding, knowing the force I was dealing with. A force so powerful that genuine anger and hurt; could have caused us to hurt each other.

§

I hurried to tidy up my desk before leaving work, knowing that Rudolf would be waiting for me. Before I reached home that evening, he had called numerous times to find out where I was. I arrived home at about 12:45 A.M. Just as I walked through the door, the phone rang again.

"Where you at?" he asked.

"I just this minute walked through the door."

"Okay, I'll be right there."

In about five minutes, he was at my door. "You got here really quick."

"I was over at Rudy's place."

Rudy is his friend who lived across and down the street from me. He is a tall, skinny fair-skinned Italian man in his forties. One day he had called numerous times for Rudolf, so much so that I just allowed the phone to ring without answering, and that is when he left a threatening message: "Tell Rudolf if he does not pay me back the money he borrowed, I am going to chop him to pieces, and no one will know where he is." When Rudolf was told about the message, he could care less, but I knew he was hiding from someone when he told me he could not be seen downtown. His attitude had made me laugh out loud before ending our conversation.

"Rudolf, if you keep contact with that man who likes yourself or is even worse, how do you expect to quit smoking that poison?"

"He has his ways, but he's a good man."

"In what way?" Disgusted I sucked my teeth. "He walks the street cussing at the top of his lungs like an insane person."

"Maybe he is!"

I turned from what I was doing to look at him. "And that's the type of person you want to constantly associate with."

"We assist each other in times of need."

"Oh, yeah, I can see that... the con and wiser con. I don't know who is fooling who." I had to laugh.

"You are so sweet when you laugh. You make me get hot right away."

"Sex, it's always on your mind. There's more to a relationship, you know."

"I know, but I always tell you how I feel." He began to roll a joint.

I continued to prepare something to eat and would glance at him ever so often. Looking at him, I see a man trying to keep his head above water and from drowning. It is written that if errors were what God counted, who of us could stand? He has made many, and it is safe to say that his maker was certainly not counting, as time and time again, he has been given chances to make a better life for himself. Perhaps he is lost, or perhaps he has given up on trying. It is difficult to go past some people's perceptions of you, especially if you have done wrong in the past. And this is true concerning one's nationality. He was also in a situation that drained him emotionally as it did mentally. His child's mother read the cards and always seems to know more about him and his activities than he did himself. Therefore, in some ways, he depended on her guidance. She is a tarot reader; how good I do not know.

I know this much: the tarot is a collection of seventy-eight images representing ancient and universal archetypes. The Major Arcane cards are the twenty-two trump cards of the tarot, representing archetypal qualities of human experiences. The numerical order of the cards is also significant in showing the path of spiritual development and personal growth. The collection is arranged in the form of a pack of cards used to gain insights into psychology and metaphysics and foretell the future. To get a reading, a person selects five cards from the deck, and as the reader flips each one, he/ or she can tell things of the future to be expected. The problem lies with the reader one has, as each card gives a few transformations. Therefore, the reader needs knowledge of Karmic Astrology. The understanding of Retrogrades appearing in Houses focuses on the process of an individual experience of that which the House represents. Interviewing the person to find out certain things about their life helps to give a true reading—as anyone who has studied the cards can give a reading.

However, he failed to realize that as circumstances changes, so must our reactions, and even the cards cannot stop the occurrence of circumstances. For who is there knowing the spirit of humankind? I saw the game she played, and Lilly, his child's mother, knew I saw her for what she was, an ambitious and creative individual who would not think twice about taking a bribe from the very bosoms to get her way. It can be said that she saw me as a threat because when one is doing wrong, they do not like their wrongs to be revealed. He lived in the paranoia of her, and the smoking of marijuana and cocaine left him fragile and unable to hold on to reality for any length of time; this resulted in his homeless state, being from one home to the next.

"Would you care to have something to eat?" I asked as I looked at him.

"Nah, I'm good," he responded as he lit the joint.

I smiled. "You look like Popeye, the sailor man, who is always seen with a pipe in his mouth. So, what is it you wanted to talk about?"

"This is embarrassing, but I'll come right out and ask you if I can stay for a few days."

I did not mind him staying, but his smoking was in the way. Knowing what I must deal with at work, I do not like to smoke or even smell it during the week. His being with me is what I will have to endure because no matter how often he is asked not to smoke in the apartment, he ends up doing it, causing words to be said that we both regret. "A few days, you say. How long is that?"

"Until Thursday."

"Today is Tuesday. Rudolf, please don't make me have to get angry with you on Thursday to leave."

He took a draw from the lit joint. His eyes had a wild look as he inhaled, then slowly let the smoke out through his mouth, causing a clouded design. He spoke, "No, Thursday it is."

I never liked him when he looked the way I had just observed. He looked like a person in desperation. As much as I wanted to help him, I knew that his actions would implicate me to some degree, and I would have to battle with him at his game.

He stretched out his hand to me with the joint. "Here, have a smoke."

"Rudolf, I don't like to smoke during the work week."

"Oh, yes, I forgot. Sorry."

"Look, it's late. I'm going to get ready for bed, and please be ready to turn in when I do, as I must work tomorrow—today, that is," I corrected myself.

I left him sitting on the porch with his thoughts. The next few days were incredibly stressful, as I had an idea of Rudolf's activities. I would leave him asleep when leaving for work and return to find him still lying around. Rudolf was in and out of my life, and his actions were the same each time he returned. This annoyed me, as I felt like his whore, someone he came to when he needed money, food, sex, and a place to sleep. As much as I was willing to help him, I knew I was battling a lost cause. I had cried myself to sleep many nights over my own situation and his, too. I saw a need in him that wanted to assist me, but he could not, not even for himself. He had not a job, he had too much of a callous attitude, and certainly not with him being an addict. Every dime he made from what little he sold went right back to repurchasing more cocaine until the little amount of money remaining was picked up by his child's mother, who read the cards, knowing he had some money in his possession. Then he will ask for a few more days to recuperate his physical strength and money. I was tired of his excuses. So, on Thursday, I insisted he leave when he asked for a few more days. It did hurt to have to insist he does, but at times, you must be cruel to be kind—so the saying goes. And some who have found themselves in such situations can honestly say it is a saying that is true.

My life was, and is not all, peaches, and cream; I worked extremely hard alongside my mother before and after she died with my sister Veronica. Veronica is the fourth of seven children, and I was corrected by her that it was eight of us, of which I agreed to disagree. In my quest for the truth, Monica did confirm my childhood memory of a death scene. A memory that has remained to this day lost in time and space as to what had happened after the sight of my sister lying lifeless. Edna did give birth to one I witness in an aluminum basin lying on its side. When I got into the room where two adults were having a conversation stopped upon sight of my entry. The child, still a baby in my eyes, would have been close to a year old from the size, and this would be Paulene, the child who died while in the care of Monica, who slipped out of the sink while being given a bath. Confirmed by Monica was the last she knew. Monica got married in 1960—confirmed by her husband, which would put me between the age of three and going on four. The photograph seen of me at Monica's wedding showed Paulene absent. Both growing as twins, to this day, she is missed as my close and confidential playmate. After her death, I am now in the position of the last of the family. I later in life exhibited what the last child developed from the fall. I suffered from tummy aches and inflammation. To ease the pain, my mother mixed an ointment with rice placed in a cloth. She tied it like a pouch, the tip soaked in oil and placed on the navel of my tummy, the end of the pouch is set a fire and then covered with glass; when extinguished, the glass is pulled away from my tummy, like suction it magically pulled the pain away and I will get some relief. In brief, I lived a rich but challenging life. I was a maid by choice, never a slave; we lived poor but were never lost; I was a mother, I sacrificed; I am a princess, called by a higher power.

Chapter 6

SAYING GOODBYES ARE NEVER EASY

I CAME HOME from work to a strong scent of flowers. The scent was that of a funeral home. Immediately I knew someone was going to die or become ill. I could smell danger, or in this case, death, before it happens. At the time, I thought the water in the vase probably needed changing, so it was emptied and refilled with fresh water. Two days after, the scent was still in the home. My apartment often had a light scent of flowers as every two to three weeks as funds afford it, the vase will be refilled with freshly cut ones, but this was a sign; the scent was powerful.

It was September 8, 2003. The phone started to ring. I never expected to hear that it was news of Mr. Grant's death—a close friend of the family, though I knew he was sick in the hospital. The morning before the news of my mother's death, the household had woken up to a strong scent of flowers, and Monica even had said, "Something is wrong with Mommy." That afternoon, on November 19, 1971, I was picked up from school to be given the news of my mother's death. She lived a day past her birth on November 18, 1924. As I got into the car, I passed out but could hear my sisters' voices, one saying to the other we must get to the pharmacy. Later I came to consciousness from an inhale of smelling salts (a liquid that brings a person to consciousness purchased from the pharmacy). Since then, every time I get a powerful scent of some kind, I know something is about to happen to someone I have a close connection with, or I need to be cautious around people. With each experience, I am now able to distinguish the scent of each; flowers indicate a peaceful death or meeting, a scent that is rank— murder, a funky or unpleasant scent—confusion or betrayal.

"Hello!" "It's me, Monica; I called to tell you Mr. Grant passed away last night."

"I knew something was going to happen. For days, I smelled a strong odour of flowers."

We did not talk awfully long as I was getting ready for work. In a spiritual satire, this was a year I felt an overwhelming inner peace. For the first time, I experience the awe of nature before my eyes, a wonderful display of a lightning storm I had never witnessed with the naked eyes, only saw on television. The parking lot cleared of shoppers and most employees' cars, except for a few here and there; I walked through from my place of employment to get to the train station. With each flash of lightning that lit up parts of the night sky, I peered into the sky as if about to go through a tunnel. Still, before being able to observe much ahead, darkness fills the view as the light disappears, leaving me in total darkness and anticipation of another spark to get another view of what lies ahead. Like a thief with seconds to spear, I peered deeper into the clouds with each flash of lightning, but the light was soon gone, leaving me in darkness. I laughed out loud; tears of joy filled my eyes at the beauty above. The display was so breathtaking I had to tell someone about what I was witnessing, at least some of it. I took out the phone from my backpack and called Leila.

"Hello!" She answers

"Hi, Leila. Are you looking at the lightning storm?"

"No, sa'. I'm scared. My curtains are drawn."

"Oh, Leila, you don't know what you are missing. It is beautiful. It is the first time, other than on T.V. shown someone else's view I am witnessing such beauty with my very own eyes. You really should look."

So, overwhelm I am sure Leila could hear my joy as I vividly described the scene. "It's okay. You get home safe."

I laughed. "I tell you, it's the slowest I've ever walked. I cannot take my eyes off the sky. I'll talk to you later, but I'm telling you, you should look. Bye."

Leila is an elderly Jamaican woman I have known for over fourteen years and the only one from the Kingdom Hall who has stuck with me throughout my trials and temptations—truly a friend. She is about 5'3" tall, has short hair, and has a thin build.

During the summer of the same year, 1997, Monica decided to visit Kathleen, my older sister. That same month she left, I visited the zoo, as I do yearly. It was a sunny Sunday afternoon. The skies cleared of any hint of falling rain, and the day itself was mild, with no overpowering heat. I got myself together, packed a few things, and left for the zoo. I took the bus to the train station, hopped on a connecting one to Kennedy Station and a bus from there to the (Scarborough) Toronto Zoo. The Toronto Zoo is known to be the largest zoo in the world, with 287 hectares of land with over ten kilometres of walking trails; it houses approximately five thousand animals and over four hundred and sixty species of animals.

A little after two o'clock in the afternoon, I walked through the gate into the zoo. A Mexican band greeted the visitors as they entered. Although I loved Spanish music, I only stood to listen to the band for a short period, then walked around to the stalls where a few women entrepreneurs sold jewelry. After a quick look around, I walked off with the decision to start at the camel's quarters and work my way around. After visiting the camels, as I started to walk, suddenly, from the sunny sky mist of rain began to fall. I took the umbrella from my bag and, as I stood to open it, while looking at another set of animals, one that stood outside of the gate from the others. In a blink of an eye, the animal raised its head, looked around, and walked back to where the others were. It stood by the entrance, and the others came through onto the open field one by one. The one that stood at the entrance then followed, and as they walked, its head turned towards me. I swear as there is a God above, the animal was looking right at me. (Perhaps, who knows I do have a connection with the animals, as said in my complaint to the building management of Lawrence Mall on the sight of the washrooms and unable to find sanitary napkins on all the floors searched.) I watched and marvelled at its action, then suddenly, it began to copiously rain, followed by thunder, and lightning. An almost silent afternoon became noisy as families and others screamed with laughter running for cover. I walked and stood under a tree with an umbrella too weak to withstand the force of the rain. In a matter of seconds before my eyes, the walkway had become a stream, and just as it began, it ended— fifteen minutes later. Excited over what I had witnessed, I called Leila and told her of my experience.

§

PHOTOGRAPHS, reminders to others of the things done in our past, which reminders can soon be destroyed by earth's elements; with the lens of our eyes, things seen that are told are our memories forever. Past down to generations after generations. Yes, I have many photographs—memories of things blessed to have witnessed.

§

Finally, the day of the funeral had arrived. I got up incredibly early, unable to sleep. The funeral was at nine in the morning. I looked through the window and up to the sky. The sun can be seen trying to shine through slightly dark clouds, warning that a storm was happening elsewhere. The atmosphere smelled fresh from the showers during the night. I stood at the window with inner peace when I heard the phone ringing.

"Hello!" "Paula, it's me, Monica. I am calling to tell you that the funeral is at nine, not ten. It's going to be crowded."

"Monica, I said that I'll be there."

"Okay. Then I'll see you at Kennedy train station." We hung up.

I spoke out loud, "They are always so excited and think people are forgetful." I repeated my sister's words: "It's nine, not ten o'clock." She must think I am a typical West Indian; always late." Completely dressed, I took one last look around the apartment to see that it was left in order; I glanced at the mirror and was pleased. I closed the door behind me and left for the funeral. I arrived at the train station and awaited my family's arrival. Everyone was greeted as I got into the van. On the way to the church, Val stopped to buy water and a gum pack. Valerie—the last of three children, was about to find out it pays to listen to one having experience. She offered me a stick of gum, but as she was about to open it, I told her thanks, but no thanks. Val insisted it was okay, as it would not stick to my partials (known for only having a few teeth on the plate dentures). Having had experience before I found a gum that would not stick, warned her that any other than Wriggles chewing gum sticks to the denture. Some dentures are made of metal. Hers were not.

A few minutes after chewing it, she, being warned, confirms, "Girl, you were right. It does stick!"

"I told you it would, but oh, no, you would not listen." Valerie no longer laughs at me, teasing me about getting old; that is why I am losing my teeth. Having had to remove two of her own, she now knows, as she has made to understand, to judge without knowledge or facts is to conclude one as being ignorant. I had to remove two of my teeth, the ones side by the side of the central incisor known as the canine. The incidents leading up to removal occurred in a few dreams.

Often said, a woman's scorn is your worse bite, is a truthful statement. One night Rudolf had slept out, and that evening in a dream, I overheard a woman's voice as she told another, "Let her come over here and let me have her taste my—buttercup," to be respectful. I never related the dream to Rudolf but constantly tried to warn him that some people don't like me, hoping that he would be faithful as I was with him. The other occurred when I saw my reflection in the mirror one night during a dream. As the reflection in the mirror smiled, the canine teeth of the image in the mirror were missing. I would later have to remove exactly what I had seen in the mirror as a visit to my dentist revealed that I had gum disease. The dream was never related to my dentist; I kept this to myself as I have many others.

§

LEGEND has it that dreaming about tooth loss points to a loss of energy and sometimes even impotence. Ancient Egyptian dream researchers believed dreaming about teeth falling out indicated bad luck for the dreamer or that a family member could die. Mirrors in a dream are rare when they do appear; their meaning is usually serious. In Egypt, people believed it stood for death or an accident because the image in the mirror was outside the person, and the person's soul had slipped into the mirror image. Modern interpretation sees it as the person's real self that is being recaptured. Like touching up a photograph, we often try to improve our image. 10,000 Dreams Explained states that dreams' mirror suggests self-realization, reflecting spiritual wisdom. Looking in a mirror can mean we have concerns over past behaviour. In addition, dreaming of a mirror suggests concern over our self-image.

§

We arrived at the church on time. As we walked up to the church, I was admiring my sister as she looked beautiful, which is not very often, as she is mostly a home person not constantly seen dressed up. "Girl, you are looking good. Mr. Patoir better be careful; you may walk out of here without him." They started to laugh. I must say I was good at putting a smile on their faces whenever I visited them. The church bells rang softly as we entered. People were going up the stairs, so we followed. The room, not large, already had many seats occupied. As you walked into the room, a bit off to the side were mostly old photographs of Mr. Grant, his birth date and length of time on earth. The casket was at the front of the room. Leon—my sister's husband, and brother-in-law, Valerie, Kienna, and myself walked up to view him. His complexion was darker than the way I remembered him. Val left to take a seat with Monica after a quick view.

"He looks different, Grandpa," said Kienna.

"He does, and that's because he's dead," I respond with a smile as Kienna looked up at me with a chuckle and a smile on her face. Leon looked him over from head to toe, and to be sure he was no mannequin disguised as a human, he pinched his hand. A wise decision, as some people were known to be buried alive. If you have not read the Serpent and the Rainbow, written by ethnobotanist and researcher Wade Davis, reading it would have you educate family members to be sure you are dead before burial. Satisfied he was not a mannequin, he requested that they take their seats. As we sat waiting for the program to begin, someone announced that the room was for the viewing of the dead, and the funeral would be taking place downstairs. All got up and moved to the main floor.

I stood looking at the photographs as the room cleared and pondered on man's existence with the thought. *We are here for a moment, yet it seems forever. Forever searching for love and happiness, peace, and contentment. Making the best of each situation that comes our way, fighting to have and to hold, only to realize at death, fulfillment is rest; rest from the wars among ourselves and the hassle that comes from the need to satisfy. If only we had learnt to love and understand ourselves, we would have been able to win the battle of the evil force's intent to destroy.* He was the only man other than my father seen with my mother. Some people get lonely, and my mother did, and she could not be blamed for finding comfort in someone else's arms when my father would be away for months.

§

Reginald is my father's name; tall, and slender build, with handsome features, and a sailor by occupation. He was often away from home. He was born on February 2, 1908, and married on December 27, 1941. Having a quiet disposition, I only ever heard my father yell once and never was I going to put myself in the position I had to hear him yell again.

This is what happen… It is funny now that I reflected on that day. It was a sunny day, and Mom needed some money, so she asked me to go to Dad to get it. He was staying at my aunt's place. I got to the house that was on Station Street. He was in his hammock as usual. I would assume peacefully resting when I approached him. "Dad…" I called. He opened his eyes.

"Hello, sweetheart, what's wrong?" he asked.

"Mom sent me over to ask you to send some money for her."

My father's quiet, gentle voice made me jump. "Get the hell out of here!"

With that, I turned and hurried down the street, never looking back, just wanting to get home as quick as my feet would move me. I finally reached home; it was about a good twenty to thirty minutes' walk, and I wondered who that man was. One minute he was the dad I knew, and the next, I could not tell. "Mom…" I called out for her. "Never again do you send me to Dad for money?"

"What happened?"

"He yelled at me. I swear the whole street heard him."

"I'm sorry, dear, come here." She puts her arms around me, giving me a hug and letting me know once more that she was sorry and it would not happen again. In addition, true to her words, she was.

As I reflect on when he died, I recall Mom and me sitting at the window one night, looking out at the star-filled night sky, the cool temperature on our faces, and enjoying the peaceful bliss of life. "Look!" exclaimed Mom, with her hand pointing up at the sky. My eyes followed the direction of her hand and, to my surprise, saw someone on a broomstick. Now, we were used to hearing stories of witches, and if what I saw, I am witness to the fact they did exist. There is a command that says we should not swear by heaven or earth—Mathew 5:34-37. This is due to memory loss that one may not be able to testify to a past incident. So that scripture says to let our yes be yes, and no be no. Therefore, by God's temple, I swear!

§

I walked down the stairs into the room, now filled as most visitors and friends took their seats. Time was given for all to get seated. Seated at the front, to the left, were those who would give their last thoughts and the eulogy. To the left of them in the first row sat his widow and her sons, and to their right, a few rows back, sat me and my family. Some who could not get seats stood at the back against the wall. I sat next to my brother-in-law, who did look stunning. At some point, he had removed without my notice. A few minutes after, the music began. Two by two members of the Guyana Police Force—friends of his, marched in and took their seats. With every hymn that played, I sang out joyfully until one woman in front of me bellowed in sorrowful sounds, "No, no, my sister, no." forced me to sit down, collapsed in tears from the woman's words. My body trembled as I cried with thoughts of saying, What the fish-sticks are you crying and shouting for? In your confused state, was it not that you accused me, saying, "I'm pretty sure she encouraged him?" You judged me, and you were not even there. Because of that, the "gods" dealt with him as they will now deal with you. I, (Marlene Paula, Bernadette, Lustol), have no reason to lie. Further, to those who think I am not all there, let me say this to you bunch of ungrateful, deceptive, money-hungry takers who believe they are better than others are; I walked in every-one's shoes to understand, to conclude, to judge. You pass judgment on me, that which you see and yet have no knowledge. That is why you pass judgment on yourselves. Unable to stand up, I kept seated, possessed by some unknown force; no one dared intervene to console me as I was burdened by grief. And you, my eyes raised towards the direction of a woman friend of his, a fair-skinned woman. You broke my heart and tried to destroy my confidence in my hope, which was spoken. To think that you had my best interest in mind, only to have your sons and daughters keep taking it without appreciation for where their help came from. Yes, I shouted within my mind. To write, to act, to manipulate those lives I cared for, and to stand there with tears in your eyes, what for? I answered my own thoughtful question. No, do not tell me, it is tears of joy to think you won, but it is tears of joy I laugh this day, to know that all that was done and concluded of me, I won the battle against the "gods" because they have made fools of you all.

The casket, now held by six members of the Guyana Police Force, slowly walked out of the church. The widow on the top of her voice shouted, "Oh, no, no," with tears as she walked behind the group. Turning to face my sister, I smiled, tears still flowing from my eyes. She walked out of the church; the program ended. Many stood outside the church as they greeted those they had not seen for some time.

Three things bring people together: a wedding, a funeral, and major disasters. Leon and Monica left with a few others to the funeral home, where he would be cremated. Leon pressed the switch that took the casket into and through the furnace, told by Monica.

§

Shelda, Monica's firstborn, who could not stay due to her having to attend classes, drove me, Valerie, and her daughter to the reception held in a spacious basement of a building. On coming to Canada after completing high school, she went straight into medical school, graduated, and worked as a nurse; now retired. All her life, she has been the responsible one in her family. If Monica can always count on one of her children, it would be Shelda. A bit eccentric at times, I at times have to shake my head and let words pass my hearing. However, there are moments she causes me to rethink my actions.

The basement accommodated everyone who was there with a view of those entering and leaving. As you enter, straight ahead to the very back, tables lined across the room with prepared food, most of the Caribbean. To the left, a few tables were for the family of the dead. To the right were the bar and the restrooms. I walked in to see that quite a few were already there. Some hugging as they greeted each other. I was about to cross the room with my niece and great-niece to be seated, when I heard my name called and wondered who it could be. When I looked in the direction of the voice, I could not recall the face. "You and Kienna go ahead; I'll join you later."

As I walked towards her, the woman's face became familiar, but I still could not recall where I had met her. "I know, I know you, but I cannot recall where from."

"I'm Li. We met at Sears Photography Studio. You had taken pictures of my son."

"Oh, yes, I do recall." A feeling of embarrassment overcame me, and I could not quite understand why. However, I braved the feelings with a pleasant smile. "Yes, I recall now. It is nice to see you. How come you are here?" I asked, surprised.

"I came with a relative of mine who knew Mr. Grant."

"I see," her appearance now made sense. Wanting the meeting to be over as fast as it had begun, as I was not in the mood to explain my past to this point.

After Li informed me of her son and his present activities and her knowing Clifford, we exchanged numbers and arranged to call each other very soon. I excuse myself and join my family. I felt helpless, overpowered by the things heard, and like a stranger among people I knew. It had been so long since most of them were seen. As I walked to where Val was seen seated with Car-Myra, I contemplated on feelings earlier during meet Li. Perhaps it was the foreknowledge of her being acquainted with Clifford that brought about the feeling experienced, or could it be my conscious accusing me of the past?

I arrived at the table, greeted Car-Myra, and took my seat. Car-Myra is a Jamaican woman about 5'2" tall, with short hair and a brown complexion; she is soft-spoken and has a drag to her speech. I looked passed her to a dark slim fella. His face, so small reminded me of a cartoon character; I smiled broadly as I greeted him. He returned the greeting with a welcoming smile. A conversation began; the topic was food. As the conversation continued, I appeared to be listening, disguised as I was in thoughts of my own. I looked at my niece with full facial features and wondered what had become of the beautiful child I once knew. As time and unforeseen circumstances change our reactions, so does our appearance. I glanced at my great-niece, who was looking at me and felt hurt as a memory flashed back to a past incident with Val and my conversation with Kienna.

"Auntie, do you think I'm crazy? Mom said only crazy people sit and cry."

"No, sweetheart. It just means you are a very emotional person, like me. There are times when I will be looking at a movie, something on T.V. or having a memory flashback that affects me emotionally, and I would start to cry or burst out into laughter. Naturally, some of us have emotions that are stronger than others."

My memory of our walks remind me that counting on tomorrow is never assured as I educate her on appreciating the simple things in life. When she smiled at me, it took away the hurt I felt inside with a touch of joy, and within, I prayed that she would grow up emotionally strong, believing in herself and her abilities. Still, in my thoughts, Val interrupts with encouragement to get up and get something to eat before it was all gone, so eventually, I left the table.

A dark, good-looking man approached the woman standing ahead of me standing in line. He is seen as a flirt and one who could be encouraged. When the conversation switched to him not getting enough sleep, I joined in, as I am now knowledgeable on sleep disorders. And did so by drawing attention to the physical evidence on my lip from lack of sleep caused by running into a car. He then started a conversation about drinks, and his description of one mixed with beer sounded so refreshing I wanted to have one. He insisted on getting me a glass, so as the line got closer to the buffet table, he slipped off to the bar. I rejoins my family members with a plate filled with what I wanted. Soon after being seated, a member of the Kingdom Hall I once attended showed up. I felt the presence of a friend... Sister Clapton. I recalled on many occasions we faced the world as we did house-to-house preaching and street witnessing. I enjoyed street witnessing; meeting people of different backgrounds and nationalities enriched my life spiritually.

A time recalled…One weekday at Donlands train station alone witnessing, a young black fair-skinned woman with a breaded hairdo walked up to me and asked, "'Do you know what faith is?" Taken back for a moment because not too many people stop to talk on their commute, and with so much to say as I had seen the spirit of God in my life. Before my response, she spoke: "'You are preaching, and you don't know what faith is; it's the assured expectation of things promise.'" And with that said, she walked away. She did not dampen my spirits; I just looked at her walked away into the train station. I found that scripture, like so many others, guided by my Heavenly Father. I also never forgot Hebrews 11: 1.

We talked for a short while, and then sister Clapton was gone, unaware at what point she had left after my sister and her husband arrived. The woman, who conducted the funeral program, then arrived and joined the table.

"You did a great job in arranging the funeral today. What caused you to choose such a career?" Monica asked.

"'When my dad died," she began. "I realize how important it was to have things organized. The work that needs to be done can be tiring, especially consumed by one's emotional state. From my experience, I wanted to make things easier for those who must go through the same situation…'"

As she continued with her explanations, my thoughts drifted off to the people one associates with during times of illness or mental distress. People have a lot to do with one's overall mental state and how well one can fight back to a state of good health. Miracles do happen. It happens from a love of self and others. The degree to which one is open and loving, is the degree to which miracles come to you. His belief in his ability to win was lacking. One's beliefs create one's reality. Our mind is the projection of our body. We can change the beliefs told to us and, thus, change what we experience. I kept looking at their faces before me; the joy of what a friend I have in Jesus allowed me to accept people's foolish talk and ignorant actions.

I recall... I was unable to stop thinking of my mother's funeral. On the morning of her death, the household woke up to a powerful scent of flowers. I was at mom's bedroom door when Monica was at the doorway of the room next to hers said, "Something has happened to Mommy." Little did I know later that day, I would be informed of my mother's death; years have passed, and although the pain of losing her still lingers, comfort is found in the memories shared. The distance between my sisters, who were once so close, made me harbour a bit of anger toward Veronica regarding her attitude. A very generous person, she causes one in receipt of her kindness, left with feelings of worthlessness. When she speaks, she causes those who do not know the truth, left with the impression that she is the only one who did all that was needed to help the family—no one else did anything to help, and the only one who has suffered. Sometimes I wonder if she believes in God's word, that there will be a resurrection of the dead—Revelation 20:5. Because the lies told will be revealed at some point. When the family responds, she feels they are talking bad about her, but it is only about her attitude. Hearing the truth is not something she takes with grace, as giving credit where it is due is not one of her selfless attributes. If only she knew the trouble I have gone through, but she will never know because as she was for me when Mom died, this is what I am for her now in silence. God judges us from the heart, and according to our deeds, rewards.

Valerie interrupts, making mention of how tasty one of the dishes is. "I have to go and get another plate before it is all gone." If it were an all-you-can-eat banquet, it would not be impolite to go for seconds to eat. However, I kept the comment to myself for fear of a confrontation I wanted no part of, especially in public displaying thoughtless words drawing attention to us. So, I smiled and called her name as I continued to complete my meal. Just then, the cute fella passed and, within a minute, came back with a drink in his hand.

"Is that the drink you were talking about?"

"No," he replied. "They hadn't one of the ingredients needed for the drink." He introduced himself.

As he kept talking, I wanted to interrupt to ask if he was married, but just then, a fella passing briefly stopped and mentioned something about his wife—my question was answered. After he walked off, still looking at him, "I wanted to ask you a question, but I just received the answer."

"What was that?" he asked.

I responded with a smile as I thought of how slow some men could be in their thinking. "Never mind; I got the answer."

"Now you have me thinking."

The conversation was going well, but I felt uneasy expressing myself the way I wanted to. Too many people were at the table. Just then, the cousin of the dead was going to sing a closing song, and the conversation switched to the ability to sing. Valerie interjected with laughter.

"Have you heard her sing? She can't sing."

Now she really hit a nerve. I looked at her with thoughts of saying. *You have never heard me sing and had the chance today, but because of the Indian woman's boisterous yelling that made you leave, you missed out on hearing something wonderful.* "Look, girl, I can sing; you haven't heard me."

"Ha, ha," she laughed. "Sure, Paula, you have to cover your ear when you start to sing..." she responded with laughter.

I looked at her as I continued with unexpressed thoughts. Instead, I suggested that perhaps we join the cousin who was about to sing. After the singing and some information about the work done by Guyana's Police Force organization here in Canada, the reception was called to an end.

Compton then told me that on meeting a nice person, such as myself, it is not a habit of his to leave without a number. I was hoping he would ask for my number, as I needed to get out and socialize. He seemed to be the perfect person to start with. He looked like the type who likes to party—which I later found out to be so. However, as much as I needed the association, my life was complicated, not a road I wanted to take another. At this point, one person in my life is all I want to focus on. Despite being single, I was not the type to play around; relationships were always given much time. I love meeting people; it is my philosophy that contact with others, regardless of whom or where they are from, brings greater knowledge of awareness and enrichment to one's life and the world we live in. Something my sister did not seem to agree with, as when she was introduced to Compton, Monica just flashed her hand in a gesture that said, "Ha, get away from me." I felt confused about my sister's discourteous act and a bit embarrassed. *What could I say at this moment to get over this feeling of embarrassment? If only there was a hole that I could drop out of sight? I have to say something real fast.* I blurted out after thoughts; "My brother-in-law loves beer; I'll give him the recipe." It was all I could think of saying. Numbers were exchanged and a few minutes later, he left. It was time for me to do the same.

As I got up to walk over to Mrs. Grant, now a widow, I saw a grief-stricken woman who seemed to have suffered much during the months of his illness—a corpus body was her appearance. I walked towards her *with thoughts* of how can I console someone whose beliefs were so different from mine? How do I say or begin to show her that life experiences one day connects us to places, people, and situations, where the other had been before? How do I tell her that her old man had put his hand into my buttercup? The reason for my anger with my mother on my way to school one day. Having told her, she should die as she had caused me to feel like a liar. But as I rode to school that day with tears in my eyes from my hurtful words, I knew deep down she believed me because even before we had moved to South Rumvelt, there was no contact with him? To tell Bernice that we are born into this universe for a purpose. No matter how short or long we live, we fulfill those purposes which were intended for us. Each one with a story from one's past life lived (we), each told through songs, poetry, or writing. Stories build friendships at times with a bond so strong, as strangers, we become closer than one's immediate family member does. Unfortunately, blinded by our love or anger, we fail to appreciate the lessons taught while we are here. As I stood by her side, taking hold of her hands, I kissed her as I said, "Everything will be okay, and you take care of yourself. Bye for now."

I walked over to where Li was to bid her goodbye and took the stairs to the parking lot with Valerie and Kienna, who were being driven home by Car Myra. After a brief conversation with my niece and her child, promising Kienna the biggest birthday party on her turning eighteen, I kissed them both bidding them goodbye. Compton did call, but twice and only the good Lord knows what happened after, for he never called again, and I never got in touch with him due to chaotic circumstances in my life.

Chapter 7

PUT A BAG OVER YOUR FACES

USE OF OUR SPIRITUALITY can cause connection with others. But unknown to many due to the distances that part us, this spiritual connection is only realized by a few whose fate has joined them or who has become subconsciously awake to their circumstances and surroundings. Dan Millian, in his book Body Mind Mastery, wrote: "Spiritual training is a secret school, and only those who have gone through the trials, received the glories which have reached out, leaped, danced, stretched, and sweated for it, know the sweetness and promise of meeting the inner challenges," I ate, slept, and dreamt about work.

One evening as I slept, I saw the image of myself in the Director of Operation's office—Zelda. All that was heard was Zelda telling me that this could not be tolerated any longer, and with that said, I responded, "You know what, Zelda?" And with a cuss word used, walked out of the office, leaving Zelda and the quality manager, Aden, in the office. The following day at work, I related the dream to Reann. Reann is a dark, brown-skinned girl with shoulder-length hair and feet like a pair of chopsticks; having a great personality and is married to a man from her hometown—Trinidad. "Someone needs to stand up to her," said Reann. "Good for you." We both laughed and continued with our day.

I certainly did not foresee this coming. A week later, after I had dealt with a call, this would be the call that would cause me to be summoned to the Director's office. It was the second call of the day. "Thank you for calling Citi's acquisition line. This is Paula speaking. How can I help you?"

"My name is Katie. I spoke with someone yesterday who I completed an application with and would like to make a change."

"I'm afraid you have reached the inbound department. You need to speak with the outbound department, and I cannot transfer your call from here. I...."

"What do you mean you cannot transfer my call? Is this not Citi? I just want to know the status of my application."

"Madam, this is a different department. Further, you need to speak to Citi concerning your application's status. All we do on behalf of Citi is to complete the applications."

"You know what?" she responded. "Forget it. I find your customer service confrontational, and I'll take my business elsewhere."

"Madam, that's your...." Heard is the click of the phone. My last words trailed off quietly, "Your choice." Before I had completed my sentence, she had hung up.

It had been over a week since I received the call. I returned to my desk after having lunch with a man who asked if he could sit at my table because no other was vacant. He is a new immigrant from the Soviet Union and filled me in on his life here and a bit on the politics of his country. As he spoke, I found out that the President of his country was slowly being poisoned by members of his own staff. I remembered the story from an article in the newspaper, a picture showing how different his skin complexion had changed over the years. Upon returning to my desk, a message requested my presence in Zelda's office. On many occasions, I have seen my dreams unfold before me, and yes, I have suffered and felt physical pain, but never did they involve me physically. I left my desk and walked around to Zelda's office. A person doing no wrong intentionally, a worker having nothing to be guilty of, stood at the door and knocked before entering. A small room with glass partitions all around. Inside a desk having a computer, phone, and papers laid around, pictures of Zelda's family and other stuff hung on the wall, at the side and back of her desk. Zelda is seen looking down at a folder in front of her. "Come on in," she requested. "Have a seat." I looked at her appearance, facial expression questioning and serious look as she flipped through the file. I wondered what trouble I could be in now. She looked up from the file.

"Paula, how often have I talked to you about your abruptness on the phone?" She did not wait for an answer but continued, "It's been numerous times, and you continue to do the same thing repeatedly. Your attitude will cost me my job if Citi does an audit and listen to calls such as this one."

"Look, Zelda, I'm not being abrupt. I am just getting to the point of the customer's question. I am not one to do much talking, especially lately. I am...."

She interjected and asked me to hold my thought while she got Aden into the room. Before Aden entered the room, she called my attention to a report from the quality department of a call received by me. I remembered the call very well. As we discussed what was and was not said, Aden walked into the office and took a seat across from me.

"I was talking to Paula about her abruptness on the phone and about this call. She was not only abrupt but, in addition, very rude by telling the customer that she has a choice to take her business elsewhere."

I took the floor as I explained my actions. Back and forth, Aden and I responded to each other. "I could have, but did not see the need to say, 'madam, I am sorry to hear that, but you have the choice to take your business elsewhere.' That would have been too many words. She was unwilling to listen to what I had to say, so I made my choice of words brief by saying, 'That is your choice.' But she did not hear that because she had hung up before I could finish my sentence.

Aden's conclusion was to end our business relationship. I hates confrontation, especially when I am not being understood. With all effort tried to explain my troubles at home, and my sleeping condition, the two people before me, whose attitude was set on terminating my employment, were not hearing my words. I shook my head in disgust and frustration with my life. Wanting to cry, but not in front of them, when Aden was asked to leave the room, and Zelda asked to be told what was going on, I broke down in tears. Once more, I tried to explain to be understood, and so did Zelda, letting me know she, too, had been having a bad day from a meeting with her boss who was very loud with her. After all, the decision to find me another department would be investigated. The company will terminate my contract within four weeks if nothing is found. I left the office red-eyed and red-faced as I walked back to my desk.

"You look like shit," said Reann as I was about to pass her desk.

"I broke down because they just don't understand. I'll fill you in another day." I knew she was right in how I looked—terrible, as exclaimed, and I just wanted to get back to my desk as fast as possible. Who would know if not told, the facts of past abusive experiences showed on my face? Not long after taking my seat Gerry, one of the supervisors, came over to ask if everything was okay. Not awfully long after being told I looked like shit, I was very conscious of my appearance, so I replied with my head slightly down with my eyes on the computer screen. "Everything is fine. I was crying, she was crying, and we hugged each other in appreciation."

"Okay, then," he said and walked back to his desk.

Gerry was becoming an emotional attraction in my life. Some days I could not wait for his arrival. The very touch of his handshake gave me the energy to look forward to another day. However, I felt within my heart that he will only be in my life for a reason, as for a season, as all other relationships have. Unforeseen circumstances that only I was able to see, and at times hear, are what would cause divisions in my relationships. Unwilling to fight for what I wanted, I will instead allow the people I loved, to walk away; holding on to the words of my father, Reginald: "It is best to have loved and lost than to have never loved at all." Some days as I looked myself over, I knew that when the Master was making all things beautiful, he took it from my appearance, and wondered why. But liken to strength, where greatness lies not in the appearance, but rather in the right use of strength, so it is with the beauty of appearances that fades. Another week had passed, and I heard nothing from Zelda about an alternate position.

§

Westley had called one evening after I got home from work. He was told of the incident and suggested I should leave the company. This was not good advice currently. I knew if I left, there would be no problem getting a job, but one that offers benefits, that will take time to find. Besides, should I leave, coming up with a valid reason why I left the company would pose a problem in getting unemployment insurance benefits. I would have to have doctors' notes every time I had a headache, back pain, or not feeling well by being overly tired due to mental stress. To leave, would also mean I would have to wait four to six weeks before receiving any benefits, and this length of time without money was not a luxury I could afford. Westley seemed to understand my situation and wished me all the best. I sat and pondered over our conversation, thinking about the price we pay when we go against the Bible's teachings. I felt sadden, tears then filled my eyes. If only we could pay attention to His teachings and inculcate them into our lives, what peace and good health would we have. Whatever lesson is taught, good or bad, we sure learn eventually from our association with each other. Jesus said: "For I am come to set a man at variance against his father, and the daughter against her mother, and the daughter in law against her mother-in-law." - Matthew 10:35-37. Should we expect any difference from strangers, especially those who applaud bad for good and good for bad? I do not think so.

Westley is a songwriter and musician born in the States, and at the time we met, he was married with two children. He was with a production playing in town and attended a nightclub that I would occasionally visit to get a break from being at home. One evening, whiles there to be entertained by the band that was playing; during the band's intermission, he came over to my table, and we got to talking. I was informed of his reason for being at the club. He seemed very respectful and kind and had an aura that attracted him to me. In some ways, he was mischievous as I am and was taken by surprise by his boldness when I was put to his test but took up the challenge. "Kiss me!" he commanded. I looked at him with a smile and asked, "Here...right now?"

"Yes!" he responded. My head lowered in a shy girlish motion; I looked around to see those around were occupied otherwise. Satisfied I had some form of privacy; I raised my head. Now directly facing him, I leaned in and kissed him. He responded, *not wanting to let go*—so I thought, embarrassed of being seen by someone in the media, my intention was just to give him a little peck on the lips. As this is an action, I had not done in all the years I had visited the clubs. Publicity show is not part of my personality. Although I love anything having to do with the arts, the lack of privacy that comes with the lifestyle is not desirous of me. He was in town for a week after that evening, so we got together occasionally. By the time he left, he had occupied a place in my heart. Still, on tour with the production, I believe to be the title—Four guys one called Mo—he sent for me on a few occasions once he had left. I had a wonderful time on all occasions spent with him. However, one day I woke from a dream where I saw my image as a bride but could not see my husband-to-be. After brushing my teeth and washing off, I knelt. *Dear Father Jehovah, in and through your son Christ Jesus I approach you this day with much appreciation for having me wake to see this another day. Father, is it wrong of me to be in love with a married man with two children depending on him? Is it wrong to want to hold on to the best thing that has happened to me in my life? If I am wrong, please guide me with*

the decision I must live with. Oh, Father, you have been good to me, patient with me, and you have given me all the experience and exposure I need to grow to maturity. There is nothing more I can ask of you but to continue to have your angels watch over me. I pray for all my brothers and sisters around the world that your angels will protect and guide them, too, and I pray for my friends and those who are my enemies that you will cause a change of heart within them. Amen.
Not long after that week, I somehow lost Westley's number and so lost contact with him. The next time we spoke was a few years later. This time I discovered that he was no longer with his wife and was living with someone he met at a club he was performing. Her children were the ones who introduced them to each other.

One year during our conversation he extended the invitation to visit. I took him up on his invitation, wanting to get a break from Canada. After spending most of the day leaving Canada at a stop elsewhere before California, the plane finally touched down. I was nervous as I walked down the corridor to the elevators that would lead me down to the waiting area. It had been a long time; life circumstances change people within the blink of an eye; I had no idea what he would look like or what his circumstances at home were. I walked down the corridor, conscious of being looked at, with confidence and thoughts as to what this man was sending for me when he was with someone else? How do I pretend for a week that I am okay with his decision? Lord knows I need to get away, and it does not matter where to, just as long as I do not have to spend too much money I do not have. Oh, heck, what will be, will be! I reached the escalators and looked down to see him standing right in front of the stair, waiting for me. We recognized each other. As I stepped onto the escalator, my tummy did some cartwheels that told me, after all this time, the feelings were still the same, and this was going to be one exceptionally long week. He extended his hand to mine, put his arms around me and kissed me. "Hey, it's good to see you. You haven't changed."

I was trembling and did not want him aware of it. With forced words, I replied, "You, too. So, how are you?"

"At this moment, anxious to finally have you here. Girl, you had me waiting all day."

"Not of my doing."

We finally reached the car. He lifted my luggage into the trunk, walked to the passenger side, opened the door, made sure I was seated, closed the door, and walked to the driver's side, where he got in and pulled out of the parking lot. We drove for a few minutes in silence, and then I broke the silence by asking. "So, tell me... what has happened with you?"

"As I have told you, I am living with someone. My wife and I are no longer together."

"I wished you had called." Oh, yes, I wished he had called. I could have seen myself in a position better than where I am now and with everything I wanted, mostly a child.

"I hadn't your number; it was misplaced somehow. However, I was busy trying to get my life together."

"So, why did you not give yourself some time before jumping into another relationship?" Sure, this would have given us some time. Time to make a go of something we had already been on the burner for a few years.

"I needed someone to help me with things, and she was there...."

I guess I was good to have a lay in the sack, not good enough for you to try to find me, I thought to myself as he rattled on about how they met.

"Life with her is interesting."

I asked with curiosity, "In what way?"

"I must let you know she likes women, too."

Hot damn, I do, too. Does she in the sense of sleeping with them? Interesting life indeed, *I thought*. What is he saying? Is he saying what I am thinking? If this is the case, this visit will make for a long week? As he spoke of her, I interrupt. "Are you saying she sleeps with women?" The truth is I cannot recall if he said yes to my question. For what other conversation went on after that was forgotten along the way to his home.

We finally arrived. She opened the door and greeted me with a friendly smile. Not awfully long after our introduction, I discovered she was allergic to strong scents as Westley informed me that my perfume was a bit strong. It was a beautiful little home, but now dark, I would have to wait until tomorrow to see what the surroundings looked like. For the rest of my stay, they took me to many places and restaurants and even had my cousin and his wife over one evening, which they did not spend much time with as they thought I needed the time alone. One evening while he was away on a night gig, Vivian and I experimented with making candles. It turned out, though, that I was allergic to one or more of the ingredients used to make the candles, and on the next day, I woke with a fat lip, the after-effect of the ingredients used. One day a peaceful midafternoon walk alone around the area and through the cemetery give some insight. It was a wonderful visit, but everything must end. Therefore, I left in tears as the plane took off. Vivian was very hospitable and seemed to be nice and the one to do most of his business for him.

Once in Canada, a bit disoriented after getting onto the bus as it drove off, no sooner everything came to place in my mind then I was able to make my way safely home. Wanting to tell someone of what a wonderful time I had, when my friend Chelsi—who lived in the neighborhood, called, it was a perfect opportunity to invite her over to tell her of my vacation. It was about two to three weeks since I had been home when I got a letter from him with some upsetting news. "What the hell?" I said out loud as I continued to read.

A few days later, Chelsi came over. "Would you like some tea?" I offered.

"Sure; black, no sugar."

"You have got to be kidding, right?"

"No. Black, no sugar," with laughter in her voice.

"One moment," I responded and disappeared into the kitchen, to return a few minutes later with two cups of tea in a tray. "Girl, I have to tell someone about my trip. I was excited about my visit until I had to see my doctor this week."

Curious, she asked, "What for?"

"He wrote me to tell me how they both enjoyed my visit, but Vivian was experiencing some discomfort, and when she visited her doctor, she was told that she had contracted Chlamydia. I could not believe what I was reading, so I visited my doctor immediately, who put me on antibiotics for a week and ran some tests. I am waiting for the results, but I have no symptoms."

"You haven't seen the man for some time. I'm sure they are the ones that give it to you."

"I'm not passing blame; I'm just glad he told me, so I can fix the problem...if there is one before it's too late."

Chelsi then informed me about the new home she had purchased and would be moving out of the neighborhood very shortly. I congratulated her and wished her all the best. I smiled as I recalled my last visit with him. Why it is some people talk or criticize before having knowledge, I do not know. Whatever had caused the problem was sure not my doing, but I gave them both the benefit of the doubt through my visit to Dr. Noah, who later confirmed I did not have Chlamydia.

§

Chlamydia is the most frequently reported infectious disease in the United States. Caused by the chlamydia trachomatis bacterium, the disease does not produce noticeable symptoms in 75 percent of women and 50 percent of men, so an infection often goes undiagnosed. People who do not know they are infected with Chlamydia may not seek medical care and continue to have sex, unknowingly spreading the disease. When symptoms do develop, men may experience painful or burning urination or a discharge from the penis. Women may experience bleeding between periods, burning urination, vaginal discharge, or mild lower abdominal pain. If left untreated in women, Chlamydia can cause severe health problems. Chlamydia damages female reproductive tissue, causing pelvic inflammatory disease, which can cause chronic, debilitating pelvic pain, infertility, or fatal pregnancy complications. Experts estimate that three million people become infected with Chlamydia each year. According to the CDC, only about 660,000 infections are reported yearly. However, Chlamydia is treatable with antibiotics. Some additional information during my research is this: Sexually Transmitted Infections—STI, formerly known as venereal diseases, more than twenty-five infections passed from one person to another, primarily during sexual contact. The most common STIs include Chlamydia, gonorrhea, syphilis, herpes, AIDS, hepatitis, genital warts, and trichomoniasis. Some STIs, such as gonorrhea or Chlamydia, may cause no symptoms. Some STIs are curable with a single dose of antibiotics, but many such as acquired immunodeficiency syndrome (AIDS), are incurable. STIs are transmitted by infectious agents—microscopic bacteria, viruses, parasites, fungi, etcetera, that thrive in warm, moist environments in the body, such as the genital area, mouth, and throat. Most STIs are spread during sexual intercourse—vaginal or anal—and can spread by oral sex. Unlike many serious diseases, simple measures can prevent STIs. The most effective prevention method is abstinence—refraining from sex completely. Latex condoms are effective, although not perfect, protection from STIs. However, condoms do not cover all the genital surfaces that may come into contact during sex, and the possibility of transmission of some STIs, especially genital herpes and warts still exists. Cases of STIs are increasing despite higher rates of condom use since the onset of the AIDS epidemic. Results from a study reported in 2008 showed that one in four young women in the United States between the ages of fourteen and nineteen are infected with at least one of four diseases monitored: HPV, Chlamydia, genital herpes, and trichomoniasis. The United States has the highest STI rate in the industrialized world; roughly half of all Americans become infected with an STI before the age thirty-five. This is because the study shows that younger people are more likely to have multiple sexual partners than a single, long-term relationship and more likely to have unprotected sex between the ages of sixteen and twenty-four.

§

Back at Gelid Communication demoted, was Hilda from Team leader and back to customer service representative. A few had quit because of the supervisor's constant harassment to make sales, and a few were fired. Despite my condition, I tried extremely hard to maintain my composure for the rest of the remaining time. My dreams were becoming more and more visible before me. The image of two of the supervisors kept appearing in my dreams constantly. I told Carmen, a co-worker, of one of them and gave a hint of who the other was by a question asked. I wanted to approach one of them to ask a few questions that may or may not confirm my thoughts, but I declined. An office romance was the last thing on my mind, and as the private person I am, I felt there were enough people looking into my life and wanted no one else. Especially the ones from the office doing so. I knew that my personality, friendliness, accommodating attitude, trust, and confidence in my abilities, attracted others and what I needed in my life. However, the time was not now to involve someone else into it, although I could not see how the relationship with Rudolf developed. "Everything you attract comes to teach you something and to contribute to your aliveness and growth," wrote Saniya Roman and Duane Packer from a book I once read and have in my collection, entitled Creating Money—Keys to Abundance. You will find throughout this book that references made from books I have read will be mentioned as they validate my thoughts and experiences; books I also will recommend reading. I found her quote to be true as we handle our encounters with others. We will avoid the bitter dispute of words that embarrasses or may eventually end a life. We need to remember each of us bears our own truths. Therefore, arguments can be avoided if we should listen before responding.

This was the third week since my meeting with Zelda. An email to Mitch, one of the team's supervisors, were read, "Let Paula know that a position has come available in editing. The time will be from three to twelve midnight, and if needed, the latest being one o'clock in the morning. The pay will also be a little less." Mitch related the message and asked me to report to him when I arrived on Monday. He was going to introduce me to the supervisor for editing. I felt a little less stressed after the news, so after work, that day decided to go to the gym for a good workout.

The gym located on the second floor is a girls' gym with many programs to fit a working person's lifestyle. In the past, I attended a co-ed and found the competition to catch the attention of the males to be more like a pickup joint instead of the facility's purpose—to get one's body and mind in shape. As I was on the treadmill, the one closest to the window enabled me to see up to the third floor, as I often would, to stare out as I ran or walked uphill, focusing on the distance. On this day, an office meeting was in session on the third floor—viewed from the window in front of the equipment I was on. It is assumed most, if not all, the staff attended. As I did my uphill routine on the treadmill with my mind on a dream, I had the night before, feeling unwanted and not belonging where I was, the paper bags over the faces of the staff seen ignited a spark of anger. Words heard the night before during my sleeping state. Wanting to leave, I instead completed my routine and left the gym drained of my energy.

To fight against inculcated thoughts, which may have entered one's mind during sleep triggered by actions during our wakefulness, one must think and act positively that benefits self. Reacting negatively will only harm self, if not another.

§

AFTER THE WEEKEND

On Monday morning, I could not see Mitch where the arrangement was made to meet—the lunchroom. Arriving earlier than the time arranged and had passed, a message was sent by one of the workers in his team to let him know I was waiting in the lunchroom. After giving him another ten minutes to arrive, I walked over to the editing department myself. I introduce myself to the supervisor and apologized for being late. "That's okay; I'm a bit busy today. And I must wait on someone else," she responded. I took a seat as I waited for the person to arrive. A young man walked in wearing a smile; apologizes for being late.

"Have a seat and bring your seats closer to mine." She turns to the young man as she gestures, "This is Paula, and this is Phillip. He is coming off the floor."

I extended my hand. "Nice to meet you."

"Same here," he said.

Lilly explained what she expected of us and inquired about the campaigns we knew. Lilly is about 4'4" with a pale complexion, very much overweight with short hair. Over the years, I would send a Christmas card to her department wishing her and her staff a happy holiday, so I felt somewhat acquainted. After a quick brief about the campaigns and her expectations, we were thrown into our position without much training.

It was happening again, just as it was at the start with the company. Many things I had to find out for myself, at times being made to feel incompetent due to lack of knowledge. Alice, a short black girl about four feet or a bit shorter, having a body like a sculptured piece of art, with a birthmark on the right side of her face, dresses with the latest fashions; is fortunate to shop at the children's clothing stores due to her being very petite. Having a quiet disposition, she trains me. Within the hour, I was shown how to navigate around the computer with shortcuts to get things done quickly on multiple campaigns. Alice was thanked for her assistance, expressed in a postcard. Over the next few months, I would get to know Alice a bit more as I would all the other workers, including Kate, who is the assistant supervisor for editing.

Chapter 8

THANKSGIVING

IT WAS THE DAY before Thanksgiving. I left the office with Tommy, who at the time worked in the editing department. Tommy is a tall slim fella, married with twins—girls. His appearance was always clean, his hair combed back with a touch of gel or moose to keep it well laid down on his scalp, which reminded me of my father's look. I imagine what his younger days must have been like with the women as I looked at him; he is one of Jehovah's Witnesses. Before coming into edit, the supervisor wanted to fire him, but after pleading his case with Zelda about his age and the difficulty of finding work, he was sent to the editing department. It can be concluded that Zelda saw her future, found pity within her heart, and found a place for him. As we walked through the parking lot to the train station, Tommy looked towards the sky and commented, "My, I have never seen the moon like that before." I looked up towards the sky to the moon hidden behind a curtain of fog. It illuminated a dim, romantic lighting. I expressed, "It's beautiful!" We got to know each other during our commute from work, and he was quite taken with my experience as a child.

I woke up at about 7:00 AM, from the door alarm to the super's office next to my unit to a rainy morning. I loved it when it rained, especially if I am indoors. Not wanting to get out of bed, I turned back and forth, the cell phone in my hand, and mischief on my mind. The phone turned on, and a message was typed. I looked over the message and thought of how long it had been since I saw a man having sexual desires. Desires mostly to give an answer to the nagging force within me, brought to the surface from my dreams. Memories of Damion, Westley, Rudolf, and those in the office, especially to set things straight. Unfortunately, I did not want to use the hurt I felt unselfishly. His invitation to take me out I accepted in kind, though I saw beneath the surface the intentions of the force. *Perhaps faith will allow everything to fall into place*, I thought. With my finger still on the tab to push send, the decision put on hold, instead a call to Tanya to invite her over I made. As the phone rang, I realized I was in a position that was perhaps a blessing, not having a child or a companion that could cause further stress in my life. I had the time to think and do all that my heart desired; if only those with their intrusiveness would leave me alone and let me live. Today the desire to make mischief was present.

"Hi, Tanya. I called to invite you to dinner," I said once Tanya picked up the phone.

"Thanks, Bern, but Cynthia is supposed to drop by to pick up some clothing I'm giving her for the baby. If she leaves early, I'll come by."

"Okay, then, call me after she leaves. I've invited someone from the office."

"Okay, I'll call when she leaves."

After we hung up from each other, I received an inculcated thought that said, "I can take your man away." I shook my head with a smile and pushed the thought out of my mind as I removed myself from the bed. I tidied the apartment and left for the store, as I needed a few last-minute items for the meal I was about to prepare. After returning and putting away the groceries, I stood on the porch looking out at folks passing by and wondered if I should call or send a text message. I did not mind the age difference between us. We were mentally connected, and that was currently important. I mentally reasoned: Getting involved with someone older makes no difference. I laughed at the thought. Sometimes the older ones take longer than, the younger ones in their understanding of how things are. I shook my head. People will always find a reason to criticize you no matter what you do; in the end, doing what pleases you is the key to making oneself happy. However, the gossiping of others is what bothers me. I pressed the tab that read—send. I was still within thoughts when the phone rang.

"Hi, you got my text?"

"Yes, that's why I'm calling."

"The new technology we have it's amazing. Look, if you are not doing anything, why not stop by for dinner?"

"I'd love to; what time?"

"Around six o'clock."

"Okay. But it will be a little after six o'clock."

"That's fine," I replied, and as we were about to hang up, I raised my voice. "Are you still there?"

"Yes," he replied.

"You will need the address."

"When I'm about to leave, I'll call to get it."

"Okay, then, I'll see you later."

Thoughts to myself as I kept looking at the phone in my hands; when a man is not anxious to have your address, he is probably expecting another invitation. This way, if the other invitation he wants comes along, he will have an excuse about not having your address, and if it falls through, he has a reason to call. Or it could be he is very private and does not want to be followed. Dinner for the evening was King and Red snapper fried fish, peas and rice with a seasoned stew and mixed vegetables on the side. For dessert, I baked a rum cake, also known as black cake in my country—Guyana. The meal was prepared within an hour. I took a shower and sits with a novel by Timothy B McCann, entitled, Until. As I try to focus on the story a part of me wants him to call, and another does not. Nevertheless, the man within the boy I wanted to get to know. However hard I try, my thoughts kept drifting from the novel to him, back and forth. Then suddenly, the phone rang. I picked it up and looked at the display. It was he.

"Hi." I paused. You know the kind of mental pause you get when you are unsure of a respond to an taken action, that kind of pause. "I'm into a book where I can't stop turning the pages." This was true, but not at this moment. All I could see between reading the book's words was his image. An image I had been fighting for a few nights now. Unable to wake from the dream overpowered by his sexual touches, my body would climax from the pleasure. "The book is wonderfully written." I continued, "I'm at the part where this guy who had lost his girl to cancer was finally on a date with his co-worker. However, the way the meeting is set up and the chemistry between them, I feel how it will end with them."

"So, are you ready for me?" he asked.

I wanted to answer him with more than just the word "yes." I wanted to hold him, kiss him, and do everything I wanted to do to feel. To say what I felt, the units in my building were not soundproof. I could hear the neighbor's conversation on my floor and above at times. The private and shy person I am, as to how ready I was to entertain him, the words were kept within. He arrived within thirty minutes of his call. we talked while waiting on Tanya's call. After ten or fifteen minutes of conversation, I called Tanya to find out if she was coming or not.

"Hi, Bern," she answered with laughter in her voice. "Cynthia is still here, and we ate so much I'm filled. I don't think I can eat anything else."

"That's okay. I guess another day. You all have fun, and I'll talk with you soon. Fate had worked to my advantage. I now had the evening alone with him.

"Who is Tanya?" he asked.

"Tanya is a girl I met at Georgeson Share Holders, a company we worked. Over the years, we became close friends. She now has a baby boy, not quite a year old. The girl she spoke of also worked there and is now pregnant."

"Do you have any children?"

I looked at him with a smile "Sometimes, I feel I do, but no, I don't." I after got up and walked into the kitchen.

"Would you like some help?"

"I would not mind at all." I was experiencing a feeling I had before. It is a feeling where your emotions are all over the place, and you are unsure whether this is lust or love. Whatever it was, I was willing to indulge myself. He was asked to say grace but declined and asked me to do it instead. I began, "Thank you, Lord, for this meal before us and the opportunity of spending this time together." We ate with little conversation. After the meal, I packed some for him to take home. With the dishes cleaned, we sat to watch a movie. About five minutes into the movie, which I was not really enjoying, I got up to serve dessert.

"This looks and tastes like a wedding cake," he commented.

"So, you like it?"

"Yes, it tastes good."

"I'm glad. I was trying to finish everything on time, and I had forgotten to put some food coloring into the mix. I'm surprised it turned out as dark as it should be." After the movie ended, he wanted to leave as he was thirsty for a drink, and I had no alcohol in the home. Therefore, before leaving I packed him some of the dinner to take and I decided to walk him to the train station. As we left the building, we walked into a blanket of fog. The beauty seen above the previous night was now here below. With the atmosphere fogged, the streetlights gave a dim glow of the road ahead; the top of the buildings was only visible by the lights barely seen through the fog. The night's ambience, the lack of pedestrians and him at my side were nothing less than romantic. My eyes are my camera, things seen, heard, and related are passed down from generation to generation. Still, I needed a physical picture to remind me of our second social outing.

"Oh, this is so beautiful. I wish I had the camera with me."

"Would you like to go back for it?"

"Would you mind? I really need to get a picture of this. I have seen so many things lately, but as you know what people are like; without evidence of facts, they don't believe."

He laughs. "You are right."

We turned back to get the camera, one which was inexpensive and was purchased from the photo hut. He now insisted that I go home with him. Therefore, when we returned to the apartment, I packed a few items away before we left. On our way to the station, drops of rain began to fall. Lightening flashed a few times without the sound of thunder that usually follows. He laughed when I commented. "Oh, the blessings and warnings of Jehovah, we could be slapped by nature for heading into mischief." We were forced to take shelter as the droplets of rain now began to pour down. The moment reminded me of the day at the zoo. An Indian man approached smiling, trying to catch his breath, to take shelter where we stood, but just as I was about to make room for him, he shouted to the others running behind him— on the sidewalk. "Don't stop; one more over." He points to the restaurant next to the office building where we stood, their laughter reminding me of children playing. The rain seems to do the same for adults—bringing out the child within. On our way to his apartment, he was entertained with stories of my observation of people on the streets. I even enacted the actions of a drunkard that caused one of the pedestrians to smile as we left the train.

We got to his apartment, which was quite a way down the hall, to a self-contained bachelor. Across from the door was the laundry room. His unit faced the parking lot, but you could see the street and across to the units above the shops. It was smaller than my unit, but I was comfortable with how he decorated it. My first impression of him, as I looked around at his electrical gadgets, was he really enjoyed good sound as he does a good view. I took a seat after I observed the unit as he got us a drink. The Million-dollar baby—a DVD was inserted into the television, and he rolled me a joint as I preferred, rather than drinking. A few incidents were recalled from work triggered from the movie, was told by me had us both laughing. It was time to leave, I indicated this by getting up from my seated position, and he told me he would walk me to the bus stop but then decided to call for a cab. Before we left the apartment, he took hold of my hand, pulled me into him and began to kiss me. I indulged his action by responding. As we kissed, *man, boy, darn could you kiss, just the way I like it,* were thoughts running through my mind. Once we got to the bus shelter, a person very observant of my surroundings noticed a taxi parked at the corner for some time as we busy conversed. I brought his attention to the parked cab at the corner for the past four or eight minutes we were there. We walked to the cab; he leaned into the open window to ask the driver if he was waiting for us. The driver said yes, and opened the door for me to get in. We bid each other goodbye, and the taxi pulled off. A loud whistle is heard from someone as the cab pulls about a car length away from the curb.

The driver, who sounded West Indian, asked. "Is he calling you?"

"Calling me?" I replied to the question that sounded silly to be asking.

"Well, it seems like he is calling me."

"Perhaps the person is because they can't see if you have a passenger or not with these tinted..." I stopped short of what I was about to say and asked, "Are your lights off or on?"

"It's off." "Then the person is not calling you."

"Stupid," I whispered in an undertone. That will teach him a lesson of remembrance, light off someone's inside, light on no one's inside. The cab pulled up to the station, and the fare was $5. I thought I had given him exactly what he asked for, but as I was about to exit, the driver turned with an outstretched hand with $15.

"Did I not give you $5?" The driver looked back at the cash in his other hand, flipped a few bills, and turned around in response. "You are right."

"That is alright; we can both use it. Have a good evening." I pushed the door closed and walked into the train station. Once at the ticket booth, I was informed that the trains had stopped running. Some tickets were purchased, and one was thrown in the box. I entered the night, leaving a young fellow standing behind me, speaking to the attendant. *Lord, if I go back, how do we stop the temptation between us. As much as a part of me wants his touch, I may regret this in the morning. Not from giving myself to him but because I would have let the ignorance of the forces get the better of us.* Those were thoughts going through my mind. I walked back into the station to notice all eyes were on me. With a smile, the ticket attendant is told I had dropped a ticket and must pass through. We exchanged a few kind words before I passed through the gate to take a seat to wait for a bus, which would take me to Yonge Street in changing for another to King Street. A young black woman in her thirties approached and sat next to me. She began commenting on how pretty my feet looked in my shoes. This, being the second time, a complement is given about my feet; Westley had once given the same complement, but unknowingly, changes were occurring, which would be realized in years to come. As we talked, I frantically searched my handbag for my cell phone.

"Well, girlfriend," I responded as the girl continued nonstop. "I hope your feet look as good as mine when you get to my age." We both laughed. "Ah, this is what I was searching for; darn thing so small at times it's difficult to find." I took my hand out of the bag with the cell phone.

"I know," the woman responded.

I dialed his number. "Hello, I'm at the station, and the trains have stopped running. I may have to come back."

"I told you to stay."

"Yes, but..." I stopped short of what I was about to say. "I tell you what if the bus does not arrive within ten minutes, fifteen minutes tops, I'll return. I'll call."

"Okay," he replied and hung up.

The bus arrived after five minutes. I pressed redial, and he picked up after the first ringtone. "Hi, I'm on the bus. When I reach home, I will call. I will let it ring once. Bye." Between us, I had set a signal. One ring means I have reached where I said I would be and is safe; two or more rings mean to pick up; this is important. Once at King Street, the last streetcar was missed, and as dawn approached the morning, I decided to walk home, embracing the cool, refreshing breeze on my face, with a feeling of accomplishment of something given my enemies about to talk. The dark SUV spotted two persons that looked like females staring at us as we stepped out of the building. I knew they were there for one or more reasons. This story is about the meeting of the minds that caused a meeting of our souls, earlier mentioned in Chapter 4.

Chapter 9

SHALL NOT LIVE ON BREAD ALONE

THE FOLLOWING WEEK, I woke up with the sunshine upon my face. On the radio, the weather woman warned of it being a hot day. I pushed off the covers from my warm body. More now than before, I needed to lie in bed a little longer in the mornings as I relieved my mental thoughts of my night's dreams. The super's office next to the unit made it even more difficult to relax. On many occasions, angry words were exchanged as to why they would locate the office from the first floor that had no tenants to have it on the second floor. It was in violation of the lease, but I had not the time or money to take them to court. I knew a bit about the Law, even spent hours researching parts of the Canadian Law, and found gaps in the making of the laws when compared to man's circumstances. However, I continued to occupy the unit due to my tiredness from moving so many times. I maintained the thought that God never gives us more than we can bear. In addition to the circumstances, I saw slight fairness in their dealings with me. My Lease: The lease is written in duplicate on the below date.

RULES AND REGULATIONS

The Tenant shall comply with the Rules and Regulations in Schedule 'B' attached...that the Landlord may make and communicate to the Tenant. The Tenant shall ensure that other occupants of the Leased Premises or persons who are permitted observe the rules and regulations in the Residential complex by the Tenant.

LANDLORD'S OBLIGATIONS

Reasonable Enjoyment: The Landlord (promises) shall not at any time during the Tenant's occupancy of the Leased Premises and before the execution of an eviction order, substantially interfere with the reasonable enjoyment of the Leased Premises or the Residential Complex for all usual purposes by the Tenant or members of his household.

TENANT OBLIGATIONS

Respect: The Tenant is obligated to respect the rights, privileges, and interests of other tenants.

Written this 3rd day of this month October the year 1994. Tenant: Witness:

§

A man has to live and do so not only on the bread he eats—alone. He must have other things, such as the opportunity to get an education, a job, a roof over his head, clothing, and things that make life worth living. Not having some of these things, a person will do what they must do to survive. I did not condone what Rudolf did for his survival. I understood to some degree and so allowed him to be with me. Unfortunately, his knowledge of the activities of other tenants in the building had him under the impression that it was okay for him to do the same in my unit. On many occasions expressing my concern about his activities in the unit went past one ear and through the next. I was busy working and was hardly home to keep an eye as if a child on his activities; he was a grown man and treated as such. However, he cared only about himself. On the other hand, I was dealing fairly with the company; any time he stayed with me, the company was notified. Not disturbing the tenants, I did, and all else that was required. However, when some people have their minds about causing chaos in your life, you do not have to be born with a curse or blessing to have your every move blocked. I left my circumstances up to a higher power, knowing that what a man does to another will return to him, good or bad. Eventually, his offspring will experience what it was like, for the individual they had dealt wrong to, as some members' vendettas are carried on through generations. Some vendettas lacking understanding of the actions took by a family member. Vendettas that could be cured had communications done instead of secrets kept. Again, I'll repeat my Heavenly Father's words: Always learning and never coming to accurate knowledge. Dancing with words that sex the mind not taken seriously.

I had this dream before, where I saw a person's hand and the image of myself sitting on top of a suitcase with other luggage beside me on an open tarmac. After lying in bed contemplating what the dream could mean, not being able to come to a logical meaning for the image of the hand, I got out of bed, took a quick shower, prepared a Last Will and Testament, and got to the gym later than I wanted to.

A few steps from the entrance to the building on Young Street, I ran into a co-worker who recognized me. He called out, "Hi, Paula!"

I looked towards the sound of the voice. "Oh, hi." I paused, looked at him, and then asked, "Lamar, what are you doing around here?"

"I'm coming from the doctor."

"Who's sick?" After the words came out, I realized it may have sounded silly, as he had just said he was coming from the doctor.

"I am."

"What's wrong?"

"I can't sleep."

"Neither can I, but I was born with this condition where I always have visions—an act, a faculty of seeing, or imaginative foresight. More so than before, my sleep is consumed by dreams—thoughts or images occurring during sleep. The medical term used by doctors is insomnia. You should join a gym; I find a good physical workout and eating the right foods help. In fact, that is where I am going now. I'll see you in the office; take care."

"Okay," he said as we walked away from each other.

I just do not understand why he would say he is sick. I guess that maybe he is. Whatever it is, I hope he gets over it. I must work with him and what I must endure (the psychological effect of my dreams) and manage during my time in the office. I would not want someone striking out at me for incomplete thoughts that cause reactions that could have been avoided. *I thought to myself* as I climbed the stairs to the gym. I changed and began my workout, which lasted over an hour.

Tanya had invited me over for lunch, so after the gym, I dropped off a few things at my apartment and headed off to Tanya's place.

My day was going as I wanted it, too. Tanya came out to meet me. As she walked towards me, two men stood in front of an open restaurant, talking. As we passed, as if the words meant for our ears, one of them, a fair-skinned fella, turned to the black fella next to him as he made a comment, his eye meeting mine. "He's a young guy with a big hook." I threw the thought, Man, thank you for letting me know that. "There are so many sick people around with no sense of decency; it causes me to wonder." Tanya apparently had no idea what I meant by my comment, so I said nothing.

On the way to her place, I could not help thinking of what people of today do. Scrutinizing people's lives. Utilizes hidden cameras (so small it is difficult for the eyes to detect), listening devices in homes to eavesdrop on conversations, or illegal searches of one's personal items, destroying individuals little by little. The eagerness to harm others is so out of control, and many lack knowledge, insight, and self-control. They give themselves to the one whose ambition and the goal is to create division, to destroy. Technology slowly controls man's lives; it is advantageous to the wicked one's goal.

Lunch consisted of Chicken Slovakia with Greek salad. During our conversation, Rudolf's name came up, as always.

"So, how is Rudolf? Have you heard from him lately?"

"I suppose he's doing well. I haven't heard from him in some time."

"So, you don't know if he's working or not?"

"No. The man has a problem as I do. We are both mentally challenged." Tanya turns from what she was doing to look at me—a questioning expression on her face, so I elaborates on what I meant. "By this, I mean our ability to entertain thoughts while maintaining our reactions. Unfortunately, in his case, his strength to control his situation is not exceptionally good. *He destroyed too many of his brain cells with that smoking of his.* A thought I withheld. He has had many jobs, but the man's strength to keep them is weak. In this world we live in today, it's too expensive for one person to carry another one's weight."

"You are sure, right."

We watched television for a while, and then I left.

Everything we do in life involves the Law, says Paul when he wrote: All things are lawful for him, but not all things are advantageous for him. Yes, this is the whole obligation of man if he intends to live a peaceful life. And again, Paul reminds us to: "Be obedient to government and authorities, be ready for every good work." As we keep in mind Satan, the ruler of this system, let us keep praying that those that render judgment will be balanced in assessing the evidence presented before them. Those rendering judgment based on their own political agenda, vendettas, or accepted bribes will eventually pay the price.

Chapter 10

BLINDED BY LOVE

REPEATED OFTEN IS THIS, love is a hurting thing, and it sure is. We wonder why we put ourselves in the position of being hurt or why we keep accepting their treatment of us that hurts or accepting their actions that show disrespect for our dislikes. On contemplating these possibilities, it is evident that when our desires take over, our sense of self-worth is lost in the battle for our sanity. All we see before our needs are met through the insanity of our mind; we logically rationalize what is wrong as right. It takes strength to not only let go of one's emotional hurt that causes us to act insane but to maintain one's true character. Love no doubt makes you feel happy, and from within, it shows on the outside. The contentment felt and the self-confidence gained from the other believing in you and what you stand for is like a flame that keeps your energy flowing, but love is also painful, as it is stressful. Yes, getting to know someone is a task as it is a joy. It is a joy from the little games played just to see how the other would react and stress from habits the other may have that irritate you.

Being able to recognize lust—a strong desire to possess and enjoy, or love—a strong feeling of affection, or passionate devotion, is important. Taking time to examine the feelings of the differences is crucial to one's happiness. Make no mistake: Come see me and live with me are two different situations. Another, what you see is what you

95

get. For years I have watched my sister's relationship with her husband and felt for her the loneliness she must feel, though her emotions she hid "like mother like daughters," goes the saying [as mother was the same]. My observation has concluded that perhaps she appreciated the little moments they shared more than worrying about his absences. Perhaps, life is to live this way—acknowledging that nothing is forever, except for the air we breathe; appreciating the time spent, short or long, the conditions—good or bad—we treasure, taking something learnt with us.

A television show called The Maury show. It is a show that interviews partnerships, among other topics, and repeatedly shows how people will lie to one another to keep the person or break up another's relationship. Jealousy, which plays a part due to the other's action, is not always a sign of weakness. A person incited to jealousy is one fit in mind and body who doesn't necessarily care about the result of their reaction. Truths are only being revealed because of guilt of having kept a secret from the person they "claim" to love, friends with or doubt of the other's sincerity; that truth is sought by either a DNA test or a lie detector test. Sometimes, the outcome hurts the individual seeking the truth, and their actions are often deplorable. Yes, there is no avoiding hurt in any relationship, and it hurts even more when your family betrays your love or trust. Remember that all relationships, whether business, romance, or mare friendships, are a learning experience for us to grow—not in height, but in mental, emotional, physical, and spiritual strength. As never before, there are many books written, as there are talk shows, such as Dr. Phil, that give advice on relationships. Relationships today are likened to looking for a job. Remove the blinders, so speaking, check the other's lifestyle and compatibility with yours, even family inherited diseases—yes—preparedness is important down the road of growth together. Some of these things are overlooked in many cases due to our love or fascination felt for the person. Before entering a relationship that eventually hurts or destroys you, think things through. Marriage is not a game; it is a commitment to another of your deep emotional feeling, called love.

To conclude, be mature of mind when entering a marriage relation-ship. It is a commitment for life—not a game, to cause some other significant one's jealousy; each one needs to be there for the other in sickness, in health and in love.

§

Summer transforms the City of Toronto "City of the Dead," a saying mostly heard from foreigners—to the city of the living. This is the start of all kinds of festivities, such as the Jazz, R&B festivals, street parties, and family barbeques, all leading up to the Caribbean festival and then to the Canadian National Exhibition, which reminds us that it is the end of another summer.

I awake from a dream; my body felt hot under the covers. I had not yet looked through the window to see the beginning of the day. One that told you from the sun's illumination would be a hot and dry day. I removed the covers and turned on my cell phone. After a min-ute, the phone began to ring. I picked it up and looked at the display to see who it was, but the ring was calling my attention to messages. I dialed the code that would allow me to retrieve the messages. One was from my sister, Monica. She called to find out how I was, the message was deleted, and another was retrieved. I put the phone on the table next to where I lay. My sister's message replayed in my thoughts. I smiled and said aloud—families. I rolled over unto my back and folded my arms under my breasts. Again, I smiled as the image of a conversation with Gerry about his family crossed my thoughts. A sound of laughter escaped from my closed lips as I pon-dered on our conversation and thought that through families, we really discover how deep our love or how strong our resentment of them can be or how their support of us gives us the energy to push forward toward our goals.

It was during a week in April when my cousin Annette called to inform me that she would be visiting for the day. She could do so be-cause she lived closer to the border that separates the U.S. from Canada. When they arrived, it was after twelve noon. It has been a while since I had seen Annette or her family. Annette and I were like twins growing up; we did and visited most places together. One day, Annette had me playing with poison ivy, which I had no clue that would later leave me scratching the daylights. Annette laughed and thought it was funny, but I was a bit annoyed to the point of getting some more and rubbing it all over her, but then thought that if I did, this would mean having to endure the itching all over again, so I declined. Another day while playing under the bed just as I got on top of her— as a mother would her child while she speaks or plays with her (a position done with Debra-Ann as I played with her on the bed during a vacation in Florida, last memory of her as a child), Cicely came into the room and caught us in that position. Years later, it was known that Cicely hung up on a feeling that she had not entered the room when she did, of something else about to happen. Our thoughts are funny; they can cause us to jump to wrong assumptions of others as it causes us to doubt our own abilities and sense of self.

The door opened to the sound of their voices before they could knock—yes, this was my family, noisy as their known to be. Annette, her new husband, her son, her daughter, and her daughter's friend entered the apartment. She introduces her husband for the first time. Annette had remarried since we last saw each other. Her first husband, after their divorce, married her older sister. Not many in the family approved of it, but their intentions worked out well for many reasons. Her new husband is Irish and Italian, the same age as her, but he looked a bit older. The fact that he was mixed, I thought, could not be all-bad. I have had my share with the Italian culture and found some of them to be loving, cruel, deceptive, and know how to buy their way in and out of situations. They brought out the best and worst in me; therefore, I would rather keep my distance from some of them.

Annette was now a homemaker, looking a bit older, as does me, and had put on some weight. I was surprised to see her looking as she was—tired—but found out as we spoke her days were quite hectic with the kids, and her mother, who is not as well or active as she was once. The huge home to take care of and her husband's needs; I could not think of why she was a bit overweight after being informed of how much she had to do. Her visit was also an opportunity to give a letter that contained personal information about me, should anything happen. She is called to the porch.

"I have done a Will and Last Testament, and here is some information you need to know should anything happen to me."

Annette laughed as she said, "What do you need a Will for? You have nothing." A comment made deceived from what the eyes saw. A comment she made that could and may have applied to her. For the things seen are temporary, but the things unseen is everlasting.

"Don't be an ass. Once a person starts to invest, they should make a Last Will and Testament. This way, the little material or financial wealth they have is not taken by the government. If you are smart, you will do the same, and lord knows how they are."

"Who are you talking about?"

"The government, that's who," I responded, laughing. "They give with one hand and take back with the other."

Annette laughed as she replied, "You are so right." She stretched forth her hand to accept the letter, and that is when I saw her scarred hand.

"What the hell happened here?" I asked in a fear-filled whisper.

"I was cooking a dish I saw on T.V. The oil in the wok was too hot when I threw in the ingredients. It flared up, and I jumped, knocking the wok over unto myself."

"Oh, my, look at your hand." I felt so sad for her.

"Third-degree burn!" she exclaimed.

"Gee." Then I said playfully, "You should have been more careful trying to cook China man's food."

She smiled. "I should have." She says before putting it in her handbag. She took the letter and showed her husband, who briefly looked it over.

I took them to the Eaton Center, and after a meal. The children and her husband spent some time looking around the mall, while we had more time to talk, catching up on past times. After the mall, they drove back to the States.

I got to work an hour later than the usual start of my shift, which was at 3:00 PM. Annette's visit had left me with feelings of sadness and fear. Fearful because of the hand I saw in my dream. It seemed to be the right hand, the palms outward open; perhaps a foresight, but because most of my visions were becoming more and more apparent lately, the fear for others was becoming more real to my senses.

10,000 Dreams Explained: The hand is the body's most expressive part and denotes power and creativity. The right hand is power; the left is passive and receptive. An open hand represents justice... A raised hand indicates adoration, prayer, or surrender if turned outward, a blessing is given. Then, I was given a blessing. Thanks!

Chapter 11

CRUEL ACTS

FROM KINDERGARTEN TO HIGH SCHOOL, to college, to university, to the business world; as we enter these facilities, there is always one person that will not like us from the moment they lay eyes on us. That one individual can say and cause division between you and others, and how you handle that individual through the actions of others is vital to your genuine forming friends. The ones that are wise in their thinking, to the safeguarding of oneself. Then there is the group whose ideas, philosophy, and phylogeny, can be difficult to change. These ones can make or break you in the arena you find yourself. For, the way of the wicked is like the darkness; they do not know what makes them stumble—Proverbs 4:19. A Chinese philosopher says, "Who the gods first make mad, those they destroy." Yes, from that one individual to that group whose goal is to make your life miserable, you must develop art in how you handle such one or ones. As you become aware of your surroundings and personal items because a hungry and angry giant (man) care not whose life is destroyed by illusions, bribes, or manipulation.

Due to my many occupations, I had many dreams. Apparently, this verse had slipped my mind. "For a dream cometh through the multitude of business, and a fool's voice is known by multitude of words," wrote Solomon in Ecclesiastes 5:3. I started to believe—according to some, who insisted my talking was foolishness. Still, I was staying true to my vow that, Until My Dying Day, I will make others aware of my experiences to bring about awareness. I had to look back to move forward. I had to let others know even if they did not believe in a higher force or power. The things we are experiencing as individuals, as a nation, and as a national group on this globe are not all due to man's selfishness and overly ambitious attitude—stopping at nothing to accomplish one's goals. Whether that be a revelation of beliefs, of gaining material and financial wealth, or one's own inner will to control others, misguided by this (our) limited power, thinking one oversees one's destiny. Is an unaware fact most are being guided by the spiritual forces of this world, and some guidance is not in the best interest of humankind. I had seen and experienced the fragility of the mind: that it does not belong to even those who possess much strength or financial wealth as the ones in charge. As one has accomplished or given material or financial wealth, it can all be taken away in seconds. This can be by a natural disaster, theft, a killer disease, or even taking one's own life—overpowered by evil (or cruel acts) that causes one to lose all faith.

§

Sunday, the first day of the week, some believe it to be God's rested day, while others claim God's rested day to be Saturday, known as the Sabbath day. Whichever day, hopefully, all are gathered in unison for one purpose, that of giving thanks and singing praises to God.

I was hungry for spiritual food, but on this day, the memory of a sister I met at one of the Conventions held by Jehovah's Witness deterred my intentions. A person who always tells the truth, even to strangers I just met, could not understand the action of the sister one Sunday when I approached her to say hello. After the meeting, I excused myself from Leila and Moana, who visited the Hall I was supposed to be attending, the location being in the territory I live. I walked over to the sister I had met to say hello. As I approached, hands outstretched in a gesture of hello, the sister loudly exclaimed. "No!" While backing away. "Don't you touch me!" she further exclaimed. She turned and walked briskly over to a brother next to the door. I felt like I had a disease, was dirty, or smelt funky, but was mostly embarrassed over the sister's actions. Having already bid goodbye to Leila and Moana, I walked over to where the sister stood with the brother. "Someone had better speak to her." I said and walked off and out of the Hall. Surely, the child lacked knowledge, and was overpowered by her eagerness to practice what was right and had no understanding. Clearly, she lacked hospitality, perhaps even forgetting the scriptural instructions that state: "Be hospitable to one another without grumbling;" or the other, "Do not forget hospitality, for through it some, unknown to themselves, entertained angels." Although, at times, some do not deserve to be entertained. I had no idea of being disfellowshipped. When the sister did inform me of this knowledge and her reasons for not being able to return, she was informed I had no knowledge of this, but if that is the way she feels, then there was nothing more to say. She left with another sister who had accompanied her and was not seen until that Sunday.

That was not the only incident pushing against my mental state. I was never informed by an Elder if I was allowed a seat on the bus to the Convention. When Monica was told of the incident, she commented, "I don't know why you put yourself in the position to be embarrassed." Far from my thoughts was putting myself in that position. Denied was my Medical Directive card. My disfellowship status had not changed my conviction and commitment to our God Jehovah. So, that night when told that due to my not being an active member of the congregation, I would not receive the card, it really hurt, mostly because of their lack of understanding. However, one day looking through my belongings, the old card was found. Overjoyed by the find, I thanked God for his guidance. Since I was in God's house, I felt some form of encouragement instead of discouragement should be given. After all, we are all sinners appealing to God for the forgiveness of our sins. Furthermore, Biblical scriptures looked at for disfellowship persons, I felt, were not all against my actions. I sincerely tried to keep the congregation clean by my adherence to the scriptures and was looking for a marriage mate—not being a habitual fornicator. Further, my relationships were not with baptized brothers, and I avoided church activity whenever I was in relationships. This, and other incidences that followed, were the beginning of my separation from my friends out and within the congregation. Cleverly orchestrated by those in authority and the enemy I have made along life's road. We will eventually meet again in a battle of recalled memory.

There are a few things in life that put some ahead of others or give them a false sense of power: being in a position of authority, money, and having friends in high places. However, it is only a matter of time before the scales become balanced, allowing them to realize that being in a position of authority, money, and having friends in high places means nothing when disaster strikes. And what the world is experiencing with COVID-19 is of a real point.

Chapter 12

THE ENEMY'S TRAP

ISOLATED FROM MY FRIENDS in the congregation found a friend within my co-worker—this I thought. I arrived a little after nine o'clock at his home. We talked for a while, mostly about my day and his plans and left after having had a beer and a joint. He decided to walk me to the bus stop, so I walked ahead and turned back as he closed the door. As he turned around, his face met mine; I held his hands, leaned in, and gently kissed him. I needed someone to talk to, and he was there.

The word Isolation means to place alone. Many today live in this Palace of the wicked one— known as Isolation—the Devil being the head of the household. Many living in this Palace are unknown to you and me, moved to be there by members of a group, by family or those held as friends. One in this position only means of reaching out is done by using social media. Their cry for help only caught by a few from their content posted. Only by a few because they are observant, caring, loving individuals who are awakened to man's manipulation. Isolated with feelings that they may be contributing to a group be-friended on social media. Soon they are deluded by the Devil's workers manipulated content of personal information posted, guided and unaware of foolish actions. Their posts remove even before viewed taken down before the legal time permitted. Used by the manipulator's friendly actions, some are left with the only escape option, which is to use the wicked one's manipulation to their advantage. How done must be carefully thought out, for a man of violence will seduce his fellow and certainly causes him to go in a way that is not good. –Proverbs 10:29. A scripture proven to be truthful within the world today. Hackers into computer networks disguising as someone they are not mislead innocent ones. Actions that calls for awareness; for "It is as a sport to a fool to make mischief: but a man of under-standing hath wisdom..." –Proverbs 10:23.

Oh, when will you stupid ones turn to do well toward each other!

SYMPTOMS OF ISOLATION ARE:

1. Level of Self Confidence drops.
2. Feelings of worthlessness.
3. Entertainment of negative thoughts becomes stronger.
4. Person begins to feel body aches and pains from stress.
5. Alcohol and Drug use becomes a daily habit.
6. Memory loss begins due to the tampering of...illegal access in...and stealing of a person's possessions.
7. Schizophrenic tendency comes in, and may not be all this in-volves, but the individual becomes withdrawn, truly captured by being isolated.
8. Attitude toward others becomes callous; at last, he or she be-comes the Devil's worker.

SOLUTIONS

1. Study and meditate on (Bible scriptures) God's word. Read, Observe, and Listen to motivational writers and speakers.
2. Breathing exercises relax the mind. Physical exercise strengthens the heart muscles and keeps the body mobile—many exercises can be found at Pinterest.com or on Google

apps. Also, long walks not only relax the body but also increase mental awareness.

3. Do mental exercises, like puzzles and games. Such mental/ brain exercises can be found at Lumosity.com.

4. Meditation is very relaxing and eases body and mind stresses. Using Google search, many apps can be found to assist in releasing stress with recorded tapes for meditation. Stay healthy by keeping yourself and your living surroundings clean. Eating a balanced meal, including vitamins A, B, C, D, and E, iron, calcium, starch, nuts, ground provisions, veggies, and fruits.

6. Get immersed into someone else's world by reading romance novels, mysteries, or biography of their lives, as you allow yourself to be taken away from your troubling situation.

§

"Thank you for another lovely evening. I really needed this."

"That's alright; anytime," he responded with a smile. Still holding hands, we walked out of the building.

He is so shy, *I thought to myself*. I really need him, a man, someone, to make me feel alive by tenderly and boldly taking me. I wish he had pursued the kiss as he boldly did the first time. Perhaps we need time to be comfortable with each other. As we stood awaiting the arrival of the bus, I kept bobbing my head to a tune playing on my Walkman that Westley had recorded. Often, when I listens to the song, I wonder if it is an experience of his.

"Could I listen?" he asks.

"Sure." I took one of the air plugs and pushed it into his ear.

After a moment, he asks. "This song has meaning to you?"

"Yes, a past experience." I left his mind wondering when I said, "Yes." It was the experience I had felt when he ran his finger down the palm of my hand. He had ignited a hunger I had been holding in for a long time, and given the right place, the right time would be happy to show just how starved I was. The bus arrived. I bid him good night and promised to call as soon as I arrived home.

The train pulled into the stop bringing with it a cloud of dust. I spun around to avoid contact and was taken into a cloud-like sandstorm. I saw myself dancing with a man. We held on to each other ever so tightly when out of nowhere appeared, an older woman. In an angry voice, she said, "You want him; go ahead, see if you can have him." The dream ended as I turned my body away and was a bit fearful when I woke. I looked at the male conductor as I passed my hand over my face in a fan-like motion and entered the train. I remained standing. One, who had experienced all sorts of feelings when I smoked, could possibly write a book about hallucinations, but what had just explained; reminded me of a dream. The bell sounded, and the doors started to close. Standing with one arm around the pole, the other hooked into the other, my feet slightly apart and my head leaned against the pole; this position giving me control, the train pulled away from the station. The ride to the next stop took unusually long, it seemed. I felt like being on a bullet train that goes extremely fast, like the ones in Europe. As the train moved through the tunnel, the sound and experience were like being in an airplane having a bit of air turbulence. Each time the train mounted what seemed to be a hill, my imagination lifted me higher in the air, as being on a Ferris wheel, and with each descent liken to being in an airplane, I tried to catch my breath. Finally, the conductor announced my stop as the train pulled into King Station. I got off and caught the streetcar over to my destination.

§

MARIJUANA, made from the hemp plant's dried leaves and flowering tops, provides useful fibers for making rope and cloth. It is a very potent drug and is often classified as a hallucinogen. The experience depends on the dose. Small doses create mild, pleasurable highs, and large doses result in long hallucinogenic actions and are known to relieve pain. The positive and negative effects include a sense of euphoria and well-being and distortions of time and space. Other negative effects include fear, anxiety, and confusion. One of the main reasons the legal system now has...and doctors have approved it only for medicinal use—of course, with restrictions on amounts individuals can have in possession. Research shows that learning and memory problems persist for at least a week after you have smoked marijuana. This fact is the case for some people.

Science Digest provided these details: "Regular marijuana puffing may, in the long run, widen the gaps between nerve endings in the brain that are necessary for such vital functions as memory, emotion, and behavior. For nerves to perform their functions, they must communicate between themselves." March 1981, page 104. Former U.S. Secretary of Health, Education, and Welfare, Joseph Califano said, "Today there can be no doubt that smoking is truly slow-motion suicide." -Scholastic Science World, March 20, 1980, page 13. Given these known facts and now legalization of it are reasons for my sense of fear when I see young ones smoking. Some have no knowledge of the damage they can cause to themselves and others. Their only concern is to experience a high to forget their troubles, which are always present the next day. Acting careless, jeopardizing their lives and opportunities. Now, mixed with a street drug called ecstasy and opium (or uppers), the cause of many deaths in 2017 and has escalated due to COVID-19. The foolish ones care less to take caution.

§

After a warm shower, with a cup of tea and some cookies, I turned off the kitchen light and curled up on the couch with a few lit candles in the living room. As I sipped the tea while looking at the glow of the flame that swayed from the evening wind coming through the open window, sending shadows that danced around the room, I thought of how short our life experiences are. The cup rested on the coffee table, I started to massage the palm of my hand below the middle finger. As I did, I recalled a religious program from 100 Huntley Street. The preacher had said, "Pain is good...." *What good result could come from this pain I am feeling?* I thought. "It not only alerts us that something is wrong, but it lets us know that we are alive." That I know; I am alive. "We can learn from pain...." The sensation felt was both joyous as it was painful. This a reminder that difficulties in life, though painful at the time of experience, end up being joyous when you look back at what was taught or gained. My thoughts wandered to past relationships as I smiled at the idea of twenty questions to ask your lover. Questions that allow seeing compatibility and self-interests.

1. When it comes to others, does he favor one nationality over another?
2. Is politics a strong subject of conversation or one he tends to avoid?
3. Who is the Prime Minister or President of (his) country?
4. Who is the mayor of his Province or county?
5. Which countries make up the G7?
6. Is money an important part of a relationship?
7. What is his favorite sport that he likes to play and why?
8. What he sees as his strength or weakness?
9. When angry, does he react first and think after?
10. What are his thoughts on religion? Does he believe in a higher power?
11. Does he know the first two sentences of the 23rd Psalms?
12. What are his views of Bible counsel on man's problems in view of changes in the world?
13. Is he very, somewhat, or not possessive in negative situations?
14. If put in a position of jealousy, is he willing to use the opportunity to further the good of the other?
15. When faced with delegate situations, does he, in all cases, most cases, or never at all look at only the evidence or further than what is not placed before him?
16. Does he love animals, and what is his favorite? I laughed at

the thought of four other questions came to mind.

17. Would he tell a lie if he felt it was not hurting the other?
18. Is pornography a pastime relaxation or not a relaxation?
19. Does age really matter in a relationship? and What is his definition of beauty?
20. Is he ready or willing to make changes at any given point in life?

The candles had now burnt to their finish; a small flame remained in a pool of melted wax that would soon consume it. My eyes now used to the partially dark room; I got up, took the cup to the kitchen sink, washed it, brushed my teeth, and went off to bed.

§

CALM REWARD

I had experienced a good night's rest despite actively tossing from side to side during the evening from my visions and dreams. It had rained most of the night. I lay in bed looking up and out the window at the grey skies, the echo like that of an open faucet drips of water from the roof above, taking my imagination to be on an island. In a hut dimly lit by candles, surrounded by coconut trees, and exotic plants, the shadow seen from the flame of candles that dances around the interior reminds me of things past and the peace and calm that will soon end. The serenading sounds of the birds, who had all been given a bath from the rain. Taking me to the city where traffic congestion on the streets and pedestrians stop to take shelter from the rain. Yes, the rain always causes a temporary pause in our busy lives with an attempt to clean the city. A comparison of all things beautiful done by nature

I removed myself from the bed and to the window and saw two homeless men crossing the street below. They stopped at the garbage cans on the sidewalk for the pick-up truck. As I looked at them going through the cans, the realization of the struggle we all go through, some having a tougher time than others, touched me emotionally that caused a teardrop to trickle down my cheeks. Within the moment, one shouted to the other, who was about to go through a woman's handbag beside her car, as she was on the other side. "Hey, that's her things!" There is a pause. "Look!" he exclaimed from the other side of the trashcan with a cigarette in his mouth as he said again, "Look!" They both started to laugh. They had found a few bags filled with empty bottles. They both lifted it out of the trashcan and placed it in the grocery cart they had with them. With smiles on their faces, which caused me to smile, they left in search of other treasures.

The life cycle: one man's trash, another man's treasure. I removed from the window and started to prepare for the day ahead.

§

On this day, I did not take lunch to work. Usually, once a week, I eat from one of the outlets in the food court. I seldom eat out due to my diet. However, today many do not have to worry about where to eat, as restaurants cater to all types of diets. It was early in the afternoon; some employees had left for lunch. I was a bit hungry and so decided to get something from the vending machine in the lunchroom. As I stood looking out onto the floor through the glass partition, Alice, Ronda, and another co-worker were seen returning from lunch. I knew there was an attraction between Alice and Jim—a tall brown- skinned, good-looking fella with an attractive body and lips that would have a woman on her back for weeks and begging him not to leave. As I admired him, I often thought he ought to be modelling instead of working for Gilad, but the bankers were being paid well for their investments, so he, like a few others, was not being let go until their profits were realized. It is hilarious when people try to hide their feelings with little reactions, which they think will go unnoticed by observation, trying to be inconspicuous as they check you out. Jim stood with his body facing the position of the door to the editing room as he conversed with members of his team as the girls entered the room. Just then, Jim happened to look to his right and saw them walking towards the editing room; with motion as a golfer in the position to take a swing, he glances at his watch. His facial expression showed delight—which man would not when looking at Alice. She has a way of making the old men wish they were young again—as he turned to watch them walking into the room.

It was about five in the afternoon when I decided to leave for lunch. My choice was a cheese bagel with tea from the Second Cup. On many occasions, I had spoken to the Chinese girl that seemed very friendly and worked there. She is of average height, has a short haircut, with delicate features. I placed my order and observed her as she prepared the bagel. One known to be very outspoken will tell you if I am not pleased about something. On a few occasions, I had to ask to have the bread re-toasted, the toast will be dark to the point of being burnt, and she would be buttering it to serve. For a person seen as cheerful and friendly, her customer service did not complement her disposition. On this day, I had, had enough of her catalyst treatment.

Would she treat another the way she treated me?

I never like looking at the color of one's complexion or nationality to draw conclusions; in my opinion, people should be treated with respect regardless of how they treat you. The owners were also amiable, but the wife sometimes seemed a bit unfriendly. I thought it was perhaps her jealousy of her husband's friendliness towards me and would soon dismiss the wife's actions or facial expressions from my mind's impression or intellect. Unfortunately, it slipped my mind into being aware of smiling faces. With the power of understanding—not of a child, I stood talking to the counter clerk as she prepared the bagel and could not believe her actions. Before cutting the bagel, the knife passed back and forth over the unclean counter without washing or wiping it; she cut into the bagel, buttered it, put the cheese on, cut it in half, and served it, then wiped the knife. There is a saying, "What you don't see or know, don't hurt." This saying is true. For what you see can hurt or make you sick. Images of such and worse actions by employees, shown on television by hidden cameras in restaurants, are why I prefer to cook instead of eating out. However, who is to say what I am trying to avoid is not happening to my home-cooked meals? Access to my unit was often detected, and I would aloud testify, "I eat with...and sleep having faith." I paid and took my order to the table on the side. I said a little prayer within my mind and began to eat, but the image of how the sandwich was prepared made me nauseated. With limited funds not enough for another meal, I continued to eat, not without thoughts of judgment, with every bite as to the server's intentions. *I know that you may be having problems, and your actions are your way of expressing that, but I am paying for a meal. It is not like I am being given it free, and I have not done anything to merit such actions from you. This is a business, and you keep serving me in a way as if to tell me my business is not needed, girl, the owners had better say something to you, or I can cause them to lose a lot of business. I am so tired of how some people treat me as invisible, someone...* "Hi Paula," a voice called out. The voice sounded like one I know, awake me from my thoughts. I look to my side, and as always, with a smile on his face, a short dark young man about thirty plus of age meets my stare—it is Mitch. Undréa accompanied him—a Chinese fella, tall, with dark-hair and a huge head; sometimes I wonder when looking at him what a time his mother must have had pushing him out into this world—has a friendly manner, had just walked in together. Andrea's attention was focused elsewhere.

"Oh, hello, Mitch," I respond, acknowledging his presence.

"Undréa!" Mitch called. "Did you see Paula?" he asks.

I turned to face their direction as our eyes met. "Hi," I said to Undréa, who responded with a nod of his head.

"Will you be here tomorrow?" Mitch is overheard asking the Chinese girl. "Yes," she responded. "Then I'll see you tomorrow." I completed my meal, cleaned myself up, and returned to my desk.

From that day forward, I had seen many changes in that food outlet, to the point that it sold.

§

Shortly after arriving at my desk, Lilly calls me over. Now, what is wrong, *I thought* as I stood awaiting Lilly's attention. Lilly looks up at me and calls my attention to a sale dealt with earlier. An editor's responsibility is to listen and correct information on product knowledge given.

These reasons: any misleading information is given, mispronouncing words that change the context of the sentence or paragraph, collecting and giving of the right parties' contacts information for all questions asked, holding any sales with discrepancies or for second reviews or sending a coaching issue to the supervisors informing them of an issue, that an agent is not following.

Kate-Lyn, who mostly looks after the French group, does second reviews. She is about 5'4", give or take, with shoulder-length blond hair and an average build. She loves to hear gossip, as she likes to tell one, and knows well how to instigate a conflict; she often sees an advantage and takes it. A person not extremely comfortable with the competition will accommodate you—the impression I was given and is married.

"Yes, I recall that sale. It was okay. What's wrong?"

"What's wrong?" repeated Lilly. "You pass the sale with incorrect information."

"What do you mean?" I look questionable at her, lines forming on my forehead.

"The customer told the agent..." she explained.

"No." I paused for a moment. "That is not true. I listened to the call, and everything was done correctly, and further, why would I change the information. If there is one thing I detest, it is people tampering with my work, so I would not do it to others." Not only that but having worked on the floor, I know all too well how difficult getting a sale can be at times, and having it held how frustrating it can be.

"Are you arguing with me?"

"No, I'm not. I'm just letting you know what I heard and would not do."

"Well, don't argue with me."

"As I said, I'm not. Just letting you know what I heard."

"That's all; I'll have to hold it." She grimaces as she keyed in something on the computer.

"You do what you have to do," I said as I moved away and back to my desk. Shortly after that, Lilly got up from her desk with the sheet the sale was on and walked out of the room. Ada overheard the conversation and came over to ask what was happening.

Ada is a stout Indian woman, as outspoken as I am, brown complexion and a friendly disposition and is married with children. Her outspoken words left me with feelings of dislike, especially when others were allowed to do what I should not. A situation that would later fade as we got to know each other, but an incident that will always remind me of how to address Ada—no endearments. I explained what had happened and was about to get out of the room for some air.

"Don't get up." She paused, slightly pushing me on the shoulders. "Sit."

"I know, but I don't like her accusation. Why would I pass a sale with wrong information?"

"It could happen."

As much as Ada was right, she pushed a nerve. "Look," I replied. "My hearing is excellent. I hear things I wish I didn't, so don't go there."

"Calm down. Don't worry about Lilly," she responded with a smile.

Most of my free time was spent educating myself, with Business books of all kinds, which left me intelligent enough to know that being on a computer's network, communication can easily be tampered with, the reason for the many problems today. In addition, recordings are edited to suit a person's goal. Therefore, I was slowly beginning to see the deception of most of them in the room. Was Lilly using me as a punching bag to make a point? She did say twice, "Don't argue with me." Was she sent with lies to test my memory?

Eventually, I got up from my desk and took a short break to clear my thoughts, which confused me. I was getting to know the woman who runs the editing room. This was her turf, and no one new was coming in to take over her seat. She would see to it if she had to send you crazy.

§

MEMORIES EFFECT

I woke as the dawn was breaking to a new day; heard are the crickets chirping below the window. The birds' shadows on the sunlit ceiling are seen as they fly back and forth, serenading each other with their various sounds, playing like children in the falling rain. The streets slowly come alive as early-morning commuters head off to work. I lay in bed, consumed by the sounds. I turn on my stomach, the comforter still covering my warm body. My mind like clockwork, not skipping a beat as the thoughts of the night before rehearsed. The conversation was overheard when I entered the bus and took a seat, after leaving Gerry's home. He was a dark fella with a cellphone, very loud with laughter in his voice. "Ah, ah," he said to the person on the other end of the phone, laughing as he listened, then comments, "No guy, not this one, not this one at all." He listens to the person's response, then continues, "Looking like that, no, no." Once again laughed aloud, and the conversation went low-keyed. My thoughts switched to the conversation in the supervisor's office. "People are treated with the same respect I see given to me." Then to a dream image of Alice and the voice telling me of my appearance compared to hers. Dreaming of co-workers or colleagues involves issues at work. I thought about issues at work, that is true. Recalling this information from the internet. The focus is more likely on traits this person possesses that mean something to you. Traits, um...she is friendly, has a birthmark on her face, like the mark on my face. It also says if the person is loud or is speaking to the dreamer, the dreamer should pay attention, as this could be significant. What significance could her words have to me other than to incite negative feelings? I shook my head, turned, and pondered on the day when I would take the words that were like lemons and turn them into lemonade. I am not a habitual smoker, so I was not hallucinating. This was my life, consumed by negative inculcated thoughts and physical feelings I daily had to fight to stay sane.

I was battling with forces beyond my immediate control and had to find a way to escape the thoughts, although I could turn the negatives into positives. The image of Shon—the superintendent, entered my mind. His voice irritated me, to tell the truth when he implied, I was crazy to be complaining of noises. I bit my lip as I looked at him, in disbelief at what he had just said. I then recall the image of Shelda—my niece, holding a gun pointed at me as I found myself pleading with her to put it away, as I shouted, "Shelda, it is me; what is wrong with you?" My mind turned to a dream book Ada had given me. I had read in the past and information sighted on the internet. Guns are a symbol of physical passion. If the dreamer is the victim, someone is angry with the dreamer, or something important could be coming up, implying a need to get out the big gun. I recall— being threatened by a weapon, which hints that the dreamer feels that everyone is against him or her, and the solution is only deduced from other symbols in the dream. I smile as I recall Shelda as one with a passion for expressing herself, so much so that she talks around a subject that confuses me and others that listen. I ponder over my thoughts as I whisper, *I was not a victim. She held the gun at me but did not shoot because I shouted to get her attention. Perhaps, I am not trusting of anyone, as stated, about seeing any kind of a weapon as a threat in one's dream.* That being true, having been disappointed so many times in the past. So much so that I have closed the door to my heart so no one can get in to hurt me again. Still, within thoughts, I realize the ability pushed aside from lack of insight. Is the ability to send thoughts and to see past the appearances in front of me. The faith I hold is this, in time, people's attitudes will change as they look within themselves at their grudges and lack of self-assurance to that which would allow them to save relationships rather than destroy them. My thoughts switched back to the night before.

Alcohol and drugs are a chemical mixture for disaster. To start drinking at such a young age, what problems or stress could Gerry be having that would drive him to the point he is—that of drinking daily. Maybe, this was the effect of traveling from city to city. In some ways, his life experiences were similar to mine regarding stability; we constantly had to move from residency.

Some of the effects of alcohol are impaired judgment, loss of eye-sight. In time, liver problems, lung disease, and shortage of breath. When mixed with drugs, one has severe illusions, mental impairment, and suicidal tendencies, slowly becoming addicted to the emotional effects. Although both alcohol and drug misuse are effects of mental and physical damage. Both; are known to boost one's creative abilities; for this reason, the laws give the Liquor Control Board and the Police the right to control the public's use of them.

My thoughts switched back to a few days on my arrival at work and seeing the paramedics removing a person who had passed out, and thought the situation, such as witness, had often been happening. Mentally drained, I saw their actions as making them appear, zombies, leaving me fighting to call them back to an awareness of self. Something the forces did not intend to allow to happen.

§

The ringing of the telephone snapped me out of my thoughts. "Hello. It's your quarter... speak."

"Bu..." It was Rudolf; this he sometimes would call me. "It's your quarter... speak," he repeats what I said, laughing. "You darn right, it's my quarter, and I'll speak. What's up?"

"Oh, I'm still in bed. I was just contemplating on some people and circumstances."

"Was I one of those people?"

I laughed. "You're at the top of the list."

He laughs. "You darn right. I'm at the top of the list."

"Oh, Rudolf, if you only knew."

"Knew what?" There was a second of silence, and then he said, "Anyway, look, I want to see you on the weekend."

"What for?" I ask.

"Look, you are my girl. Can't a man want to see his girl?"

"I keep telling you to stop saying that. I'm your friend, not your girl." I emphasize my tone of voice in the last sentence.

"Just shut up; you are my woman," his voice rises.

"My woman," I repeated, laughing. "Of course, you have the freedom of speech, but it still does not make your words true. I'm telling you, snap out of it, as I'm..." my voice lowered as I completed my sentence, "not your woman."

"Shush. I'll see you on the weekend."

"Call me, please."

"Okay, I'll call." With that said, he hangs up.

With words of thanks, I petition God. *Oh, Jehovah, how deep your thoughts really are. As I review my ancestors' words, I see the wisdom in their actions. In innocence, I spoke, and in my innocence, you corrected me and caused me to see. Oh, my loving father, what is there that I can give you—nothing. You have given me the world, the lives of those I saved through the power of my mental strength; the emotional and, at times, the physical pain I bear for them, without their knowledge, while some made a mockery of me, as they have done your son. I will forever be yours and dare this body of mine to forget your loving kindness—never.* I turned on my back, pushed the covers off, and got out of bed. I tidied the apartment and prepared myself for another day's work. On closing the door, I recall Rudolf's phone call with a smile, as I mumble to myself on the way to the elevator. I know he is just coming up with some story to get me to give him money, with the promise to repay it, which he will never do, and to play with my head if I let him. Then he will be all confused in search of some rich, preferable White, or Indian woman, who will take him in. The elevator finally arrived at the lobby. I exit with the thought of how many times I had asked myself if he really loves me or if I am just his opportunity—a means to an end, but I never seemed to get an answer or perhaps I am just in denial of not accepting my feeling. Situations were getting to me. I had exercised much patience with people having foresight with acknowledgment of "spiritual" actions. I recognized the demons' position on this planet and was willing to let matters fall where they may, with the outcome as it should (perhaps) be.

Chapter 13

LOOKING AT YOU LOOKING AT ME

I ARRIVED AT WORK ON TIME, cleaned my station, and began another day's work. Today I was going to put some of my experiences to work. I had heard enough to realize that the images seen were just their clever disguise to cause separation between me and those still asleep spiritually. Having had the opportunity to see much in life, I knew that **Beauty** is something anyone can achieve through the proper use of make-up and surgery. **Love** is something we are all capable of giving if we look deep within to appreciate each one's role in our lives. **Laughter** we unintentionally share with others, done by our lack of knowledge or innocence of the situation. **Sorrow** is something we all feel at some point in our lives due to the loss of a loved one, the cruelty that was done to others, to us, or people's misunderstanding of us. These similarities are the reason for my generous disposition. Young or old, disabled or mentally challenged, I am able to see something; each can teach the other. Given a few suspended days off from work due to an innocent mistake, saying something without the use of the word (upon approval) took me to the Science Centre. To a bookstore where I purchased a Dictionary of Psychology, a Dictionary that opened my mind to a greater understanding that we are truly a people of faults, as it contained many phobias and phobic stimuli we suffer. So many they were I could not believe that everything a person consciously overindulges in or feared was known as having a phobia; this is not to mention the many emotional and psychological problems shared by most these days. This caused me to see that no matter how perfect one's outer appearance is there is some fault, as the Bible so often stated on many accounts as a reminder that we are imperfect humans, and that we truly are so as not to get puffed up with pride.

§

Most times, I carried a dictionary with me. This was a weakness I have of not being able to spell correctly. A weakness I have tried extremely hard to overcome with little success due to situations in my life. And for some like me, the computer became an advantage, in that it helped to cover our weakness as it did a disadvantage for those that know our circumstances, to make fun of our work behind the scenes. Often repeated is, if you have nothing good to say about someone, say nothing at all, and the other, think before you speak. However, this may be wishful thinking, as some find others' disabilities, weaknesses, and personal life, as reasons for entertainment. So, many times, people speak without understanding due to not having facts or attempting to place themselves in the position of the other. Or they become very defensive because some action by another or something said hit them at that tender spot—their conscience.

§

A few incidents to clarify...

On this day, a few sales held were for the length of time, as information taken was not necessary, others for misinformed information given. One agent in particular, whose sales held, was not only clever; she was facetious in how she presented the material. It was an issue of timing, which was brought to the attention of the supervisors, who failed to inform her about her much longer calls. An outspoken person and to the point, being tactful in how I say things, I decided to send a message within the context revealing the reason for the held sale. My intention was to compliment the agent on the clever way she handles the sale and credit be given where credit is due. My comment was well intended, went out with spelling mistakes and was seen by a few I wished did not. Not only is my situation a reason for my weakness in spelling, but the computer's dictionary has contributed to the weakness of many in spelling correctly. And for this reason, those hiring will put you to the test. Not long after, an email with a joke of the day circles around the office, having to do with a lad applying for a job whose cover letter and résumé contained many spelling mistakes. Then one day, a similar post appeared on Facebook, informing those who can read it are smarter than most. Yes, through our mistakes or faults, living can become creative, as our flaws give laughter to the world of others.

§

On returning from lunch, John's comment overheard regarding the mistakes moved me to call Kate-Lyn's attention to my accommodating of others. John is a fellow in his early fifties with speech impairment; he stammers and daily reminds me of a friend—Noel—from my homeland, who has not been seen for some time due to my constant moving. John was a church minister but left due to his personal choice. He is unmarried and cohabitates with a partner. When I started with the department, he took it upon himself to inform me of all those within editing, some not with the immediate department. I listen and remind myself not to pay much attention to all said but rather to let me know each one.

"Kate-Lyn, can I speak to you for a moment?" I call out.

"Sure!" she responded and removed from her desk into a little room designed for private meetings. I followed behind.

"Look," I began, "I am very patient with people. I was just back from lunch when you asked about a sale, which I could not recall, but I have. The reason it was held...." I explained and then added, "One more thing. Because of my personality, when people make a fool of me, they make a fool of themselves. That is all I wanted to say. Thanks for your time."

"Thank you for bringing my attention to the situation," she responded, and we both walked back to our desks.

After each meal, it is a custom of mine to brush my teeth. One day at work, I went to the washroom after a meal. As I entered the room, I left the door ajar. As I stood at the sink, two Indian girls walked in, one wearing a niqab, a burqa-like garment that covers everything except the eyes, and the other wearing a hijab that covers just the head. Their religious outfits told me they were Muslims. The one wearing the Hijab went to the door and was about to close it. I said to her, "Please don't close the door." She ignored my comment, for the door was closed when I looked. I immediately commented: "I understand a bit about your religion and about you being seen without your headdress. People talk about accommodation but don't seem to understand the word's meaning."

"Madam, there are two doors, and one is closed; that is accommodation," said the one dressed in the niqab.

Instead of responding to what was said, I left it at that, as there is a Bible verse, I try extremely hard to recall daily: to let anger alone and leave rage. Another reason for not commenting further is to allow her time to think about what she said. You see, the outer door she could have completely closed that was left ajar by my entry, but instead, she closed the inner. Upon leaving, the inner door was open, and the outer left closed.

"Thank you!" one said.

"You are welcome," I responded as I walked off.

Later that year, the one wearing the hijab who worked as a monitor joined me in the editing room. We had lunches together and little talks allowing us to know each other. She eventually left the company and me with a smile whenever I looked at fashion. You see, accommodation is not what we can see but what we also do not see. Accommodation is also respecting the inner emotion of others. Although

I knew one, the other that wore the burqa, I did not—appearances do lie. If something did go wrong, my screams would not go unheard with the inner door open. Besides, it would be easy for me to run to the outer door to escape; I was fearful, not stupid. Acceptance, on the other hand, must be done with caution given the world in which we live. Acceptance is something, if we all practice, would eventually bring us to a greater understanding of self. Unfortunately, some see themselves as better than they see others due to the other's lack of financial wealth, cultural differences, education, and one's simplicity, and so within society, treated with indifference.

§

I had to be back to work on Saturday, so after work on Friday, I just wanted to get home as soon as possible to get some rest before getting back into the office, which seemed to be within a few hours. I bid everyone good night and bumped into Gerry on my way to the elevators, walking towards me just out of the men's washroom. He was the last person I wanted to see. After our last meeting, I felt that time away from each other would be best. Nevertheless, one may ask, did fate cause us to meet or was it the timing from the camera's view? A feeling of love emerged from his presence.

"Oh, hi Paula," he calls in a cheerful tone. "Where are you off to?" He opens a pack of Tic-Tacks, retrieves one, and pops it into his mouth.

"I'm on my way home. I have to be back in the morning. Look, I'm going to need your help in moving the couch." It was not a question, as he knew about my moving from where I was.

"Oh, Paula, about that... I will not be able to assist you. I have plans. It would have to be some other time."

I look at him, thinking, why is it when I need help, I can never get it? "I'm disappointed. I can never depend on you, men. All of you are the same—never available at crucial times." Had he paid attention and been sensitive, he would have noticed a touch of anger within that sentence. Unfortunately, he missed it. Instead....

He laughs. "Don't say I will not help you. It just has to be another time."

It could not be another time, I must get out of the apartment before a certain date, but already feeling the rejection, I contained my thoughts. My playful nature was active as we stood waiting for the elevator. However, he had just disappointed me, so all dissolute imagination of what I wanted to do with him faded with the pain of his rejection. The elevator arrived, and we bid each other good night.

As I walked in the rain through the parking lot to the subway station, the need to hold and the fear of having a man in my life, someone to call my own, lingered on my mind as my mind's fantasies played around my head.

Chapter 14

THE GIFT

Oppression may make a wise one act crazy, and a gift can destroy the heart.

Ah, take the cash, and let the Credit go. And heed not the rumble of a distant Drum! –Lustol.

THANK GOD IT IS FRIDAY; the weekend has begun. One of the outbound campaigns needed help, and all those willing to work extra hours were welcome to do so. A few days into the week, I went to Zelda's office to ask what time I needed to report to Mitch, who oversees both the inbound and outbound teams.

After a knock on the door, I enter the room with a different approach. "Good morning, Zelda. Are you okay?"

"Yes, I am," she responded with a smile.

"Then let us keep it that way. I came to ask what time I should report to Mitch."

"Whatever time you want to start before your shift."

"Okay, I'll start tomorrow."

"Thanks," she says before I turn to leave.

"You are welcome. Have a good day. By the way, you are looking pretty today." I meant it.

"Thank you, Paula."

I waved my hand as I continued out of the office and back to the editing room.

Not awfully long after listening to a few calls, Lilly requested my presence at her desk.

I walked over. "Lilly, you asked to see me?"

"Yes, I did. I want you to listen to this call. You remember this call?" She gestures to the air phones to put them on.

"Yes, I do. I held it because the agent did not get a clear response from the customer," I responded as I looked at the sheet on her desk.

"The agent did get a clear response, that's why I want you to listen to it."

"Okay," I reluctantly said with disbelief as other thoughts circled my mind. Lilly picked up the recording at the point where the customer answered the agent. "Please rewind a bit further back." The tape was rewound. The question asks, and the customer's response was clear and correct. How could I argue with this fact? Anyone who knows me, knows me as not one to back down when my integrity stands in question. "That's not what I heard. The recording listened to three times before I decided to hold it." This was true. I was speaking the truth, but how could I prove otherwise with such proof that doubted my hearing. "The customer's response to the question of her age was, 'I think so.' She spoke so fast and exceptionally soft; it was difficult to hear. The reason for me reviewing the call three times within this segment, to which I held it after I was satisfied with what I had heard."

"Okay, I'll release it."

"Okay, then, is there anything else?"

"No, you can go back to work."

At this point, I wanted to quit. I knew the strength of the forces I had to deal with and some whose underline racism I dare not overlook. Once again, I sat in contemplation of the day, up to the point of speaking with Lilly. Why are they doing this to me? I know what I heard, and that was not the response on the recording. Were Zelda and Aden testing the equipment due to my comment about people being able to tamper with recordings? I am tired of being accused of incompetence at my job. To listen and not say anything is accepting responsibility for the wrong done, and I will not do that. I will stand by my word. After all, a rich man has money and uses that as his honor, and what good is it when your truths are shoved aside by the person. However, a poor man, all he has is his word; that is his honor, letting his yes mean yes and no means no. If one cannot be true to one's word, what kind of person is he or she? I left the day behind with most of my questions unanswered. I opened the door to my apartment. A shelter I can come to that is mine, with no one to answer to and no one to care for except myself. After a long day taking care of someone else's work other than one's own, the limited energy left to focus on yours is truly taken away. The weekend had begun, and I wanted to be in a different atmosphere. I called Gerry, who was happy to have me join him at his home.

§

ANOTHER WEEKEND BEGUN

On Saturday morning, I arrived early at work and was able to pick up donuts for the group. Before starting the day's work, I cleared my desk and composed a letter. Gilad procedures change so often that workers do not know what is going on, including the supervisors, except for the ones who seem to be running the show. Held on this day were quite a few sales. One agent I listened to had not only made mistakes in presenting product knowledge to the customer but was very unprofessional. During lunch, the agent was seen sitting in the lunchroom; I approached her to give some friendly advice after giving her some input from the call. The agent's eyes, still on her meal, responded. "It could be the way you were listening to the call."

"It could be," I responded as she continued to finish her meal without further comment. Dealing with people of all cultures for a long time, I am very much aware of their behavior and so wanted not to continue with any further comments.

After lunch, I returned to my desk and was seen speaking to Kate-Lyn, Masui. I entered my log-in password and began to listen to a sale. In the background, an agent is overheard.

"Who does she think she is? I asked the question, and I got an answer. What difference is it how I...?" Suddenly an interruption. "Shush." As another said to her, the voice became a little lower. I smiled as I recognized it was Angel's voice. "The girl can hear you," she said. Angel is a great salesperson with a personality to match. She knows how to engage people in conversation and has knowledge of her products. Something went wrong along the way with her and her good friend, and since then, her attitude toward those in the position of authority was not friendly. One day, on my way to work, I stopped to chat with her about missing opportunities due to her attitude, which she needs to work on, especially since she has a young daughter who depends on her.

"Girl, what are you talking about? Those people owe me monies." I smiled and responded, "Even so, you need to act wisely."

During our conversation, I was informed of being seen in the neighborhood where her mother lives. I seldom visit strange places unless I had gone to an area for some reason, so I asked where this was. To my knowledge, once informed of the streets and was nowhere there. However, Angel insisted that her mother said it was me—I had never met her mother, but her mother knew me. Thoughts surface back to the night I was with Gerry and the SUV seen in front of the building. "Perhaps I was seen." After our brief conversation, I left Angel with her friend having what they bought from Tim Horton's, never to be seen again. Her employment was terminated.

The day had ended, and as I walked through the parking lot to the train station, I realized that criticism, whether constructive or personal, people get very defensive. Perhaps this is because of the attitude that one is not standing in their shoes; and, though this may be true, correction taken gracefully can produce better friendships, as it does a better you. Instilling the attitude of listening could improve one's life, keeping in mind that some people say things from misinformed knowledge. Listening before responding, in many cases, eliminates the embarrassment of self and conflicts with others. For it is better to be swift about hearing, slow to speak and slow to wrath," advises James 1:19.

Chapter 15

A WORD SPOKEN AT THE RIGHT TIME

IT WAS THE END of another week's work. As I left the building and walked to the train station, the scripture at Proverbs 25:11 came to mind that reads, "A word fitly spoken is like apples of gold in pictures of silver." I recalled a comment about a call during the week that sent a message that though actions speak louder than words, words spoken at the right time could cause an effect. Looking back on the day's activities, I wonders if Masui had done his job again—what is required of him. *Perhaps,* I thought. *Maybe I have found a worker like myself that do what is required, at the right time, on most occasions.* Individuals of mature minds pay attention to words and things in detail. Children, on the other hand, overlook things and words spoken. More than ever before, we should not want to be like children and not dwell on every word uttered with the intent to argue. However, to overlook things and words spoken without questions are actions that could cause conflicting thoughts among each one, leading to different conclusions. Each must know when to react, as there is a time for everything. Sometimes one may walk away having concluded that they were not heard—that is okay. At another time, another place reminder of the past day for clearer understanding can be taken.

I opened the door to my apartment, a bit tired but content and to some degree, happy within. I was surprised that the phone was not ringing off the hook, as Rudolf called to find out where I was. As I closed the door and removed the bag pack, the phone rang from within the bag. I quickly struggle to retrieve it before it stops. I flip it open. "Are you following me? I just walked in, and here you are calling."

"I have eyes everywhere!" he exclaims.

I was not about to doubt that. Everything I did seem to be gone unnoticed recently, and I wished I had some privacy. "I am beginning to believe you do. Look, give me about half an hour before coming over." I wanted to wash off the day and all the cares of it.

"Okay, I'll see you about ten o'clock."

"That sounds good. Bye," I respond and hung up. He was on time. At ten o'clock, I opened the door to the knock, which indicated it was he. He had a special way he knocks when on a mission that let me know it was, he. "Come on in."

"You are looking good," he comments as he enters.

"Oh, please, Rudolf." A word at the right time, as I needed words of lifting but drawing attention to myself is something I does not like and tries to discourage others from doing. Beauty is in the eyes of the beholder—why? Because man can only see the outer appearance. I knew I was not looking as good as his protest. My eyes would always show how tired I am, as much as I tried to hide it. So conscious of this, I continue, "I know you need glasses; talking about glasses, have you had your eyes checked?"

"No, but I'm meaning to."

"Ah, ha." There is a second of silence. "One day, when it is too late. You better pray to God that you don't lose your sight because if you do, you had better be with someone who really cares for you." That I said with much concern for him and anyone in the position lacking sight.

"So, how is everything with you now that you know I haven't checked my eyes?" He laughs as he finishes the sentence.

"It's not funny." I stop myself from laughing as I look at him with a smile. "You see, that is what I keep talking about. Life is just a joke to you."

"People make it a joke, so I laugh with them."

"You have undoubtedly taught me much, but I can't live my life like you. This is why I need someone serious."

"You want someone serious?" There are a few seconds of silence, which cause me to look in his direction. "Here!"

I kept looking at him on the couch, his facial expression all serious. I started to laugh. He had this ability to cause me to laugh, if not smile, at his words or his antics. Still laughing, I shook my head as I respond. "Boy, you sure know how to get me out of a bad mood."

"Well, you said you wanted someone serious. So, I'm giving you someone serious."

"Okay, Rudolf, I got your point." Did I really, or was I just saying this to continue the conversation on a serious note? To the point of hearing what I was hoping to hear from him, from his own lips.

"I know you got our point. As a matter of fact, he wants to pop out to say hi to you." He began to slowly unzip the material.

"Rudolf, stop!" I plead. "You tell him I don't want to say hi to him." This was the reason for my concluded thought regards dealing with him. Rudolf was serious about Dick. He not only talks to him, but at times, he claims his reactions are to Dick's thoughts and actions. How could I deal with a man whose presence is absent at times? Having no recollection or taking no responsibility for his actions. With the zipper open and Dick looking straight at me, the head clean and shining in the glow of the dimmed light, a picture-perfect hard candy ready to do serious decay. He looks down, and with a slap of the hand, he sends the head to one side as it returns and settles smack dab in the center. Could I keep a straight face with the sight of what was occurring in front of my eyes? To avoid laughing out loud, I bent over in silent laughter.

He looks at Dick. "Stop that. You see, she doesn't want to speak to you."

"Rudolf, I'm serious. Put Dick where he belongs and zip it up."

"Perhaps she'll talk to you later, but for now, you got to leave." He put Dick where he belonged in his pouch, zipped it up, and proceeded to take a joint from his pocket. "Okay, let's talk," he said and walked over to the cabinet; he opened it in search of a lighter or a box of matches. On finding a lighter, he places the joint in his mouth. He flicks the lighter at the joint's tip as he asks, "How was work?"

"This week was most interesting, and when I'm finished at work, I have to come home to deal with these."

"You mean the superintendent?"

"Yes. The people keep ignoring me with all the letters and talking to them about the noise. It's like talking to stones."

"You should move!" This was easier said than done. I had moved so many times; the thought of moving again drained me mentally, causing my physical strength to do the same. "Why should I? Locating the office where tenants live is just not a wise idea. I'm paying rent for a reason."

"And that is?"

"What sort of a question are you asking me?" I look at him, my eyes ready to cut him. Then again, a person in and out of people's homes, not knowing one of his own, such a comment is expected. I stretched my hand for the joint between his lips. "Give me that." I pull it away from him. "You are an idiot." Words used in a term of endearment. I took a draw. "For the same reason, others pay rent. The payment for a roof to be over them, a place for peace and quiet and to recuperate." I use his famous words: "To *recuperate* one's strength and sanity from the chaos out there." I took another draw of the joint.

"When last you heard from Tanya?"

"I spoke with her the other day. She and the baby are doing fine, she said. She and Cynthia are no longer speaking to each other...."

"Who is Cynthia?" he interrupted.

"She's a girl we both worked with, but a close friend of hers. There was some mix-up about her being at Cynthia's baby shower. I doubt whether I was told the full story. According to Tanya, she feels Cynthia's attitude is related to her hormones."

He laughs. "Hormones," he said and then asked for the joint. He repeats himself, "Hormones. You, women, are something else, always blaming your crazy mixed-up moods and attitudes on hormones or PMS (post-ministration syndrome). Why can't a man blame his crazy actions on hormones?"

"A man's and a woman's personalities are different. Let us look at sex, for instance. In most cases, a man would have sex to ease his frustration. A woman, on the other hand, does so to feel loved. To conclude, a man is more physical, a woman more emotional—idiot." He looks over, crossed eyed at me, his head slightly up as he blows the smoke slowly out of his mouth with a smile. "Cynthia seems to be an altogether individual, but then again, we all do, until placed in circumstances that cause our true self to surface." I thought of the first time I took him to meet Tanya. This was my second visit to where she had moved, and not once since, at the first or the second time, did Tanya invite me into her bedroom, but Rudolf was on his first visit. If I did not know Tanya to be flirtatious, her action could have caused tension between us, so I wonder if Tanya's actions in some form may have caused the attitude between her and Cynthia.

"I need to make a small piece. Would you walk the stroll with me?"

I did not immediately respond; I kept staring at Rudolf as I re-called a nightmare. I was in a club more looking like a shop; it had a door leading out past the counter where a bar was. An Asian man stood at the back of the counter. Suddenly, a commotion began. People seemed to be talking all at once, then blood splattered. I looked around to see what was happening and saw a co-worker visiting at the time from England, a friend of Masui, being chopped up. I turned to the man at the counter; you see what you people have done to my face. I looked away from him towards the door and saw my brother, who told me to shut up and be careful what I say to these people. The scene blurred as I tried to escape. Then I spoke. "As much as I would like to accompany you, the answer is no. The last time I did, I had a nightmare, you remembered. I told you about it. It involved a co-worker from work being chopped up; the incident also included an image of my brother. The whole scene was so bloody, I woke out of it trying to catch my breath all sweaty—the answer is no, dear. Further, do you recall the night I did go with you? Those women looked like they were about to hit on me at any moment. I had to have my eyes at the back and front of me—no sir, no, no."

"That's being on the stroll. You have to be that way. You can't be looking all timid and afraid."

I wanted to laugh after his response; instead, I said, "Sorry, dear. You may or may not want that lifestyle, but nothing so far has shown me differently. You like excitement and living on the edge. I'm different, a bit of excitement—yes, living on the edge—no."

I knew how important it is to have the support of those you love, and having to tell him no, was a bit difficult, but I had others to consider—my spiritual brothers and sisters. Some will never understand my motives, for they would never step into the shoes of another. Further, supporting him this way will only encourage a lifestyle I want to have no part in.

"Well, could I borrow a small piece from you?"

I knew this was coming, so I ask, "How much?"

"I need $30."

"You know I don't keep much money on me. All I have is $20 and some change. You could have it because I'm not going out of the house at this time of night."

"That will be okay. I'll repay you."

I shook my head and smiled, knowing I would never see a dime of it, as I walked off to get my handbag.

On my return, he asked, "Want another draw before I put this in a cigarette?"

"No thanks, I've had enough. So, tell me, where are you staying?"

"Over at Robby's. Bu', that man is something else. He keeps that place dirty. He has all sorts of gangster boys coming and going at all hours. The neighbors are complaining, and Robby does not give a darn. The other day they ran him out of his apartment; he is such an ass."

I started to laugh as I asked, "Are you serious? Strangers run him out of his own apartment."

"Yes. I'm not kidding you," he responded as he started to laugh at the humor of the situation.

"The two of you are so bad that you are no good. Always covering for each other, trying to put one over me, thinking I am stupid."

"I know you see things."

"Yet you try to play me. Lilly is the right woman for you. Pimps you when she knows you are playing her."

He got up, walked toward me put his arm around me. "But I love you; forget Lilly and all the others." He lowers his voice, "I went to see a woman, a spiritual woman, and she said I need to love you in the rear."

I gripped his arms from around me as I eased away from his hug. "What the hell you just said? Are you crazy? Why would she tell you to do such a thing?" I was firing off question after question, not waiting for an answer. Not quite finished, I continued, "See what I mean? All of you want to destroy me, from child to woman to man."

"I went to her for guidance," he replies with a bit of regret detected in his response, either from relating this to me or for what a fool he has been.

"Spiritual guidance...!" I repeated. "And she told you that is what you need to do. When people dabble in unknown matters and their lives are all messed up, they become gullible to people's unfounded ideas or suggestions."

"Don't be upset. I did not have to tell you." This is true, but he did. Now what?

"No, you did not, but your actions were trying to tell me something. This is why we must end this. Your coke habit will be the end of us both."

"I love you. I would not hurt you," he said as if at the point of tears.

"I've heard those words before, and he ended up hurting me." I references Clifford. "What has happened to trust?" He did not respond. I dug into the handbag and retrieved a few notes and some coins. "Here you are." I handed over the monies to him.

"Thanks, Bu'. I will not forget this. I want to run down the stroll. Would it be okay to come back?"

"Rudolf, I'm tired. Let me get a chance to sleep. Seeing tomorrow is Sunday, make it back at a reasonable time, so I can get to rest." I closed the door behind him as he left.

Imagine the man who wants to ride through my tunnel. *I thought to myself* as I prepared the bed. He has watched so many adult movies that he now wants to practice what he sees on me if he is not lying about talking to some spiritual quack—surely one of the devil's workers. I smiled and shook my head as I imagined what must have transpired between them. Rudolf's many intimate conversations of past relationships cause me to wonder about the reason for his action to seek the spiritual woman, as claimed. In about half an hour, he was back. He took a seat on the porch and began to cut into a huge piece of white rock. Pieces, he then separated them into dollar amounts. Afterward, he puts it into a bag apart from a few pieces for himself. He had finished cleaning up, taken a hit (street talk for snort), and was about to take another. Although the door leading out to the porch was closed, my six senses were active, and without looking at what he was doing could tell he was smoking and in a world all of his own. "Rudolf," I quietly and slowly called so as not to scare him out of his intimate thoughts. "Rudolf, please, come to bed; I'm tired," I called again after a few seconds.

"I'll be there shortly. I just need to get myself one hit so I can sleep. I'm finished doing what I must." I did not respond. After fifteen minutes, I again called, my voice a bit louder, "Rudolf!" He had just lit the homemade pipe in his mouth as he drew the vapor from the crushed coke into his system. He had apparently thought that for the time he was left alone, I had gone back to sleep, so the unexpected sound of my voice caused him to jump up from the seat. With the pipe in his mouth, lighter still lit, he almost burnt his lips, knocking himself to the wall. I smiled as I could see what was happening between sleep and being consciously awake. He answered muffled as he consumed the remaining vapor from within his mouth.

"Yes!" he responds, the tone of his voice muffled from his smoked fill mouth.

"I said come to bed," my voice having a sharp pitch and loud tone. "And now, don't make me get upset with you."

In a much clearer tone, "I'm coming now, right now." He responds in a lower tone, "Right now."

His body against mine is felt as he turned, pulling the covers over his head as he drifted off to rest.

My last words to him as I finally began to drift off to rest were, "Oh, Rudolf, you are trying to live a rich man's life in the disposition of a poor man's world."

The remaining question is why people find it so difficult to understand others. Is it because they fail to put themselves in the position of the other to understand, or is it an overwhelming need to exercise power, imperiously stupid, that causes them to act like children without logic? Missing the point that power, fragile as it is in us, needs to be balanced; maintaining such balance produces a greater understanding of self among deeper love, sincerity, and peace.

The other is listening. Something we need to cultivate more in our lives. Fully paying attention to what is said to us, we gain a better understanding of that person's emotional state and intellect. Instead of perfecting our own autobiography and assuming thoughts or actions—though, at times, actions of others do validate our assumptions; it is putting oneself in the other person's space—his or her head and heart—listening to gain understanding.

Chapter 16

DARKNESS vs. LIGHT

"WHO THE GODS DESTROY, they first make mad," an oriental saying to keep at the back of my mind. The things I have suffered, done by those who seemed to be a friend or someone who cares—one has to walk in my shoes to gain a deeper understanding of what is meant. My world is not so different from the present world we share, though it encompasses others; the rules differ. As there is an interchange of encouragement by faith or discouragement by disbelief among each, I must fight to maintain my physical and spiritual well-being, as does my mental sanity. As things heard, seen, or felt and not always revealed, a person's faith and trust are sometimes questioned.

This has been occurring for years before me and will continue after me. Disbelief. Although evidence is shown, people will still be in doubt. I now fully understand the scripture that states, a physical man would only understand that which is physical, he does not receive things of the spirit of God, for they are foolishness and cannot get to know them, but spiritual men will, that which is spiritual. A song I often sing, 'At last, I am aware of love. I asked my papa not long-ago what love is, and the answer he gives is, child you got to find out for yourself you cannot learn from someone else, and if you live long enough, you'll be aware of love....' Yes, when we are mentally mature and sincerely love another, experiences are ascertained from our having faith and belief in the spiritual realm that gives light to avoidance of physical harm. One of my strengths is that to love. My love transcends thoughts and helps to cure conditions. However, this ability also can be harmful to my physical being, as it can be mentally. Eventually I have learnt to use my ability to love wisely.

§

I arrived home from a mentally challenging day. With the door closed behind me, I walked over to the couch, dropped my tired body down and laid my head back. I closed my eyes, inhaled, and exhaled a few times as I relaxed my mind. A few minutes passed, and tears began streaming down my cheeks. The day had moved me to tears as I thought of my conduct. For him, I can be anything and everything. However, I had made a vow to myself never to give of myself completely to anyone. Even my religious conviction was not quite complete. Never for a second have I doubted a higher force in operation, but there were too many thoughts beyond my comprehension; I just had to search for answers on my own for a greater understanding.

I prayed...*Good and gracious God, Jehovah, grant me insight into what confuses my mind. Help me to continue loving those persecuting me mentally, to remember the part each one plays in my life and be able to guide them through the power of loving them that you have shown towards me. Show me how to correct each one's actions as I call to mind my own done with limited knowledge now being perfected by your loving kindness. Amen.*

Unfortunately, I could not get away from a few things that were a secret to some and to others unknown. The laughter, the secret comments and eye contact made between a few of my co-workers and the supervisor—Kate-Lyn, when I answered to being called. Theodore repeated my response innocently or sarcastically, "Paula is coming!" Told me that my life had no privacy, and the group was anxiously waiting to discredit me with any faults they could further find. The day had shown me how people's lack of knowledge and desire to see others failure, will belittle or discredit them in any way they can. Even with facts, shows their own lack of self-confidence or worth. I was hurting very much. I genuinely love my brothers and sisters of all cultures, especially those in the Congregation, and being hurt by them took strength in being able to turn the other cheek, to accomplish my personal goals at the end of each day. I thought of the saying, "You only have one life to live, so live it. But what would happen after the loving—after releasing all the buried emotions to an image, which antagonizes me during the nights? Will he be mature enough to see that I was just seeking an answer to a situation he may never understand? Questions I ask myself. Some do it all the time—use each other for their own advantage, so why cannot me. However, I was no actress, not in a physical sense. An emotional individual, it is beyond me to play with the livelihood of others. I know firsthand how things are done in secret and can affect someone to the point of destruction. I could easily do what I wanted and achieve one of my desires, but I was already a part of society living in poverty. And did not want to contribute to it by adding another fatherless child, which time was about robbing me of the intention. Society already had its problems. Some of those in authority fight to keep the order of present conditions in a world that is slowly getting worse as days go by; in return, they need someone to keep them in order, too.

All realities spring from a single dream (thought or image) or idea (mental picture or thought.) The degree of success depends upon one's belief in self and how badly one wants or needs it, that the very thought of the outcome is to taste the achievement. Support of friends and especially one's family are also important. Having to stand on your own can sometimes be difficult, but it produces your inner strength, heightens your abilities, and deepens your faith. There is strength in numbers, but strength is shown when one must stand alone as God's salvation is recognized.

§

HYPNOTISM is the science or practice of hypnotizing someone. Hypnosis is anything that induces sleep, such as reading a book, watching television, yoga, religious meetings, or things that occupy a person's mind for any length of time. Our dreams are also a form of hypnotism. Subconscious thoughts of our past are often induced by what we had observed or heard during our state of sleeping or awakening. These printed observations on our minds can cause us to react consciously during wakefulness to situations productively or destructively.

It was time for my yearly physical. An appointment was made with my family doctor the week before, but I could not keep it due to insomnia that had me overly tired. I called the office to cancel and reschedule another.

I was with Shelda—my niece, to obtain a book from the library for research to gain a deeper understanding of what I was experiencing.

She turns to me. "What do you want with a book on hypnotism?"

"Knowledge never hurts anyone," I responded.

"Paula, don't you know the Bible warned against it, and don't you know the demons are more powerful than you?"

I knew where her thoughts were going, but I was not talking about practicing such things, only getting an idea of man's thoughts about black-and-white magic and hypnotism. I needed this information due to certain things observed. (Like a whicker dining-room chair—same design, color, and material as mine, as was a white marble table like Tanya's seen in the garbage area. Tanya was told of the table.

Wicked are the beliefs and practices of some people; by taking someone's material possession, they can inflict physical harm, and by cannibalism—they will become like them. I know God's word on the matter and the reason he warned: There should not be found in you anyone that maketh his son or his daughter to pass through the fire, or that useth divination, or an observer of times, or an enchanter, or a witch. Or a charmer, or a consulter with familiar spirits, or a wizard, or a necromancer. For all that do these things are an abomination unto the LORD... - Deuteronomy 18:10-12.

"Yes, I do. Having knowledge only helps to protect me."
"You are opening up yourself to a whole lot of danger."
"Maybe, but once prepared, you can protect yourself."
"You are never okay dealing with the demons," she replied.

Was Shelda, right? Some may think so, and those who do are highly intelligent. A girl a little naive, gullible, and unaware that the demons are powerful, perfecto angelic creatures at what they can do by projecting thoughts of their intentions that moves one to react in ways, not of one's personality. Shelda has little idea of the world we live in today. The angelic angels can be the voice (person) next to you. So, be aware of the friends you keep. Living in darkness is likened to having limited knowledge, compared to having vast knowledge that gives light to one's pathway. I have acknowledged that today, there are people who believe in and practice all sorts of rituals and spells, such as voodoo. A set of religious beliefs and practices of West African origin, surviving in Haiti and other parts of the Caribbean and scattered communities in the southern United States. For others, it's cannibalism, eating the person's body. A practice that has passed. The last I read about cannibalism was in the Awake magazine written by the Jehovah's Witness organization. Those who practice such ritual are believed to become the individual. For those who fall victim to these practices, pity is felt for their lack of knowledge. Some may argue that cannibalism existed in Jesus' day, and this being true, nowhere did it state that the person eating another human will become that individual. When a group was told, they would have to eat of their fathers, sons, or daughters' flesh, it was because they would not have food on account of their rebellious conduct, actions of Jehovah's disapproval and his chastisement.

An incident... I had a severe headache for almost a week and had to have a brain scan. Due to a person's act of leaving a hat with nails sticking around the crown of it, left lying on the bench of a laundry mart I frequently used (by the public), at the time living in a rented part of a home on Main and Danforth Streets. On seeing Doctor Noah for severe headaches, I insisted he send me for a scan, which he did; fortunately, the scan returned the brain's normal. A day later, after being given the news, the headache disappeared.

Yes. Of some of these practices, I was a victim. Fortunately, I came out victoriously due to my faith in (God), higher power and understanding of people (but not without some damage). And I continue to fight daily from becoming the victim of their wicked intentions with which they have captured the gullible ones. Some people's beliefs and actions can cripple you if you are not consciously aware of yourself, your surroundings, and people in general. However, the things we do have a chain reaction, and the true God himself will bring every sort of work into judgment concerning every hidden thing, as to whether it is good or bad, so whatever Lucifer's or his agent/s plans were for me, I trusted it would fall right back on them.

Chapter 17

WHEN THINGS CHANGE

I GOT DRESSED and off I went to complete another day's work. Later that day, Gerry is seen in my department. His presence on most occasions is felt before being seen. I looked up as he walked through the door. Normally he would make eye contact with a smile, but today, he was different. He walks past me to Lilly's desk. The conversation was concerning a held sale. I was close enough that the conversation could be overheard. I turn, look at them briefly and still, he ignores my presence. That is odd, I thought to myself. I know he has a reason to be guilty, but embarrassed. Perhaps having lived in India has something to do with his do not care-attitude at times. In a nation where the norm of most is war and strife, growing up in such an environment does have a way of shaping one's mind. Then again, like myself, the day's work, coupled with mentally inculcated thoughts, may have had much to do with his demeanor. However, that was no excuse for him to ignore me or not even call occasionally.

Many incidents told me it was time to look elsewhere for employment, but tough as it was at times, I was comfortable knowing what I had to work with. Further, constantly moving from one job to the next creates instability in the minds of potential employers' evaluation of you, which is counterproductive. To venture into the unknown can be scary, but until making that change, one never experiences the other lessons life has to teach. The same is said of relationships. Many stay in relationships be-cause of comfort or fear of moving on, even with the signs clearly seen. Is this due to knowing who and what they're dealing with? time always tells.

§

SIGNS, a gesture or motion used to express some thought, com-mand, or wish; any unwritten word, character, or the like, used to ex-press a familiar meaning.

People are always looking for and asking for a sign. Way before I was born, my and your ancestors asked Jesus, "Tell us, when will these things be, and what will be the sign of your presence and of the conclusion of the system of things?" - Matthews 24:3. I am sure some of you can recall your earliest years, I know I can. One consistent oc-currence is Sundays, having a donation or not, off to church, I was sent. Never have I seen my mother go to church, but every Sunday, her words to me were (God rest her soul). I often wonder why people use that phrase—however, she would say to me, "You had better get dressed and go thank your father for being here." I knew of one who, on most occasions, was never around due to his career in life, and when he was, his presence, I greatly appreciated. So, what does she mean, and why doesn't she get dressed and go, always insisting I do? These would be my self-questions. However, never did I express my inner thoughts out loud. Now grown, being in church and at Sunday school, which was held beneath my aunt's house on Station Street, in-stilled principles and morals gained and kept in thoughts that are my foundation and guide within this life I live. For some of you, it was, "Don't touch that; it will sting, burn, bite, or hurt you." Their verbal warning was not good enough, so you must find out for yourself with much curiosity that got the best of you. Sooner than later, what you told not to do, you did, for your disobedience, the consequences you received. From history down to today, we have many accounts also recorded in the Bible and Historical books of Kings, Queens and of ordinary men and women seeking a sign and did this by speaking to and seeking the services of spirit mediums and fortune tellers. There's a record of Saul doing this in Samuel 28:8-13. The funny thing is, even though a sign is given, some tend to ignore it. Perhaps this is done knowing we have the free will of choice to test our inner strengths by pushing them to the limitations—or that of God's patience with us. Guilty of this I am.

§

I awoke out of a dream. The image of a man and a woman in a seated position having sex, the woman had her back towards him. Then I heard a man's voice. Even in my sleeping state, I am alert. The man heard saying, "I love you." The sound came from below the window. No one responded. I did not remove myself from the bed to see who it was, as I was now aware of the devil's designs to discredit my intelligence. As our Creator knows our inner thoughts and desires, so does Lucifer by the manipulation of his subjects he cleverly used to have you think you are dreaming. We, more so now than before, need to be conscious during our dreams to protect ourselves both physically and spiritually. Especially in our wakefulness, as we are not left without warning, the spiritual realm will become more active in this day of increased knowledge. So vast the increase of knowledge due partly to man's dishonesty, violent and evil acts.

Here to enlighten is a recent occurrence. Many years ago, I had a dream, the image was of an Indian woman. She seemed to be angry with me as she said, "you will never get ahead." And to this day those words are seen in every road taken. I have a part-time job I occasionally do. A few days before this occurrence on my way out to the job at the last moment, I removed a phone from my belonging and put it away. I was overly tired when I got home from the job, and this was mostly due to sleepless nights taking a toll on my body. The next day as I looked for the phone it could not be found. I knew it was not left at the job, but called to find out if it was seen; accident do happen.

It was not. Walking home from the grocery store that morning, a voice is heard behind me, "You okay." I turned around to see a woman beside me with a phone in her hand held to her ear. She smiled at my attention which I mirrored. Her actions were carefully observed as I saw an actress before me. When I got home, as I did another search for the phone, my memory recalled where it was. The phone worked well the day before, but when I tried to turn it on, it froze on unlocking the pin. What could have happened? It would be a question for anyone. Lack of privacy in my unit could have moved "that one" who overheard my conversation (with contacts), having access to my phone could have been the one/ or ones that locked my phone or the chip, not mine, removed by the intruder. This is the kind of action/s we have to become aware of. Situations that cannot only stress an individual out or cost money one doesn't have but lack of understanding concludes something is off with the individual whose verbal outburst is misunderstood. One must be in the person's position to comprehend the actions of the invisible forces or a narcissist.

Now seen are technical surveillance produced and put in places that were not before. Cameras that have caused living our lives today seem to be on a stage where most have become actors and actresses. Making this song, 'I always feel like someone's watching me,' is a predicted song of our time. Some in a society whose innocence is deceived, as they cannot distinguish reality from fantasy, loose morals some live. We need to remember that dreams are often confusing. Therefore, we need to get all thoughts (or factual truths) together and in perspective chronologically to unravel each word heard and each image seen to ascertain the meaning.

I removed myself from the bed to prepare for the day ahead.

§

I got to work on time, cleaned my station, and was about to log on when I noticed the changes to the software; I was denied access a few times to different applications. The assisting supervisor recently promoted was asked for assistance. Unfortunately, he was no help, as he had not yet shown how to operate the software, so Ada was called to assist. Finally, I was able to get started on my day's work.

In this world, a minority whose six senses are more active than others, allowing them to sense occurrences before they realize; I am one of those individuals. When Ada walked off from speaking with Samantha, she looked at me with eyes wide open, her facial expression as a person just informed of something unbelievable, mumbled to herself. Looking around the department, I noticed a few others had left, and a funny feeling came over me right then as Lilly called my name." One moment... I'll be right there," I answer. Although the door was slightly opened, I knocked to get Lilly's attention.

"Have a seat," Lilly said. Kate-Lyn is presently seated across from her. "I called you to let you know I'm going to have to lay you off. There's just not enough work to keep you on. Further, I spoke to Zelda, and she said there's nothing on the floor for you to do."

I was surprised at hearing this. Gilad was currently training new recruits for other campaigns. With my skills and adaptability, why could Zelda not suggest me trained for one of the other campaigns? "I see," I replied. It was all I could say now. As my thoughts and emotions kept jabbing at me. I had the choice to speak out, but that was to control.

"Even if I want to keep you on, with your SPH (sales per hour) not being consistent, I can't. We had a talk...."

I interrupt, "Yes, I know about my SPH being up and down. Look, there is no need to go into details; we both know the reason why, as I explained to you. What I need from you is a letter stating that...."

Kate-Lyn interrupts, "She will need the superintendent to know... ." She also lived in Government subsidy housing and knew what I would require in a situation like this, but I interrupted.

"Don't even remind me of that right now. There is just too much going on. I don't even want to think about them right now."

"Your ROE form (record of employment) can be picked up next week with your cheque. That was exactly what I was about to ask when interrupted. "You can log off now, and we will pay you until six o'clock." Lilly looks at Kate-Lyn.

"Absolutely," responded Kate-Lyn.

"Thanks. Is this all?"

"Yes," replied Lilly.

I walked out of the office and back to my desk to log off. In the process of doing so, Masui came to me with a printout of held sales.

With a smile, he asks, "Paula, you held this sale without an explanation."

"Oh, it was a mistake; it should be released. We will get that done."

"Thanks," he replies and walks off.

I completed the logoff, said goodbye to those in the room, and returned to where Kate-Lyn and Lilly were still seated.

"There's a sale held by mistake." I handed the printout to Lilly. "It's a good sale; please release it. I'll see you next week to pick up my cheque."

I look at Kate-Lyn. "Kate-Lyn," I paused, "good night." With that said, I walked out of the office. As I walked the hall towards the elevator, the owners walked towards me; I nodded my head as we passed each other, and the girl smiled. Before leaving the building, I picked up a few local employment newspapers and spoke to Jackson on my way out. Jackson is a young man from my hometown who had briefly worked with Gilad.

I walked through the parking lot, my thoughts on how many times I had walked this road before—a road that never gets easier. Giving of my time and dedication to a job only to be thanked in the end by a kick in the ass—so speaking. A few minutes after entering the station, the train arrived. It was crowded with commuters returning from or going to their jobs, so a seat was unavailable, forcing me to stand. I wanted to cry but was strong in holding back the tears; after a few stops, I could sit. A brother stood beside me. I could see him looking at me, so I forced myself to look back at him—as I knew and had always been told I was like an open book, meaning I could not hide my emotions; in pretense, as though I was alright. Do not even try, just do not say a word to me, were my transcended thoughts as I looked up at him. I opened one of the employment papers and, with a pen, went through the want ads. For a time, my attention will be taken from my feelings of rejection, disappointment, and the need to cry.

Finally, home. I walk into the apartment and to the radio; at maximum volume, it is turned up to conceal my sobs. The tears, like an open floodgate, flowed down my cheeks. *Father.* I spoke softly, my voice drowned out by the sound of the radio. *Why me? Why are people used to making my life miserable? I try to please and accommodate others in my life, but in everything I do or try to do, there is a difficulty along the way. Why father, why?* The sink in the washroom was now turned on as I washed the tears away. I sat on the toilet with a cold, damp cloth to my face. *Perhaps,* I continued, *the time off will give me some time to rest. As you know how tired I am. If their intentions, especially Zelda's, were to hurt me, their actions would work to my advantage. Justice, I can see, Father, sure rests with you.* Still seated on the toilet, I recalled a religious program from 100 Huntley Street seen on television by a speaker named Dr. Charles Stanley. "Facing our Failures," he said, when we find ourselves having failures in our lives, these are some of the points to remember; he had mentioned more than five points. Still, these were the ones I chose to remember.

1. "Godly people with the right motivation sometimes fail.
2. Do not blame God for our failure or failures.
3. When facing failures, the first place to look is within.
4. Failure is not the time to fear but to have faith and
5. The opportunity to correct our mistakes, from the second chances given."

Those reminders moved me from the toilet with renewed faith and confidence. I washed off myself had a snack, turned off the washroom lights and turned into bed, putting the day at rest.

Chapter 18

OBSTACLES IN THE WAY

THE FOLLOWING WEEK I went to pick up my cheque and met Dan on my way to the office. He is also from Guyana.

"What's up? How are you doing?" he inquired.

"I am fine. I am on my way to pick up my ROE form and start looking for something part-time...."

He interjected, "So, what happened? Why did she let you go?"

"Boy, many things are going on around here that I'll rather not get into at this time."

"If you are looking for work, my lady works at American Express. I can give you her number to call and find out what you need to do."

"I know the company is hiring, but the location is too far."

"Yeah, it is. It takes her about an hour to get there. Keep in touch all the same."

"Thanks for the information, though. Take care, and I'll be seeing you." I walked off down the hall to the door that led to reception. "Good day!" I greeted the receptionist, who returned the greeting with a smile. "I am here to pick up my ROE form. Is Hanna around?"

"I'll get her for you. Have a seat."

"Thanks," I said and step back a few feet to take a seat. After about five minutes, Hanna came forth with the form. "Paula!" she

155

beacons, the form opened in her hands. I walk toward her. "Hi. Thanks for having this ready for me." I took the form.

"Take care," Hanna replies and walks away.

I sat back down to look over the form and noticed that the starting date was incorrect. I clapped my tongue against the roof of my mouth making a funny noise behind clenched teeth *as I thought*, how could they have the date wrong. They knew I was coming in to pick up this form; why did they not check the records to be sure everything was correct. Working in this place, you must do everything for yourself regarding accuracy. I stood, walked to the receptionist, and requested Hanna be called back, as the Form was incorrect. The receptionist picked up the phone, dialed Hanna's extension and told her what was wrong. In a few minutes, she was at the desk. I was mentally tired; I inhaled a deep breath and exhaled the frustration as I stood and then walked toward Hanna. "Look!" I said pointing to the section that read the starting date. "This information is incorrect. How could you have the date and year so incorrect? I started not in 2004, but in 2002, and the date is also wrong."

Hanna took the form, looked at it, and at me, "I'll have this corrected. I'll be back shortly."

I sat back down and waited with much disgust as to the setbacks in my life, wondering when it would all end. This was just a break from what was about to come next. After I received the corrected form, I decided to go to the resource Centre to update my resume. With my skills and ambition to do work that may seem embarrassing to some, I knew it would not be long before something came my way, so I held off from filing for unemployment insurance—the office was also in the building.

I got to the Resource Centre, signed in to use a computer, removed the diskette from my bag, and pushed it into the computer. To my surprise, the information on the diskette I printed a few weeks ago was now changed. Not only was the format different, but a few words were missing. I sat at the computer trying to fix that which was not touched by my hands, but the laughter coming from a room across from where I sat mentally confused me. So, pretending not to pay attention but rather to what I was doing, I typed in what was originally there and again, the sounds of laughter echoed from the room, the thought that they were probably able to see what I was doing caused me to leave. On my way home, I called Leila. "Hello!" "Leila?" A few seconds pass before I continue, "How are you?"

"I'm fine. Where are you?"

"I had to come to the office to pick up my ROE form, and I am now leaving the Resource Centre. Girl, I am so tired. I don't know why or who is doing this to me...." I explained to Leila what had just happened, and as always, she listened. This is all I needed. Yes, someone to be there in times of frustration. Not needing guidance as this, I know; eventually, I will find through meditation and looking back at the end of the day. Although interchange of experiences give guidance from the other perceptions. I understood why the roadblocks in my way of achieving my goals. The man or woman who knows my affairs and me, with truths and secrets to tell, will do all in their power to stop this revelation. I sense a lack of privacy in my home as on my computer, but it is only a matter of time before a matter becomes clear to those confused and innocent of the wicked ones actions. As I was beginning to see.

§

There exist people in this world whose faith is weak, and without seeing evidence of proof, there is denial. In addition, others without faith do not really care for shown proof—mentally pushed by others with racist and jealous attitudes to hate; the belief is each holds his destiny and has nothing to do with a higher power, and so they continue in their wrathful course. They will cause havoc in one's life, doing what comes as an advantage to attain their own wealth, failing to recognize this fact—God's eyes are everywhere, seeing the things that darkness cannot hide. The mystery remained, who is controlling the inner thoughts of those around me. Their actions pushed my mind having to control my reaction to protect my physical being. Complaint letters of attempted mental manipulation from incidents encountered at entering my unit, given to management of the housing development, went unanswered or not investigated, as a response to the complaint was never received. Because the sentence against the wicked has not been executed speedily, the heart of the sons of men has become fully set in them to do bad. Time and time again, this statement has proven to be true. Unfortunately, many forget there is a time for everything under the sun. As it was in the beginning, so it is in the end. As I quote, "Those who behave arrogantly on the earth in defiance of right-them will I turn away from My Signs: Even if they see all the Signs, they will not believe in them: and if they see the way of right conduct, they will not adopt it as the way; but if they see the way of error, that is the way they will adopt. For they have rejected Our Signs and failed to take warning from them." -The Qur'an, -The Heights, Surah 7:146.

END

Part
Two

CONTENTS

Acknowledgements

To express my deepest gratitude to all who played a part in my composing this memoir of encounters. I hope all who take the time to read my book will enjoy it as much as I have enjoyed writing it. May you be encouraged, enlightened, and creative with what life offers you.

Prologue

Throughout my life's journey, these six ethics to follow sometimes slip my memory, and they are important to do before the start of any activity is this...

Before you Pray – Believe. Difficult for some who do not detect human presence.

Before you Speak – Listen. The other person's thoughts are important as yours.

Before you Spend – Earn. Never put your hat further than you can reach it.

Before you Write – Think. Tattoo on mind before tattoo on skin or writing on paper.

Before you Quit – Try. Do not give up until all options are explored.

Before you Die – Live. We are here to explore, learn from nature and each other, laugh, dance, and enjoy this earth, our home!

Chapter 1

NEW BEGINNINGS

IT WAS JULY 1, 2006, the final day for me to move from the second-floor apartment. The move was just a floor up. Most of the day was spent moving items into the new apartment, some being packed away where I wanted them to be, except for several glasses that were put aside to be placed in the cabinet of the entertainment unit. This was my last evening in the old apartment; I got out a bottle of Malibu rum, the remainder left in the bottle. Sitting on the floor with my back against the couch, I put the bottle to my mouth and took a mouth full. The cool, refreshed flavor of coconut saturated my mouth as I swallowed slowly, feeling the liquid run down my throat; my eyes scanned the apartment, which was now almost empty of my belongings. The television played a movie that occasionally grabbed my attention from my inner thoughts. The change would be good, *I thought to myself* as my imagination pictured the apartment. It offered a great view of the outdoors and gave me a sense of freedom from the enclosed unit I am in now. I wonder who that bird belongs to; it is strange how it always watches me from the tree. I wonder if it has some sort of monitor device that is picking up on what I am doing. I must stop this. I think way too much. *I shook my head to rid of the thoughts* as I tried to focus on the movie. A few minutes passed, and my thoughts drifted back to past altercations between myself and

Samson. When the office moved next to the unit. I complained about the noise; to no avail did they acknowledge my cry for help. The constant hitting of the inner door was like being hit in the head, and some days would have me wake with a headache. After numerous complaints, they finally fixed it. Temporarily, I had some peace from the office staff's early morning activities. A few months passed, and a new tall blond girl joined the cleaning staff, and not too long after, one evening, as I came home from work, the glass door to the office was seen broken. They changed the door from that incident to a heavier type, and the noise was even worse when closed. Due to sleeping on the floor, the echo of the door when closed caused an effect. Once again, with many written and verbal comments about the situation, the superintendent had the exit and office doors fixed, but the problem still exists; as the doors closed, the sound was not as loud. So finally, I give a signed transfer form to the office. Unable to take the noise that would drive me crazy, I set out to visit the main branch to speak to anyone on the board who may be able to bring about changes to my situation. A woman, who took down my verbal complaint and promised to get in touch with Millie, saw me at the door.

Promises are for fools, I always say. Therefore, I left intending to get a lawyer to solve the problem. Fortunately, when I visited the courts, got a pamphlet of referrals, and got home, I received a call from Millie, telling me that an apartment was available, and Samson would be calling to set a day for me to look at it. I am no one's fool. I knew there were vacant units in the building, and two or three days after handing in an emergency transfer should have received a call. Instead, by their agenda, it took them almost a month or two before calling me. After looking at the unit with Samson, I decided to take it as much as I needed to move away from the neighborhood.

I was able to get Lamar that weekend to help with moving a few items, unable to get Gerry. Getting the couch out and into the elevator was quite difficult. At last, we had accomplished this. The button to the third floor was pressed, and a few seconds later, the door opened. Getting the couch out of the elevator was a bit easier than putting it in. Joyous, we were finally on the floor, with one at each end of the couch; we began to move it. As we turned, we found out we were still on the second floor and had not moved as we thought we did; we both started to laugh, as there was nothing to do but look at the funniest of the situation. We now had the task of getting it back into the elevator and to the right floor—this time. Once inside the new apartment, after a few attempts to get it up the stairs, Lamar exclaimed. "Paula, this job needs a few more hands; you'll have to call me when you get a few other people to help." We were both exhausted and sincerely needed a few extra hands.

"You are right. Let's lean it against the wall and get the entertainment unit together."

As Lamar worked on getting the unit together, with my occasionally helping, I unpacked my clothing in the closets. Lamar was quite helpful, and once done, he left, intending to return once I got a few others to help. I continued to clean and pack away items into the late evening, the apartment slowly coming alive with my touch, taking on a look of my character and that of my dreams. The pictures on the wall indicated of few episodes, can tell of the dream each belonged. To complete the decoration of the entertainment unit, I got to the kitchen cabinet to retrieve the glasses intended for it. As I got out the glasses, one by one, I realized two were missing. I was now upset, as I knew I had left several glasses of the same kind, and someone had to have moved them. Who is the mystery? Having watched, on many occasions, talk shows of psychics, and found Montel William's talk show with Sylvia Brown to be remarkably interesting. I never thought I would be experiencing the same things until I moved into the new apartment. I heard others talk and watched others explain to the world of having left certain items in their homes only to later find them removed, some of them recovering these items later, in exactly the place where they had left them. Or never discovering them at all. I never had something removed from its place(not before moving or seeing a ghost), as I have heard people talked about, including my niece. Who related seeing her grand- father—Reginald, in his hammock on her visit to my aunt's Stella's place on Station Street, turned out to be his form. As his body was not there. This brings me to this point of similarities between our world and the world above. Our elements are Fire, Water, Earth, and Air. While the elements above are Fire, Water, Earth (dust), Gases and Form. Often repeated, until you walk in another's shoes, you really do not know. This saying is a fact. Truly, through experience, we gain a greater understanding. And knowledge is cut short by deliberate or foolish killings of individuals. Without being in unfamiliar situations, we need to listen to the revelation of those who have. Although I found Sylvia Brown's explanations of psychic phenomena interesting, there is disbelief in some things, such as the dead being able to communicate with the living. There is an explanation for... as there is a time for everything under the sun. Thanks to God's Word, that has made things clear. Having knowledge of the spiritual world we live in, only then will one understand the depth of Satan's manipulation of circumstances, getting us to believe untrue things, acting like children, and having no sense of right or wrong. Removing glasses from the apartment after the locks changed was not acceptable. The opportunity for someone to enter the apartment existed. Why is the mystery?

We are so intricately connected it is a shame that this fact wrote Mikhail Angelo in a poem she wrote: "We are more common than we are uncommon." And to this fact, once recognized, there would not be so much tension and wars among us. Understanding the intentions behind the games people play is important, as when you do, you can play along with your truths. I detest one thing, which is to be played with as if a toy. If they—whoever it is—want a toy to play with, they should find the retail store Toys R Us. There they will find a variety from which to choose. We all have intentions for why we do certain things, but we must know when to stop, as pushing a person too far can and will damage them, which is crossing the line. The line of loving, caring, acceptance, of being human. Out loud, I spoke, "Whoever you are, you better put my glasses back. This is going too far. No one plays games with my mind. I remember everything I do."

I knew that saying what I did made no difference, especially since the locks had changed. The reappearance would blame one group—the cleaning staff, whose denial will surely make me look like I was losing my mind. Shifting the blame to the next-door neighbors—who had many opportunities to enter, the motive to do so, now that being another matter, what was I to do.

Later that evening, I called Leila, then Gerry. I then found out Gerry's reason for not calling. He really does not like speaking on the phone. Was this true, or was this an excuse? *I thought to myself* after hanging up the phone. I then took a shower, and having had pizza earlier with Lamar not being hungry and overly tired, I turned into bed. The cell phone beside me started ringing. It was after one o'clock in the morning when I glanced at the display. "Hello!"

"Hi babe, it's me." The voice came back through the receiver.

"Yes, Rudolf. What's up?" I asked, still groggy from the day's activities and trying desperately to enter a place where I could get some rest without being disturbed.

"I'm fine. I am at work. We are working overtime trying to get things organized for opening a new Canadian Tire store," I interrupted him.

"Oh, I saw the flyer, and one of my hair-stylist told me about that new store." I had more hair stylists than the stars…lol. I had too due to some days catching them in a bad mood or their hair cutting skill had more to do with appearances.

"So, how is everything with you?"

"Well, I'm home. I was recently laid off."

"Are you serious?"

"Yes, Rudolf, I'm serious. Don't worry; I will find something soon."

"I'm sorry to hear you are not working. Anyhow, I'm living in Scarborough on Ice Cream Lane." He laughed as he said the name and caused me to do the same.

"Boy, you are so funny."

"I'm living with a chick who has her own home." A woman's voice was overheard in the background.

"I am happy that you have found someone and are working. Perhaps now you'll be responsible."

"If you see me now, you'll want me back."

"Oh, Rudolf, please, I've had enough of you. Your lifestyle and mine are quite different."

"I'm no longer smoking, and I'm working."

"I have been told that too often, only to find out differently." I started to laugh. "Look, Rudolf, I'm tired and need some rest. I am really happy for you. Take care of yourself and be respectful to her. I'll talk to you another day. Bye."

"Okay, take care!" he replies and hangs up.

Now awake, I stared at the ceiling in the partially dark room, and through the sheer pleated curtains at the window, the abstract lines on the ceiling caused by the illumination of the floodlights from the courtyard, I thought of the conversation I had just had.

Trying to take another stab at my heart, were the angels busy at work, this I saw. Sincerely, *I thought to myself*. I am happy for him and hope that this time the chance he has given; he will take full advantage of it. He is a good man; perhaps if his child's mother was different and his life had fewer obstacles, his life outlook may be different. Being with Gerry, I did for many reasons. One reason was to show him a relationship with him is not about money or good looks. It is about communication, and support of each one's goals, and another, is to shut the mouths of those who talked negatively about me. *My thoughts tracked back* to a time on my way home from visiting Gerry. On missing the King Streetcar, I started to walk home when a car passed with its top open and two persons—I could not tell what nationality they were, but they were not black, observed as being male yelled out, "Be careful of that guy; he is going to hurt you." They were looking at me, so I knew to me, they were speaking. What do they know about him or our friendship? *My thoughts wandered back to Rudolf's* call left on my cell phone the day after being laid off. "I still love you, and you could do what you like." What was that all about? I began to believe he had eyes all over the place, as he had said. As my thought process continued about our situation, the couple who lived together came into focus. Day in and day out as she left for work, the husband would do the same. The difference was he would leave and spend the day with his buddies. At the end of the day, they will greet each other. He lies about the kind of day he has had. The man had been doing this for over a year until one day, in conversation with a friend was told the truth about her husband's daily activities. Surprise, she sure was, but she never doubted him as he brought home his pay every week. Monies earned from gambling, and he was good at what he did. In his eyes, he was working and doing no wrong, she need not know what type of work, but this he perceives to be wrong. This story constantly presents itself in the forefront of my mind when I come home day in and day out, only to find Rudolf lying on the couch. Was Trini playing me? After an hour or so had passed, staring at the ceiling in the dark with my thoughts, I finally closed my eyes and drifted into a world I would rather stay far from.

Chapter 2

WOULD YOU FOLLOW YOUR SHEPHERD'S CALL?

ALL THESE YEARS, I had lived a quiet life even after being in Westley's life for a brief period. I was not sure when I became a public figure. However, I had an idea it did after meeting Rudolf. With me, he did not hold back the anger he felt inside toward others, and when he smokes, he tends to go into intimate details of his love life I wished he kept to himself. His actions left me thinking that he would do the same about our relationship, so I held back in giving of myself completely; further, I knew it was not a lasting relationship. My father once told me, "It is best to love and loss then to lose and never love." I was satisfied that my loving him was with reservation because the truth is what I hold was still having the privacy I deserve. He would speak of the men on the other floors. On many occasions, his stories would bring laughter to my life. One of them, a client of his, lived above my floor. One day as Rudolf left his apartment after a drop, a young boy encountered him in the hallway as he left the person's apartment. The young lad looked at him and started laughing. "I know what he was thinking, Bu. He probably thought I was gay, too."

"Are you?" I ask with a smile.

"What shit are you asking?" he responds with a serious face.

"It's a question. For all you know, you could be…." I motion with my hand in the air from side to side.

He started to laugh. "You are full of it."

I am told of the time his dad died. He was asleep with MariJune, and all he could remember was spinning around above the bed. Was Trini hallucinating, or was this the truth? If he did, he most likely had an out-of-body experience. However, the only person who knows the truth is MariJune, he, and God, as I was not there. Further, I was not about to doubt him. For these facts, I know strange and unexplainable things happen to people, and for some, to experience is to believe.

Due to a few sleep disorders such as insomnia, sleep apnea, narcolepsy, nightmares, sleep talking, and walking. Understanding the type of sleep disorder can help one's overall physical and mental health. A past resident, on Sharp Street, in a house my sister Veronica had purchased, and Monica financially looked after. My responsibility in exchange for rent was looking after the yard and paying the utilities. I lived in the basement, and a couple lived above. They were a mixed couple; she looked like a Native Indian, with long beautiful black hair, fair-skinned and tall, neither thin nor fat, but just the right build for her height, about five foot six inches. The man was about the same height and a little on the thin side; he was friendly and very polite. She, on the other hand, did not say much. One day unexpectedly, I approached her to find out why the basement was so cold when the utilities were often being paid, and to get some heat has to turn the oven on. The question caused the throwing of words. I am told the home is warm enough and is accused of being a schizophrenic. In a conversation with Veronica, I found out what she meant from Veronica's explanation it was someone with mental problems; I laughed, as I was not aware of having a mental problem.

§

SCHIZOPHRENIA—disorganized speech and behavior, deterioration in work, social relations, or self-care, and often confused with multiple and split personality.

A month after the incident, I was in a library, as I often do and recalled the word. I got a medical book and looked up the word. I put down the book and studied the content of what I had just read and whispered; she must be out of her mind. She obviously sees how tidy I keep my surroundings and myself. Perhaps seeing no visits of friends gives her... I look back at the explanation and as I close my sentence—Deterioration in social relations that.... A mental light emerged. That could be it; she sees no visitors and assumes, but calling me a schizophrenic is wrong. It must be a new word she encounters... A memory came to mind that put a smile on my face. I recalled Veronica's neighbor back home that constantly fought with her and the day I used a word discovered from the dictionary: intoxicated, which the girl is told she exhibited. The full understanding of a person suffering from schizophrenic behavior; lacked knowledge.

One evening, this my first occurrence at the residence, I had an out-of-body experience. As I lay sleeping, I felt my force leaving my body. I could see myself lying in bed as I exited the window beside the bed. Yes, this truth; how could I doubt Rudolf? I was not on drugs, which would have been marijuana or alcohol.

To tell is another incident: It was in a month during the winter, at an assigned job in a bakery working the evening shift for an agency. On this assignment, during a break for lunch one evening, the decision to switch a phone from my back pocket to the front so as not to sit on it, and the keys to the back done. Minutes later, I left the lunchroom to the washroom to tidy up before going back onto the shift. As I was pulling down my jeans, I noticed the keys were not felt in the back pocket, nor was it heard dropped into the toilet bowl, immediately panic rose, and I looked onto the floor and noticed it was not there. After use of the washroom, I rushed back to the lunchroom only to find out it was not there, nor was it seen by the woman who occupied the seat. The supervisor informed of the loss, she and I did all we could to locate or return the keys by someone who may have picked them up by mistake. It was now getting to the end of the shift, and my panic worsened. I wanted to cry; action was avoided. I was called off the production line to the manager's office, explaining what happened, and he concluded to look at the cameras. Closer to the end of the shift, he came with disappointing news. "All that was explained was seen on camera, except what went on in the washroom," he says. The suggestion was then made to do another search, and this time, in the garbage bins. Why would someone throw someone's keys in the garbage? *I thought to myself.* After he left, I left the production line and returned to the washroom. I looked around and even into the garbage bin and in my coat pockets as had suggested, which I insisted would not be there as I did not put it there; I even informed those in the room that if a set of keys were found, kindly let management know. Leaving the washroom now on my way back to the floor, I felt something on the lower front of my foot; when I passed my hand, it was the keys. Did it slip my mind that the keys had been removed from the front to the back pocket—No, it did not. Did movement even feel during the shift that it was in my possession—No. Fogged memory—a temporary state of amnesia suffered made sense after speaking with my sister— Monica. How the jeans were pulled down and up should have left the keys in tack, as all the other items—which did not happen, as the situation consciously explained. The movement of the keys on my body was never felt, which could lead to asking what happens to the body when the mind becomes confused or sleepwalking. From my experience, The mind is conscious of where you are and what you are doing, but the body's nerve senses are asleep. Thus, the sense of feeling becomes absent until a part of the brain alerts the body's nerve senses and causes it to become awake, bringing consciousness of a situation. This causes panic when the mind reacts by alerting the body of heat or cold or one's in danger; causing the senses to be confused, not knowing where you are. A state of absenteeism is seen among some within society that is not readily known, only knowledgeable from news broadcasts of missing persons or killings. Many need to become aware of their circumstances; a call is so important for family and friends to communicate with each other, or a psychiatrist seen if one can afford the cost.

§

This life is filled with mysteries and mystical experiences, and before I relate this spiritual story told to me I would like to give some background information about Simon's belief and the Qur'an.

Simon is Muslim, an elderly person, wears glasses and is married with grown, now married children. I have spoken to him occasionally about his faith and found out why the religion does not believe Jesus is God's son. From his concluded explanation, since The Most High has no beginning or end, HE is of no gender—male or female (Revelations 22:13). Mary did not have a sexual relationship with HIM and does not believe that she conceived of divine intervention. In my opinion, it is a shallow belief of faith. Since ALL things created came into being through (Allah) Jehovah. For HE that says to it 'Be' and it is! However, they believe Jesus is Mary's Son and the greatest Apostle ever walking the earth. I even inquired why Prophet Muhammad never used the name Jehovah, only Allah.

§

The Qur'an was revealed to Muhammad over twenty-three years. Muhammad never received any formal education before or after the revelation of the Qur'an. He was an unlettered man who could not read or write; each revelation had to be dictated. It is written that historians have preserved the names of more than forty persons who served as scribes of the Qur'an. The Arabs were skilled in memory use, and Muhammad was no exception. He was born in the year of 570 CE and died in the year 632 CE. He was forty years old when he was called to be a prophet alone in a nearby mountain cave called Ghar'hira for meditation. He was the first recipient and memorizer of the entire Qur'an and taught throughout his life the Qur'an to others by oral recitation. As a result, many Muslims dedicate their entire lives to accurate memorization and teaching of the Qur'an. The Qur'an central theme is Divine Guidance that constantly invites mankind to follow the path of the messengers.

I found out after acquiring The Qur'an from a co-worker— Natisha, that the religion: Islam is a continuation and confirmation of the messages passed on by Adam, Abraham, Noah, Moses, Jesus, and other messengers whose messages differ to suit human society that was gradually changing; to a more comprehensive Divine Message. I also found it to be a Holy Book that inspires a higher level of faith.

This story of his friend's experience was told to me by Simon, then a co-worker. "His friend was out with friends for the evening and walked them to the elevator of their apartment. He got home to his own apartment, went to the veranda to get some air, and felt someone push him. He held on tightly to the rail, afraid he would fall. After gaining his composure, when he looked at his watch it had stopped at a certain time. The next day when he called his friends to see how they were doing, he was told of their mishap in the elevator. When his watch stopped, it was the same time as their incident."

Yes, this life is filled with mysteries and mystical encounters, it amazes me the trivial matters people tend to fight and fuss over, acting like children.

§

DREAMS—they can act as a monitor for correct behaviors; dreams help us to understand who we are, as they also give us information on what actions need to take to enable us to avoid making mistakes. They are past mental experiences, usually in the form of a sequence of ideas, images, and imagined events, often accompanied by emotions, occurring during REM sleep. There are also different types of dreams such as: reoccurring dreams, precognitive dreams, magical and spiritual dreams.

§

Somewhere in the city, in a shopping mall, I was deciding whether to purchase sugar or flour. As I looked around, I saw two young children had wandered away from their parents. A public phone started ringing, and a man looked around to see where the sound was coming from. A person approached him and asked, "Do you know where your children are?" This I heard. However, as I kept looking at the fellow in my dream who now seemed to be the children's father, He did not respond but kept looking around him as he scanned the mall. A woman then walked up to him, whispered something, and he did respond. That was when I woke out of my sleep to the ringing of the neighbor's phone, heard during my sleeping state. The clock on the wall read minutes after six o'clock in the morning. The phone kept ringing, so I got out of bed—twice. The first time to check to see if it was my cellphone left in the living room, and the second time to check at the street corner to see if someone was there, recalling in the dream the reference of someone going to the corner.

It was now after seven o'clock, and passing through the courtyard from the left, a fair-skinned man in his earlier thirties or forties raised his voice, "Get up, brain dead." Eventually, the phone stopped. I could not understand why someone would ring someone's phone for so long. Perhaps they thought that the person or persons should be awake at this time of the morning, which was now close to seven o'clock. I do not know where he was passing through from, but due to the length of time the phone was ringing, he may have heard it, too, and decided to comment as he passed. Was it he who had dialed the number? Strange!

Chapter 3

STRANGERS

I SAT ON A STOOL in the kitchen, having breakfast at the counter that divided it from the living room, steering past the tree that was almost naked of its foliage from the pressure of the wind and rain to the highway ahead. Almost all its leaves were removed, revealing its shape and age. In a trance, as I observed the passing traffic on the Gardener Express, the billboard's neon sign interval flashing colors of advertisement of different sorts reminded me of a different kind—that of a peaceful world. I am blessed to have given the many experiences I have had thus far and thankful for preserving of my life and the patience shown by God. The same I have inculcated into my own life toward others—patience.

The fall season was ending, and another season was soon to arrive—the life cycle—changes us to growth of all kinds. Unlike some things in life that remain in the same place for years until death. The difference humans have is the ability to move from one place to another, allowing us to meet others that add to our intellectual growth as we experience a different part of this world and a different culture, which adds richness to our lives. Though I sat in a moment of silent tranquility, the world around me was slowly changing, and only a few were able to observe this. In contrast, others were busy defrauding and living life in the camera's view with the feeling of immunity of what the changes can do, will do, or will mean. I was enjoying my part-time job at Research Tech but desperately trying to understand myself. At the job with one of the supervisors, I had a mental connection known by the medical field as a shared psychotic disorder—a mental disorder in which a person develops a delusion similar in content to that of an associated person, with a pre-established delusion. This was obvious on a few occasions when he came to my section, and I could not control my body's reaction to entertained thoughts. I knew I needed to find the strength from within the dreams I have to be able to react most positively to his presence. However, unwilling to seek help, I decided to deal with the situation on my own, at the same time using my inner ability to correct the thoughts of those who may be present at the time of occurrences. He is a tall, stout person with blackish-brown hair and fair skin; he reminded me of Solomon, the superintendent, only a little taller than him.

I recalled one day at work… It was five o'clock, and most that were present for the afternoon shift were getting alcohol swabs and checking what station they were assigned. I got a paper wet with the cleaning stuff they provided for cleaning one's desk, checked the board for assigned seating, and proceeded to the station. A few minutes passed, and a girl about five feet a few inches, a little on the stout side, sat in the section and station next to mine. As the evening progressed, a conversation started between us, with suggestions of different ways to approach situations that I had tried that worked for me—given the girl's response would be, 'Don't tell me what to do.' "I'm not telling you what to do," I replied. "What I'm saying is sometimes, by using a different approach, we get the results we seek. It has worked for me." I continued my work without any further comment as I thought she would not have spoken of it if she was not seeking an alternative action to her situation. I sucked my teeth and shook my head at her attitude. People are strange.

The shift was over, and me and an elderly co-worker walked to the train station. She was going in the same direction as me, so when the train arrived, we sat together. On the way, she began to inform me of her religious beliefs and even offered me some holy water she walked with. I refused and called her attention to the reputation of prayers. Prayers are done, as we were doing—telling of what is bothering us. She then started to inform me of her grandchildren. I listened for some time and then decided to give my opinion.

"I don't want anyone telling me what to do," she responds.

I had heard this statement too many times for the evening, so I replied, "Look here, I'm giving you a suggestion. One you can take or refuse as it is your decision to do. The conversation is a two-way street in case you forgot."

"I know, but...."

As she continued to talk, I was so upset that her earlier response blocked me out and I did not hear what she said before bidding me good night as the train stopped at Bloor station, where she got off to board the train below to Scarborough. The train moved off, and I smiled as the thought came of how people are strange. No wonder Jesus asked the question in Matthew 11, verses 16-19: "With whom shall I compare this generation?" Stating that when John came neither eating nor drinking, people say he had a demon. The son of man did come eating and drinking; still, people say, "Look a man gluttonous and given to drinking wine, a friend of tax collectors and sinners." I sometimes wonder what others say about me at the Kingdom Hall attending—assigned to since I do not usually converse with them. Perhaps people should say up front, I just need a listening ear to get a few things off my chest, not your verbal input. This may make life easier, and a person does not have to feel insulted. Perhaps, she had forgotten she was once a child and failed to or decided not to allow her thinking to accept the ignorance in which all grownups once toiled.

As the train drove on, I recalled Dr. Noah once telling me that I could not teach him anything. So wrong he was—not everything, but surely a few things as wisdom are proved righteous by all its children. It was my body; only I felt what it was going through. Therefore, to become wiser in his profession, he was to listen to what I had to say.

Also recalled was Shelda saying the same thing to me one day. Kienna was in the car's back seat, and it had really hurt to hear the sentence out of her mouth. I held back the tears in silence as I watched the passing cars. A brother from the congregation had also said the same thing to me, forgetting that he once lacked the knowledge to teach. We are all born equal—equally sinners with the need to learn. People are strange!

I knew the difference between knowledge and wisdom. I had knowledge of many topics but lacked wisdom in some matters. Wisdom is declared by applying knowledge; any formula (that) declaratively applied to something without a doubt one knows procedurally (how) the result is. Not what it should be. I was humble of my intelligence—or not, by the admission of some people's attitude. However, I stood amongst the group who lacked wisdom, for if those in their profession possessed wisdom, the world would be rid of deliberate conflict and diseases or prevent them from occurring. And we would be free to travel without the worry or fear of being attacked by some idiot savant—a person with 'mental retardation' who can perform at a high level in some restricted domain of intellectual functioning.

Finally, after some time of sitting with my thoughts I got up, washed the dishes, and did a chapter for the book I was writing. Each day before work, I spent an hour or so on my manuscript until one day, I received a call from Gilad asking me back to work. Research Tech was given two weeks' notice and, for the remainder of the time, discovered I had found the ability to successfully control the negative thoughts that control my reaction to certain ones around me. Tanya's visit to the office to pick up some papers also enlightened me about a few in the office attitude towards her.

Chapter 4

DRAWING MEANING FROM WORDS

AND IN THE LAST DAYS, God says, "And it shall come to pass afterward, that I will pour out my spirit upon all flesh; and your sons and your daughters shall prophesy, your old men shall dream dreams, your young men shall see visions: And also, upon the servants and upon the handmaids in those days will I pour out my spirit." –Joel 2:28-29.

I saw the visions of the experiences and revelations of what will be. As some professing Christianity are misled due to failure to understand their dreams for what they are, they misrepresent the True God by their actions. Thus, some go forth in war and strife without the readiness to declare the good news of peace, with the belt of truth, and with their (heart) having the breastplate of righteousness.

It was getting to the middle of the month, and my couch still rested on the stairs in the apartment. Getting help organized to lift it onto the floor was difficult. Tanya called not too long after I got in from trying to arrange a few folks to help remove it.

"Hi, Bern. How's it going?"

"Fine. I was just trying to get some help to remove the couch. Unfortunately, I'm unable to do so."

"So, what are your plans for the day?"

"I'm not sure. It is a great day; I may go down to Harbor Front. If you would like to, we could go together."

"Maybe I will. Guess what?"

"What?"

"I was on the internet the other day, and I thought I'll be the bigger person and send Cynthia a message just to wish her all the best, and I didn't expect her to be online. After I hit send, I later saw a message from her that said, "'Life is too short to care about everyone, so you only care about those who care about you."' What do you think she was trying to say?"

"It's a very mature message. I feel she means exactly what the message says. You know Cynthia better than I do, and if she's someone who doesn't talk much, a message such as that would be expected to be coming from her."

"I think she's trying to say she only cares for people who care for her, and because I don't care, she doesn't care."

"Tanya, why are you so negative?"

"Don't forget she told me to lose her number."

"I'm not forgetting. I heard your side, but a story has two, and my sister recently corrected me—it has three sides. That would be yours, Cynthia's, and the person who told the story, who is acquainted with both of you."

"Seriously, it all had to do with me not getting to her baby shower."

"That's what you said. It has to be more."

"Well, I don't know what it will be."

"Women who know you and are comfortable with themselves are not threatened by your selfish display of attention. Some Women, though they're encouraged by your ego with a smile, beneath lays contempt. You need to care about others' feelings, especially if they are friends."

"I can't help people's feeling of jealousy."

"True. A person's lack of self-confidence is not your fault...." A conversation I wanted not to continue since Tanya was reading way too much into the message or, without understanding, decided to ask, "Then, we'll see each other later?"

"Yes. Meet me at the subway station at about two o'clock."

"Okay," I replied and hung up.

I met Tanya after the arranged time. This gave her and Omar—her son, some time to enjoy the street festival. We walked from Dundas and Yonge Streets to Harbor Front. Something we had in common is being at the beach or the park. The ambiance of open space, water and greenery gives a sense of inner peace. The scenery is mind-relaxing, just to sit or walk around the harbor as you enjoy the sea breeze against your face, the sight of the sailboats and people having fun with their water skis, or the children rowing around in the pond. Not much was going on when we got there, other than a few entertainers that performed for a small crowd. After ordering and eating a meal from a few vendors, we rehashed a few things observed during Omar's birthday party.

"By the way, I meant to ask you about your girlfriend, who was bitching with her boyfriend. Did someone beat her up? She had black and blue marks all over her body."

Tanya gives a smile. "It's a love thing."

"You've got to be kidding. Her body reminded me of mine after moving. She bruises easily as I do."

"I don't know why she stays with him."

"Is this the guy she bitched with all day?" I ask.

"No, This is the one who came later in the evening. From the time I was introduced to him and the way I saw how he treated her; I really didn't like him."

"I wonder why she puts up with him. Perhaps she likes the danger or lacks self-confidence. Further, I do not think her sister approved of her actions. I was observing them together."

"She spoke to her about him, too. I guess it is what she wants. I was at his place once. He has a great apartment but not a place I would like to be for any length of time."

"Why?"

"His apartment is in a high-rise, way up high, with glass windows all around. When you look out, you're afraid you'll fall any minute." She laughs at the end of her sentence.

I laughed, too, mostly from her facial expression before she ended her statement. "Perhaps the height or being intoxicated, with the adrenaline of being on edge, suppresses the pain if she feels any."

After returning to my new apartment, they stayed for a brief visit and left. We both, including Omar, had a wonderful afternoon.

Chapter 5

A PAST TIME REVISIT

IT WAS NOW NOVEMBER, close to the end of another year. I came home from work a bit in a daze. Something about the cold weather causes people to become depressed, although each season shows its own beauty in ways of different cultural festivities. However, for most from the South, during this time of the season changing to Winter, one must make a big mental change to adapt to the cold.

I flipped open my cell phone and pressed the button to turn it on; a few seconds later, it started to ring, notifying me of a message. I flipped the top up and navigated the arrows to retrieve the message—it was Westley—he was attending a funeral of a musician friend, and since he was close to Canada, was thinking of visiting for a few days. I deleted the message and decided to call him later. After my visit a few years ago, it had taken me some time to accept his decision, but we will remain friends. The woman he was with seemed good nature and was good-looking—something that matters in his books, and as far as I had seen, they seemed to get along great, and if he was happy, I was for him, too. I wonder to myself if seeing him again would bring back buried feelings. My life had changed now, especially after my last encounter with Gerry; what I had learnt, I made a vow to stick to my God, the only person I know that loves me for who I am. After preparing myself for bed, getting to sleep was difficult; I tossed and turned with thoughts of how I will react to seeing him again it had been a few years. The morning had arrived, and I had hardly slept. I picked up the phone, flipped the top open, pressed the menu button, then the icon that looked like a computer's screen, to contacts; keyed in the first letter of his name that got me to his number and pressed dial. As charming as usual and happy to hear from me, I am told of the day he will be attending the funeral and the day he will be visiting. I had no idea or even entertained the thought that he would bring along the woman he was living with. The evening before he arrived, he called, but it was much too late, and I was much too tired to return the call from cleaning the house in preparation for his arrival. Therefore, the next day I called.

He answers the call. "Hello...I called you last night. What happened?"

"It was too late to call when I noticed your message."

"Vivian and I will be there around seven o'clock in the evening. I called to get some directions."

"Sure," I replied and gave him the directions to the office building to pick me up from work. Since his arrival would be sooner than my scheduled time to be off work. "Call me when you get to the building, and I'll meet you in the parking lot."

"Sure. We'll be seeing you later. Have a great day."

"You, too." We hung up.

A bit saddened by the fact that his visit would include the woman he was living with. Although I expected her to be travelling with him, I did not expect her to be visiting too. I was also annoyed that she was in the same state as he and me on our first trip together. This is childish, *I thought*, getting all emotional. Our lives are different, and I was now able to have the strength to go forward, accommodating and accepting each one's decision.

Many are the plans of man, but the counsel of Jehovah is what will stand. Truly, all the plans we make, accompanied by pain, sacrifices, fear, and disappointments to that final accomplishment of joy, are all in the master plan of His will for us. If only, though, we could trust in Him, who we cannot see, to guide us, how peaceful life would be and how less challenging our goals or plans to accomplish will be, but we are physical and believe only in that seen or felt. In addition, we still deny their existence even when things are visible or there to touch. Reminds me of a cyclist seen wearing a jacket with the words, "I want to believe." I ponder on my past life and can recall the steps I have made. The journey has left me tired and, at times, lonely, but I know that I can always count on God to see me through, and that alone is having success.

Success is defined in different ways; to some, it is having financial and material wealth; to others, it is their good deeds and the knowledge they have left behind. Yet to others, it is having peace in their lives, the lack of worrying about keeping it all.

I got dressed, turned on the light in the living room, and left for work. My shift was almost over. I had an anxious feeling all day; it had been a long time since I had seen Westley. My appearance had changed. I had lost weight due to my participation at the gym, and the sides of my face had a darkened discoloration. I often joke about being in fashion and not having to spend money on blushes, always in fashion, I would say, compared to the runway models who get their faces artistically done to having their cheekbone highlighted. This is my attitude about life and myself, always looking for the positive within negative situations, the reason for some loving me and others hating me; my attitude irritates them. My secret thought is another regards ignorance. My phone rang, and he called to ask for further directions; he was going to be in the parking lot within minutes. He recognizes me as I open the building door to exit because he sounded the car horn. However, our meeting was not an exciting one, the expectation one might expect from two people who had not seen each other for some time. This was due to a verbal altercation with a co-worker before his arrival, which had left me in the mood of being by myself, and certainly not up to entertaining. A few things I hate and one of them is arguments. Especially when the other lack logic and insists on acting foolishly; when this happens, you are no longer considered an acquaintance deserving of my respect or affection, and what I do next is no one's guess.

I got into the car and noticed Vivian sitting in the back seat, said good evening and began to explain what had occurred, taking the time needed to get my emotions settled when he asked if he was going to get a hug. On the way home, I explained in detail what had happened, having had to curse him, and ask what he wanted from me. The disappointment I felt over my co-worker's action was the beginning I would experience in the attitude of others. The evening spent with them was one I allowed myself to endure. I have the ability to stop whatever I want that's a damage to my personal health. But at times would prolong a situation to see the outcome or to gather information about the person or persons I dealt with. I rarely drink, preferring marijuana whenever socializing, but even that habit I had abruptly stopped. All it took was one drink offered to me to try, and I could not form my thoughts into coherent sentences. Unknowingly, I was a great actress and could pull myself through the evening, learning much about his live-in partner and her ability to control her anger. In return, my own by not responding to the woman's comment regarding my inability to complete my work, using insomnia I suffer from as a hindrance.

Often repeated, unless you walk a mile in the shoes of another, you do not know the troubles they have seen or endured—this is true. However, each one experiences life on one's own level of understanding and strength, thus expressing oneself from that standpoint. And here is where the competition takes one's innocence away—when we are pushed beyond our mental strength, psychologically, others take control of our lives. Therefore, it is important to be patient with oneself, as we do with the other person.

Their stay was brief, and I was much grateful that it was. So used to living alone; just entertaining the thought of them staying much longer was frustrating. After I bid them goodbye, I returned to my unit, did a thorough cleaning, made breakfast, and took a shower and a short nap before heading out to work. That evening, I slept as if a baby as I was so tired. However, during my sleep, I felt myself being carried and felt my body shifting I assumed in a coffin. I eventually woke up but felt normal and not afraid. After a brief walk to use the toilet and a drink of water, I curled back in bed under the comforter. Although it was a strange dream, the thought of Westley and Vivian at the funeral, honestly had slipped my mind.

§

I felt, after my return visit with them quite a few years back, that onlookers used our relationship. Not knowing by whom or for what reason, I tried to keep the relationship between both and myself normal, despite the negative thoughts I entertained from outsiders. Mine was not the only life that was changing. Changes were occurring in everyone's life around the globe, and I was most thankful that where I resided was not as bad as other places. Earth's natural elements also contributed to the changes in many lives, for some had lost financially and materially due to earthquakes, fires, and floods. Defrauding the gullible ones was rampant; some companies lost millions due to computer hackers. "'There is a high likelihood that sophisticated artificial intelligence will be used for cyber-attacks soon. Artificial Intelligence can be used to mine large amounts of public domain and social network data, to extract personally identifiable information which can be used for hacking a person's accounts,'" says Deepak Butt, founder, and CEO of Aighra, a mobile security start-up company.

Daily, someone was being shot, and there seemed to be no peace in sight accomplishing in the middle east, and with each new Presidential or Prime minister's election to office came controversies of a different kind. The church's hope of making changes in people's lives is overshadowed by the Bishops' or Priests' actions and acceptance of rules contrary to God's law. At last, men can now plan trips out of space. At times, it seemed hopeless that conditions would ever get to normal. Many had questions on their minds: How can you be safe in this troubled world? The answer is, now more than ever before, we need to stay awake, alert, and keep our senses. We also need to have strong faith, not only in our abilities but also in the higher force to set matters right and lovingly communicate with others, bringing peace and understanding among us. These actions need to be done at this time when the world is in transition, and people have had enough. Enough that some are recruited as human bombs to make their point, thus killing innocent ones. Others fighting mentally to save their lives in a world that is worsening.

§

The next day, after having breakfast I was cleaning the stove and decided to remove the burners to find underneath them filled with starchy water, as if someone had left unattended for a good time, a pot which boiled over, leaving a vast amount of water beneath the burners. The scene surprised me because I always cleaned up after myself and could not think of the last time, I cooked rice to boil over, causing such a mess to the extent I was looking at; under the burners water filled part way up. I cleaned the stove, had a shower, and headed off to work. All day I kept thinking back to earlier in the morning. Who could have done that? Someone had to have entered the apartment and done that, but whom? *I thought*, who is the woman we saw standing in the hallway that kept staring at us coming in from the restaurant? The voice heard as I cleaned, "Never again," "Westley, is that you? What did you say?" I asked to be sure of what I had just heard but got no response. After cleaning, I left for the store. Who could have been so bold as to enter my home to make such mischief if it was not them? What were their intentions? And the voice, was it him or had someone installed a device whereby I could overhear a voice? *My thoughts* took me back to the first evening they arrived and had dined at the restaurant not too far from the building.

After eating, Westley looked back at the waitress with an order of fries for the person sitting at the back of him. As he kept looking and commenting on how appetizing it was and wanted to have an order, Vivian stated, "She is still hungry." I pretended not to have heard and thought why she would say, she, instead of you.

At the end of the day, I was satisfied with myself by how I handled them both. Trying to understand the situation, I called my cousin and related what had happened. Greta also found the situation strange and agreed that I should speak to Vivian about it. However, what if it was not, she, and it was just someone else trying to cause a problem with our friendship? Then how do I solve the problem? The situation did call for a face-to-face discussion. This was not something to discuss over the phone, so I will let her know there is a discussion we need to have, but in person.

Chapter 6

STRANGE TIMES

THE BEGINNING OF ANOTHER YEAR, and with it for many came pangs of distress. Looking back over the past five years, each year seems to bring us closer to—some say the end. It makes one wonders if the Maya Nation is correct in their predictions that the end of the system will be in 2012. However, the year passed into another, this time with many fleeing their homelands looking for a safe haven. No one knows the day or the hour when the son of man will arrive. However, over the years, man has done his calculations to predict a date that has so far not proven to be correct. Some Jehovah's witnesses, too (direction not given by the organization), had predicted the end. Surprised, as our teaching has taught, that 1914 was the beginning of Jesus' enthronement. And, if a day (2 Peter 3:8) is calculated as a thousand years in God's timetable or calendar; and Revelation 20:5 states that the dead will come to life until the thousand years ended, this would mean that life on earth has another eight hundred and ninety-three years from the ending of 2021. Much time given to make personal changes acceptable for entry into the New Kingdom and changes to our home—earth. However, as stated: no one knows the day or hour. This means He, the one who says, 'to Be' and it becomes; no one truly knows.

However, the change that did occur was a war that ended a peaceful system into one more advance scientifically, medically, and technically; and seems at the point of this book advancing to the domination of man to their end. To illustrate—seen on the televised news, a family man killed his wife, five children and himself over a critical situation at his job. Then there was the unemployed financial manager in San Fernando Valley who, over severe money problems, shot and killed his wife, three children, mother-in-law, and self. As well as in July of 2017 Equifax, one of the consumer's credit reporting agencies discovered one of the largest breaches in the history of 143 million American personal information stolen by computer hackers. It is time people wake up to the understanding that they are unique. They cannot be like others or have what others have. Only what they, as that unique individual, can afford to have, to give, to become. While working together within a community towards a common goal and as a nation to make it realize for the country, protecting the people within the country we live will help life (we) prosper.

§

MONTHS LATER...

Into the year, I heard from Westley. We were emailing and phoning each other as often as one remembered the other. He wanted to see me, but I knew that if he genuinely wanted to, he would have made the trip. He was torn between his love for one and his fondness for the other. His life was stable, he had someone helpful to him in his career, and he would be a fool to lose what he has to run after someone in a different country of a different nationality he barely knows and who has changed since our last meeting. I knew nothing much about him other than what I was told. In addition, I was not like some possessed person to be looking into his background for evidence that may move to an unfair evaluation of him or give up on a person who seemed to be nice. Over the years, having grown past my fascination with him, I was more in search of someone mentally capable and strong to handle me and what I brought into a relationship;

I was not sure Westley was this one. The months were passing fast. It was almost September when he emailed to say that he had a job in town, and since he was going to be in the country, he thought of taking a few extra days to spend with me. Aware of his situation, I expected that he would not be coming alone, so I started to make a list of places and things to do during their visit. A few days before his departure, I was told Vivian would not be accompanying him as she could not get time off work. I was a bit disappointed because this meant the discussion, I wanted to have with her about the stove would have to wait. I was relieved though conflicting emotions rose; I knew this visit would allow me the time I needed with him to sort through my feelings as it will convince us both where each needed to be. A knock heard on the door told me he had arrived. I ran down the stairs and opened the door to my unit and my heart. We embrace each other with a hug and, moments after, ask to follow me up the stairs. Not long after finished cooking and a bit tired, and so was he from his activities, we laid in bed for a short time as he answered questions about his gig—the job he had in the city. Afterward, we got up to eat and then went for a short walk.

On the day of the airshow at Exhibition Place, we took the bus to the grounds and saw part of the show as it started; from there, we took the boat over to the Island for the day. We returned to the city late in the afternoon and had dinner at a Thai restaurant after returning home, spending some quiet time. I welcome his visit but has resolved my feelings for him in my heart but test him to see where his head is at and, in doing so, finds out that his interest is with Vivian. When a woman is alert to the feelings of a person she loves, she can tell when she has lost his interest. I was somehow happy for him that he was happy with Vivian and knew that Vivian did not feel threatened by me, as she knew what he liked and how to give him what he wanted. On the other hand, I was not like her, and would never be able to contest with her; I looked at the situation with a smile.

A day later, he left, and I knew that was the end of a season that had taught me the simple mindset of a man, and I was blessed to have found out sooner than later. His correspondence read between the lines, a man angry, disappointed, and sympathetic towards our relationship. And I was not looking for sympathy, I knew he really cared, but it was mostly me who had to fight against those that wanted to hurt me for whatever reason. I have found out that some people develop hatred towards you because of their own lack of self-love or worth, and it is no use fighting to change their intentions towards you, as they will never change until they die.

·

Chapter 7

UNCLEAR COMMUNICATIONS EFFECT

IT WAS THE LAST MONTH of the year 2007. Much had occurred during the year that had left me tired mentally. In addition to coping with the mental fatigue of those at the office and questionable incidents at home, I was also dealing with losing friendships with some at the Congregation. At a Sunday meeting attendance during a conversation with a visiting sister from England, I found out that I was disfellowshipped. Embarrassed and hurt by the brother's intrusion, after he left, I apologized to the sister. The congregation meeting concluded, and I called a meeting of the brother to inform him that I had no idea I was disfellowshipped, and even if I was, whatever happens, to be hospitable in the house of God. The brother apologizes and tells me he thought I knew I was. Not only did a committee whose rule is to consult with the party or parties whose conduct is against Bible teachings and then make a public announcement so that the brothers and sisters will take the appropriate actions towards the one disfellowship; not done. Later, in trying to resolve the misinformed situation, I was even informed of distributing propaganda literature. Because our conversations were based on one's disfellowshipped, he perhaps thought that I must have known from the two occasions we have had. His visit when I once lived on Main Street and the other occasion, on the Esplanade. My thought differ thinking this was due to being seen in public occasionally with disfellowshipped persons. Reasons given of having association with such ones he did inform, and I expressed my thoughts on the subject, and at no time during or after the conversation he mention, you are disfellowshipped.

Many people claim that the English language is difficult. It can be, especially when one is talking and the other is, at the same time, or attention not given to words spoken by the other. Because we are from different countries with different cultures, information processing is based on the type of upbringing one has had, our environment, our religious beliefs, or our disbeliefs. Therefore, understanding comes with clear and specific explanations and when people are direct.

Amused by the information and stressed over my conduct, I respond, "What a lie! Who is this person that calls himself a brother who would lie about me distributing propaganda literature? What have I done to him or anyone else on this matter that would tell a lie like that?" I knew my life was not by the organization's teachings; most importantly, my unhappy Bible-trained conscience was neither. A person, who is always seeking permanence, will not settle unless I am sure the other party was committed. Before and after leaving Bissell vacuum, I had only had four lengthy relationships, three of which were cohabited not with brothers of the faith, and all different situations leading up to my overall growth. After a relationship ends and I has had some healing time, I would resume my religious studies and activities. Since this is what I had done on separate occasions, this was my intention to do it again, only this time, the "gods" had already used me to their advantage and were about to show me the power they held to destroy. I was not going to destroy myself because of them. I was no stranger to people, somehow finding it amusing to lie about things I had not done. The question is, why. Why do people tell lies to others? I could not help the thoughts I consumed from contact with those I had faced who had lied on me, and who have made me look as the one who lies because they fail to recall incidence. And many times, glad that I was still alive to confront them. I do believe those who practice a life of lying are short-sighted and live in disbelief of two facts: first, all lies will eventually become known, and secondly, those now living though dead will come to life (the resurrection of the dead) - John 11:25, Luke 12:2. Yes, we may be dead, but when one gives one's life over to the True God, believe me, he will make you rise, he will make you stand; he will make you firm all in HIS truth of righteousness.

After meeting with the brothers on a few occasions and letting them know the truth of the matter, how I felt and how I was raised from infancy, my final say over the matter was typed and given to one of the two brothers I had spoken to on a few occasions. Indicated when last we spoke, "I have given the letter to brother Victor," he said.

"So, you have said," I responded.

"What did you say?" he asks.

I repeated myself as I threw the shawl around my shoulders, secured it around my neck, and said goodbye as I left the Hotel's reception room, where I had just celebrated the Lord's evening meal.

Good Friday is a celebrated holiday worldwide by many religious groups; the day is known as Memorial Day or The Passover. On this day, people celebrate by attending church services, some by having a feast with friends and family in their homes. In contrast, even those who do not practice any religion as a charitable action, feed the homeless. Actions done in remembrance and symbolic meaning of the Last Supper. This celebration for Jehovah's Witnesses, known as the Memorial, occurs after sundown on Nisan 14, according to the Jewish calendar. Each year is celebrated in March or early April. The only ones in attendance who do part take of the bread and wine are those of the Discreet Slave Class, whose spirit has borne witness with the Lord's that they are the chosen ones. My partaking of the meal is not a claim to be of the chosen ones, but due to my witness as a child, I must prove faithful to my calling. I eat out of having faith. As written: "And he that doubteth is damned if he eats, because he eateth not of faith: for whatsoever is not of faith is sin." –Romans 14:23. Indeed, everything that is not out of faith is sinful. And when an individual's sin is accomplished leads to death.

As I walked down the hallway leading to the stairs, a voice behind me whispered something I did not understand; using my peripheral vision, none was seen at my immediate sides; however, being aware, I responded out loud, "I heard you." I was now at the bottom of the stairs and seen wearing a mask around her nose and mouth, about to exit the lobby, an elderly woman. I looked at her *with the thought,* yes, I know. I can also smell the evil intent in the air. This thought stems from my suspicion that someone was reading my work and perhaps playing games with me, but I was not playing a game, and many times has expressed this to close ones and colleagues. And even when asked to play the lottery, I will announce I am serious; I am not playing with you guys.

All things in life are made for man's enjoyment; when we indulge deeper than our physical senses can tolerate or allow, or financial resources allow, we sin. My participation done out of fun is to see how close my numbers come to winning. I am fully aware that the money spent playing the games goes to helping athletes and some charities, so no guilt is felt. I do not believe in 'good luck, but rather, if one is deserving of something, it will be realized. As the scriptures even show, "The lot cast into the lap, every decision by it is from Jehovah." –Proverbs 16:33. Further, "The lot causeth contentions to cease, and parteth between the mighty." –Proverbs 18:18. Everything under the sun is created from someone's needed to fulfill a desire, and that of another's enjoyment; how we use the things created is the deciding factor of moral goodness.

After making a stop at the convenience store, I arrived home, cooked a meal and relaxed for the rest of the evening, occasionally recalling the difference in the taste of the wine the first time I part took the meal, attending the Congregation at its location. Mature faith does not live by answers to prayer but by prayer! I had prayed many times for the strength to be able to part-take of the meal, as I know the judgmental thoughts of others and what effect it could have. My prayer was mostly to strengthen my faith with the knowledge of my truths. Moreover, although I had knowledge of the Bible and accounts of Jehovah speaking to faithful ones in the past, of times when he spoke, those present were unable to understand. Personal study of the scriptures led me to passages of accounts where I could read this.

In my letter to the Congregation, I mention that it was only in the year 2008, in my study of Bible literature from the Congregation, I was enlightened that spiritual hearing is not something granted to all of us. Hearing with a sound and hearing with understanding are contrasted in the account of John 12:28-30, after Jesus spoke and a voice out of heaven answered him by saying, "I have both glorified (it) and will glorify (it) again." The crowd that heard it began to say it had thundered; others said an angel had spoken. Another account of the contrast of hearing and understanding is in Acts 22:6-11, about the conversation of Saul of Taurus and Jehovah and in verse 9, the scripture stated that those with him did not hear the voice. Yes, from my experience, the voice was like thunder, and I understood the words spoken as, "You people down there!"

Chapter 8

GROWTH ENHANCE THROUGH FRIENDSHIPS

THE MONTH OF AUGUST was the beginning of the end of the summer with most of its activities. Tanya called to invite me to dinner. The invitation is accepted. It was a Saturday afternoon, lately feeling unusually tired; I decided to go back to bed. The radio softly played in the background as I drifted back to sleep. I walked in on a social gathering. Tanya is standing among a few people I do not recognize, except for a person I had been introduced to at Omar's birthday party. Tanya then turned to the image of her mother, whom I had also met. She is overheard saying, "Mommy, I would like to go, but I don't have anything to wear." The sound of the radio was heard between my conscious states of rest. The voice sounded as if Hilda from the office responding to the question of where she was going this evening, asked by the host who runs a morning program, Flow. Over tiredness, I could not move my body off the bed to get to the radio to investigate what I was hearing. I assumed it was after thirty minutes had passed, I opened my eyes. The statement heard still lingered on my mind.

Sunday afternoon, I got dressed and left for Tanya's home. On my way, I call out to a fella I had met while waiting for the bus, partly blind due to an eye doctor's incompetent treatment of his developing glaucoma in one eye. During our conversation, I am informed he is being accompanied to a picnic.

Many are living with glaucoma and are not aware of this until it is much too late; the condition has damaged their vision to the extent of losing sight altogether. It is recommended eye checkups be done at least once a year. Many from the South do not think of it because of climate conditions, but to the North and especially endured climate changes, it is something we need to do. He is also Guyanese and has had some difficult times, but none tops the condition he lives with. He had to mentally accept and learn how to live with his present condition.

The bus arrived at Sherbourne Station, where everyone got off to either get the train, take a taxi, or walk to their destination. As I got off the bus, a homeless girl known to ask for a specific amount of money approached. She was wearing a dark green pullover tracksuit, her hair uncombed, her hand and face unwashed, and one of her eyes covered by green mucous. On many occasions, I had given her monies. Without approaching anyone else, she walks up to me with outstretched filthy hands; she asks, "Change Mom, change Mom?" I stepped aside to avoid her touch while wearing a white top. "Sorry, I have no change!" I quickly announced as I stepped further away to avoid her touch. However, as I did, so did her in unison of every move, as she continued. "Change, Mom." Then she asks, "Are you... ." I interject before she completes her sentence, afraid she may touch me and soil my clothing as she was beginning to get much too close for comfort. So, I said in a deep-toned voice loud enough that she would hear, "Don't touch me. I have no change." I quickly walked away from her into the train station and down the stairs to catch the train, mumbling words only for my ears. I do not know why she insisted on wanting to touch me with her hands all filthy. I should have yelled get away from me and go wash. They always want to touch me when I can feel their appreciation. I recall the other who did, one day on my way to the hairdresser's whom I had given some monies. Always wants to touch me. I repeated down the stairs as I pass the blind man and his companion.

I arrived at Tanya's later than expected to find her, the baby and a male friend who was asleep on the lawn chair. "Sorry, I'm late. I was trying to get some money and eventually ended up at the bank. So, how are you?" I ask as I gesture to Omar to come to me.

"I'm fine. Since he got here, he has been sleeping."

"Oh, hello." Her friend woke up to the sound of voices.

"I'm sorry. I am so tired," he said, raising himself upright.

"That is okay, I understand. It's good to see you again." I had met him at Omar's birthday party; his name I could not recall now.

"Would you like something to eat?" asks Tanya.

"What I need is a drink."

"I only have one beer left, and the store is closed."

"So, that means I can't have it." I paused as I looked at her. "That's okay."

"No, I'm just saying I have one beer, but if you want it, you could have it."

"Are you sure?"

"Yes, I'm sure." She calls her male friend to get the beer.

Hossain arrived in a few minutes with the beer. I opened it and was glad to have something cold and something which soothed my thoughts. We sat and talked for a while, I informed Tanya of my weekend, and we shared a few laughs over a few incidents. The afternoon was ending. She left with Omar, so she could get him ready first, as the end conclusion was to go out for dinner. Hossain remained with me as we talked a bit about the situation in Afghanistan, and a bit about his work and situation since coming to Canada and how lucky he feels having met the boss he works with.

Tanya appeared at the door leading to the basement and, with an angry tone, blurted out... "I have a child you know. I can't do this all alone."

I was facing the door, so my eyes were removed from Hossain, who immediately turned around to look at her. "Tanya, what's the matter with you? Hossain told you he would look after the child; all you needed to do was ask." My tone rose a bit.

She turns around, walks back into the basement, and slams the door. Hossain excused himself and followed her.

I remained outside with my thoughts. The force is so strong; it takes over one's mind and soul, and they become a different person unconscious of subconsciously inculcated thoughts, reacting not rationally to situations before them. Despite the situation, I did not come here to get into an argument. I ignored my dream, seeing her image with a group of people and her comment about not having something to wear to the function. Before me, displayed a similar situation to the dream. Hossain's comment about taking her to a fashion show his company is having, her mention of not having anything to wear, and then her display of the pink gown he brought for her to wear. If I leave, I will give the forces the upper hand in causing separation. If I stay, I will, hopefully, be able to bring her a better awareness of herself. Therefore, I will stay to see the outcome of the situation I have placed myself in. My thoughts were interrupted by the presence of Hossain, who came back after fifteen to twenty minutes.

"He's asleep."

"That's good; now she can get ready." The conversation resumed where we had left off. After twenty minutes, Tanya came up. I got up. "Are you okay? I need to use the washroom before we go."

"You are not allowed."

"What do you mean I'm not allowed?" Tanya smiled as I continued down the stairs. The door to the washroom closed; I yelled out to her for a key to open it.

"Take a knife from the counter, push it in the hole, and turn," she yelled.

I did as instruct, and the door opened, allowing me to use it. I stood at the sink, *consumed by thoughts* of the past minutes, washing my hands. This child's mood changes so often that keeping up with her can surely stress one's friendship. At this point, I really do feel like leaving. I walk up the stairs and out into the backyard. "Are we all ready?"

"Give me a few minutes to get Omar's bottles together." She left and was back in about ten minutes.

We left, closing the gate behind us.

"Hossain, you'll attract a lot of admirers," I said.

Tanya laughed as she exclaimed, "The image suits him!"

In addition, I continue, "Lots of admirers, but none wanting to commit. As they say, nice kid, nice guy, but I need no baggage." We all laughed as Hossain continued pushing the stroller.

Soon after, Omar started acting up as we were on the Danforth deciding on the restaurant to stop to eat.

My observed thoughts concluded of Omar. Every child born has some traits of the mother or father. More of the father or mother inculcated depending on the degree of association with either. Omar had Tanya's moody disposition. As he grows, as we all do, developing independent personalities from our parents due to circumstances that push us to evaluate one's character—perhaps he will change. As these thoughts I contemplated, Omar became more agitated; of course, he was also teething, which made it worse.

"With him like this, it's best if we just turn back," Tanya suggested.

This did make sense, but I had been around her for quite some time now and could sense ahead when situations would affect her actions. At this point, I had enough of her attitude for one day. "You are right, but I am going to leave."

"I don't know why she doesn't want to come back," she said to Hossain.

I bent over and bid Omar goodbye. "It's okay; we'll do this another time." I embraced her with a kiss and shook Hossain's hand as I said, "It was a pleasure speaking with you. We'll hopefully do this again."

"Let me walk you over to the train station."

"No, I'm fine. You stay here with them." His insisted attempts to walk me to the station I rejected. "See you both again. Bye," I replied as I cross the street and disappears around the corner from their sight, never to see him again.

Chapter 9

BODY LANGUAGE

A FEW DIZZY SPELLS occurred after moving up to the new apartment. At the start of my menstruation the following month, I continued to bleed non-stop. After Dr. Noah's retirement, my briefly new family doctor suggested that I see a gynecologist, so he went down the list. On mentioning a particular name, I told the doctor of having seen him before and would like to return to him since he had seen me before. Fortunately, the doctor worked in the clinic part-time, so my doctor made an appointment for the following week. Doctors are seen in extreme circumstances, as my dream experience-initiated fear.

Details for clarification: At the time, I lived at Pape and Gamble Streets. Earl had visited that night. Seated on the floor, having many conversations. One led to him asking how to spell entrepreneur; he broke the word down, so it spelt correctly, and I recall laughing...accomplishments bring me joy. He informed of Monica's circumstances before retiring to bed. That night I prayed that her blood pressure would fall to normalcy so that she could undergo the operation she had to have done. As my sister Monica lay hospitalized at Scarborough General Hospital, as I slept, I found myself looking at two doctors in blue gowns in what looked like an operating room due to seen equipment. Overlooking the person, a woman on the table who looked like my sister, as I heard one saying to the other, "You know, we can use these people because of their genetics." I jumped out of my sleep. From that experience, I will do everything necessary before doctor visits. Not only that, but any medications prescribed experiences severe symptoms, and immediately it's stopped. I always advise people to let their doctors know all they need to know about their food intake and medications; the more knowledge doctors have, the better they can treat their patients.

My circumstance is not that much different from others; the difference is I live more spiritually than I do physically. Doctors, not having full knowledge of the science of the mind, is not fully qualified to treat others like me. Any spiritual person will tell you that their senses are much stronger than other individuals and capable of separation from the body. This knowledge was confirmed by Phineas Parkhurst Quinby, born in the 1800s and died January 16, 1866; he was a philosopher, clockmaker, inventor, spiritual healer, early photographer, and mesmerist. He says, "The idea of separation is something not dawned upon the intelligence of the world. This may believe but not admitted among the scientific." He says, "The senses are attached to the identity of our belief, and we are affected according to the fear that we associate with our senses." Knowledge of this science is to know when an impression is produced on the senses.

Before the Invictus Games of 2017—which was started in 2015 by Prince Harry for war veterans and those who suffer from Post Dramatic Stress Disorder—I had a dream. The image of a double amputated, short haircut, fair complexion looked as if attempting to get away from someone; the facial features looked like a woman. The body moved out of a window and down what seemed to be a hallway; amazed at how she moved, I woke out of the dream, overly concerned for the individual. Then I fell back into another dream.

It was Sunday morning when I attempted to stand up out of bed and experienced severe pain in my right leg just below my knee as if attempting to put on an artificial leg; it caused me to cry out, "Oh, my God." The pain was gone when I left home for the Kingdom Hall meeting. This and other incidents (some later explained) are why visits to doctors are seldom because I fear some doctors lack knowledge on treatments, and explanations may seem crazy to their minds.

§

I sat in the waiting room until my name was called. I stood up and followed his motion to enter the room. He is of average height, has a dark complexion and dark hair, and was born in Africa. He wore a white doctor's gown. He suggested I take a seat, and he did too. "How are you today?" he immediately asks as he opens my file.

"Not so well; the reason for my visit," I respond, looking at him go through my file.

"We've seen each other before!" This was not a question, as he did recall my visit.

"Yes, but the problem this time is that I have been bleeding now for over twelve or fourteen days which is very unusual for me since I only have my periods for two to three days."

"The cause could sometime be the size of a fibroid ..." I knew this would be his first diagnosis since this was the reason, I had seen him before. "Or it could be a cyst or a few other things; however, we will find out. I will give you a prescription for some birth control pills; this type (he mentions the name) will reduce and stop the bleeding." At that point, the phone rang, and the conversation was about a passport and travelling plans.

"Look, Doc, I am not sexually active..." I said once I had his attention. This was true, for it had now been over two months since what would be my last sexual encounter with Gerry. He was silent as his eyes returned to the file, and my thoughts drifted.

The meeting was at his place. He met me in the lobby, and we walked the hall to his apartment hand in hand, talking and laughing at each one's funny comments. He opened the door, letting me in. A few steps in, the door is closed. He grabbed me by the arm, pushed me towards the closed door, took my other arm, held them intertwined above our heads as he kissed me on the ear, his tongue playfully edging down my neckline with tender kisses. His lips were close to my nipple but never on them the way I wished they would be—so wanting him to. We moved to the chair, and he put me to sit on top of him. I could feel his erection; he wanted me as I did him. He put his hands behind my head and gently drew me towards his mouth; his kisses were sweet, like candy—I woke out of the dream. My last encounter was over months ago. It was some bed exercises as the sexual act was nothing like a dream and fantasies I had before the encounter. I was curious about the dreams I had been having actions done in wanting to know the person behind the boy. As he looked up at me, our eyes met.

"And I don't use birth control pills," I reminded him.

"These are not just for sexual intercourse; it does more than prevent conception. If you have fibroids, it helps to reduce them. Women develop fibroids mostly after having children, which occur in adulthood. I will need to get a tissue sample and...."

From the moment he mentions the word scrape, the recollection of my first visit to him flashed a physical sensation of pain from my naval to my vagina. I immediately considered an excuse to postpone the procedure for some future date. "Look, Doc, I'm on my period (which I was) and really, I don't feel comfortable having you do what you need to do."

"It, it will be fine. I do this all the time, I need you to get undressed below the waist, and I'll be right back."

I reluctantly removed from the chair and slid behind the curtains as I undressed, feeling embarrassed to be examined at a time like this. When he got back in the room, I was on the table. Told to lay back and put my legs onto the foothold on the table. He inserted the speculum, then opened the cupboard and took out a long thin transparent tube about the length of his hand to elbow. He told me to take a deep breath as he was about to insert the tube. I wanted to get this over with as fast as possible. However, the fact that I did was not why I quickly shouted... "Take it out, take it out." I felt the tube was getting to my heart—that was the impression.

"I can't see," he replies. "Just a little more; just take a deep breath."

I could not take the pain for another second, so I insisted louder, "Take it out...take it out, now!" I shouted.

He pulls out the tube. "See, I did not even get the amount of sample I needed. This will have to do."

Darn right, it will have to do because you are not returning to the kitten home. I got dressed and left the office, forced a block away to take a seat due to nausea and dizziness. I called Monica, explained what was happening and began to feel a bit better during our conversation, having enough strength to get up, walk to the station to catch the train, then a bus back home and into bed.

Chapter 10

AN INVITATION DECLINE

ON THE WEEKEND, I was doing some research from a medical book I borrowed from Shelda by Judy Selfridge Thomas, Emergency Nursing—an essential guide for patient care. I compared the book's common complaints and related factors to what my body was experiencing. Ectopic Pregnancy—abnormal implantation site of an embryo. Common complaints—unilateral low abdominal pain, vaginal bleeding, and dizziness. Related factors—Ectopic pregnancies occur in the fallopian tube, and the risk factors can involve abnormal tubal structure, prior meningitis, and previous Ectopic pregnancies. Miscarriage—can be related to fever or trauma; Common complaints—abdominal pain and cramping, vaginal bleeding, missed menstrual period; related factors—termination of a pregnancy before the twentieth week (fifth month). Some of the symptoms experienced.

I decided to take a break in front of the television on the cushions on the floor, my head against the wall as I looked back to the date of Omar's first birthday party. Could I have been pregnant, but due to the lifting and jumping thorn the placenta to cause these conditions, *I sat in thought;* he did say he wanted to climax, but I told him not to, to hold back. Did that son of man could not? The phone rang, interrupting my thoughts. An acquaintance from Gilad called.

"Hello!" "How are you? This is Norma-Jean."

"Oh, hello, how are you? It has been a long time since we spoke."
We had not because she was now in a different department.

"I'm doing well." I could tell this was true from her voice. Not
exceptionally long, her friend died; he was a single elderly man financially well off. She was surprised to learn she had inherited a few material things from him. "I called to invite you to a picnic my church
is having." Me and Judy, another co-worker, had gone to one of her
church functions before and thoroughly enjoyed the entertainment
and meal afterwards and without a doubt knew; I would have a good
time.

"Oh, Norma-Jean," I respond, turning my head towards the window. "The heart is willing, but the body is weak."

Just as I spoke, passing was the squirrel I had come to adore. In
his mouth, he carried a little one. What the… I whispered with a
smile; this was the first time I had notice him in a parental role. He
often comes onto the veranda to feed and spend a few moments before heading off. He—Patches, I named him from his facial features.
Would bring others with him to feed on the nuts left for him; so often,
I enjoyed the moments we shared just looking at each other, him with
his little paw gestures as I spoke to him. Observed, he would come
early in the mornings and at sundown in the afternoon to feed and
seldom during the mid-afternoon. I guess climbing during the sun's
heat is just not smart. Patches is no longer seen as the city for the
housing complex has cut the tree shorter, so there is no access to the
balcony.

"What's the matter?" Norma-Jean asks. For a moment, my attention taken by the squirrel's actions did not acknowledge Norma-Jean's
question. "Paula!" she called a little louder.

"Oh, dear… Girl, I have been bleeding for over fourteen days and
keep getting these dizzy spells. I saw a gynecologist, and I am waiting
on the results. I'm afraid I will not be able to attend, but thanks for
the invitation."

"I'm sorry to hear that you are not doing well."

"So, how are you and your roommates getting along?"

"We are doing great."

"That's good to hear." We talked for a few more minutes and then said goodbye. I was taking the birth control pills prescribed but noticed unusual swelling in my ankles with occasional numbness in my legs and immediately thought this was caused by the pills. Further, the bleeding had not stopped, and the dizzy spells continued. I called the gynecologist's office, explained the condition, and requested an urgent appointment. Unfortunately, booked, and I would not see him for another week. Each day I felt weaker and exhausted. My bills and rent to be paid had too by me—I had no one to help. As much as I needed to stay home, I had to find my way to the office.

One evening at my desk, I started to feel uncomfortable, the air seemed cloggy, and I was having difficulty breathing. No big deal, this has happened before, and I will soon get rid of the feelings. Kate-Lyn, the supervisor, asked if I could go onto another campaign just as I was about to log off to take a break. "Sorry, I can't. I just have to get out of here. I can't breathe." Kate-Lyn looked up from her desk. "Okay," she slowly responded, the word drawn out questionably. I got up from my desk and felt extremely dizzy as I exited the office. I kept a bottle of Smelling Salts in my handbag and immediately reached for it. Unable to walk further from the office door—a blessing in disguise. I leaned my body against the wall as my legs weakened, causing me to drop to the floor in a seated position. With the last ounce of strength, I pulled the bottle out of the bag up to my nose and inhaled, bringing myself back to consciousness. Kate-Lyn approached me about five to eight minutes later.

"What is wrong?" she asks, taking my hand and placing her fingers on my pulse.

I, responded with my voice extremely low as I was tired. "I've had these dizzy spells. The feeling will soon pass, and I'll be back inside shortly."

"I don't know, Paula; your pulse is feeble. Would you like me to call an ambulance?"

"No, I'll be okay." I give a moment thought of how I was feeling and then... "Look, you go back in, and if I'm not there in ten minutes, call the ambulance."

That evening an ambulance rushed me to Humber River Hospital, the closest hospital in the area. After a long wait, various tests, and a severe reaction to the medication given— perhaps caused by a miscalculation for the amount to administer given by one nurse to another; my feet were cold and numb to the touch as my lips started to get puffy and blue. As the one who had given the amount to administer in passing looked at me said, '"You got a Pamela Anderson thing going on,'" in laughter. Had I not insisted that the attending nurse contact the doctor assigned to my case, may have caused my death. They found the problem and admitted me to the Intensive Care Unit. After being hospitalized for over a week, I asked for a release to home care. The doctor obliges, with instructions to take a few weeks off work and be seen as his outpatient; later recommended to another gynecologist.

I was happy to leave the hospital; I spent a week at Monica's, and in a few days, I was back to normal and anxious to get back to work.

Chapter 11

TEMPTATIONS

I RETURNED TO WORK on November 24 after being released from the hospital for blood clotting in my chest around the heart. a few days' rest, after returning home from Monica's I was ready to get out of the house. I had to find a job, as living on the assistance I got from Unemployment Insurance was not enough for the other things needed in my life. A few weeks later, I had an appointment, and an interview for the job was recommended. I was once again working. However, just when I thought the obstacles in my way were all gone, the devil workers were again at work to confuse me mentally. As usual, I will stop to pick up my mail on my way to work. One evening at work, I could not believe what I was reading from one of the mails opened; written in bold letters was Notice of Eviction. What the hell? I whispered to myself as I instructed my mind to take deep breaths to calm my thoughts. I read the letter twice and decided first thing to-morrow to investigate the matter—forgetting that it was Friday, real-ized I would have to wait until Monday to do so irritated me. Time will not soothe the anger I felt. This action was not the first of what will begin a chain of different other actions to cause questioning of my character.

§

Monday, after returning from an appointment with a Manpower Agency, I went to the office. Solomon, who works under Millie, answered the bell.

"Solomon, good day. I received a letter from you today, and I would like you to have a look at it."

"Why do I need to have a look at it? If it has my signature, I sent it."

"Please, I'm asking you to have a look." He walks over to the desk, draws the letter closer to him, looks at it and repeats. "I told you if it has my signature, I sent it, and it does. What's the matter?"

"What is the matter, you ask? I can't believe you folks sent me a letter like this, so I would like to make an appointment to see you and Millie to discuss this Eviction Notice because, according to this letter, I have fourteen days to straighten this matter out

"Millie is not here."

"Please leave a message letting her know I would like to have an appointment to see you both."

"I told you she is not here. Call her and leave a message."

"Why can't you just put the message on her desk?"

"I told you she was not here, and I don't have to give you any explanation."

He did not have to explain, but she was in the office, and it could not take a pound off him to rest a note on her desk. I had, had enough of his attitude at this point. Over the times I have dealt with him, I noticed him have a racist attitude and looked past this, but not today. I will have to let him know in a few words what I had on my mind to say to him for some time now. "I really don't understand you people. It seems that you are drunk or something when you people are talking to others than yourselves."

"Are you going to stop there?" he asked, a smile on his face.

"No, I'm not going to stop there; you people are probably on drugs, too." Just then a woman came in and I walked out of the office. Having a few more things to say, but talked myself into not allowing him to cause me to lose my temper further; that was almost to the boiling point.

As I walked into the apartment, I picked up the phone, called Millie, and left a message to see her as soon as she is available, noting the urgency of my call. I was most times in receipt of notices of owing rent and could not understand why when I also kept notes of my payments to the office. Their attempt to confuse my mind was working, and I would soon stand up for the gander's right.

Chapter 12

TRIALS

NO TEMPTATION I KNOW has taken me except what is common to men. This I know, God is faithful, and he will not let me be tempted beyond what I can bear, but along with the temptation, he will also make the way out for me to be able to endure it.

§

It was the month of September. I had found a part-time job, which did not last exceptionally long. During my training, I met one of Gilad's top performers. We had worked on the same team, and he left holding the title of thirty-plus sales in a day. Although he made more sales, he did not surpass me as one of the company's top three financial producers. After a week's work, the company told me, my services were no longer needed

I arrived early, so I stopped at MacDonald's and purchased a muffin and tea. I had not quite finished drinking the tea when it was time to report in. I walked into the office from the lunchroom and noticed a few new recruits seated and ready for training. Only standing for a moment, one of the trainers came over to take me onto the floor where with the others, I would begin working for the company. On my way into the room, I was told I would meet the person in charge of running the room. *I thought* to myself, this is officially the day I will show and continue to show what an asset I will be for Information Solution from Public Opinion. Left standing at the door after a brief introduction, I faced a dark woman in her forties, about 5'3".

"Please have a seat," she requested.

"Thank you," I replied as I sat on the chair.

"How are you?"

"I'm fine, thank you," I replied as I bent over to put the cup on the floor. "And I hope you are the same. I know I should not have anything other than water at my desk. It's a bit hot, and I want to finish it." She looks across at me, never mirroring the smile given.

"You have had training for over three days; it is something we don't do." Sure, what a contradiction, *I thought* to myself. "We don't have time to continue to train you. We have been listening to you, and your quality is not good, and you continue to make mistakes."

"I thought that was all taken care of. I know of the miscoding issue brought to my attention and taken care of; I don't understand." Whatever happened to the promise they made at the start about helping people to improve? My *thoughts were.*

"Yes, we told you not to side talk, and you continue to do so."

I had heard enough criticism at this point, and instead of telling her where to go, I just wanted to get out of there. English is my first language, not my second; therefore, I need to respond if a customer asks a question or makes a comment. It is not as if they are the ones calling. It is (we) the company calling them. Before responding *were my thoughts*; "Look, does…?"

The woman interrupted. "We will have to let you go. We will mail your cheque to you."

I bent forward and picked up the cup and bag from the floor. As I did, I knew the tea was a bad mistake, taken to the room. "Thank you, and good day," I replied.

There was nothing more to say at this point. As I walked out of the office, passing the room seen seated and looking out the glass window, the person who tested and hired me; I waved, exiting the room.

I had to let out of my system the anger I felt, so I called Monica.

"Hello," she answered in a soft and low tone, her mouth filled with whatever she was eating.

"You know, I have really had it with African Americans, Caucasians, Chinese, Italians, Indians...." I continue, all other nationalities forgotten in the heat of emotional passion, "Every one of them; I am tired of them. You should walk in my shoes, and then you will understand what I'm going through." The sound of Monica's chewing irritated me, but I continued to explain my dilemma *as I thought* why I was even bothering to do so. "And it is a good thing I was honest with the people at Capital One when I filled out the form for account balance protection, letting them know I was on three days training, and if hired on a three months' probation. Had I told them I had found a job and left it at that, look at the mess I would be in trying to pay that bill."

"Yes, you would be screwed. What can I say? People are who they are; just go home, take a shower and relax."

"That's what I'll do. The bus is here. I'll talk with you again. Bye."

On my way home, I dismissed the thought of calling Tanya. I felt Tanya needed time to reflect on her attitude. I was older than she was, never showed her any disrespect, and she needed to return the same respect. All is not lost; experience now gained working in research. While at the company, a co-worker had given me the phone number of another research company who was hiring. I recalled phoning the company before and was told they were not hiring—a company Tanya had worked for before leaving on maternity leave. My overall conclusion of the situation is that I failed sexually to stimulate the mind of those listening to my phone conversation. I did not like the sound of my voice on tape; I did not expect them either. They exhibited short-sightedness, a reason for many failed companies today that seek sexual gratification from hiring those with pretty and handsome looks with voices that stimulate the mind. Often, when one door closes, another opens somewhere.

Chapter 13

CONSPIRACY

IT WAS AFTER MIDNIGHT when I got in from work, and about one-thirty when I turned into bed. *Heavenly Father, I thank you for this day and for bringing me safely through it and into another. Thank you for being patient with my faults and the loving kindness you continue to show all others and me. I pray for those in countries that are having many difficulties and do not know where their next meal is coming from, and that you will give them the strength to endure their hunger, trusting and having faith in you and your word, that you will not forsake us in our time of need. Amen.* I got off my knees and onto the bed, pulling the blanket over me. I close my eyes with a sigh of relief.

BANG—a loud noise was heard; something or someone dropped to the floor. My eyes flipped open as I lay still on the bed. Footsteps—clump, clump, clump, running down the stairs, then knock, knock, someone knocking at the door. I reached for the phone and dialed 9-1-1.

"Emergency...How can I help you?" a woman operator asked.

"Look, I'm calling from...." I give my address and apartment number. "Someone seems to be in trouble. I heard a loud BANG that sounded like a shot, and someone was franticly knocking at my door. You need to send the cops over." As I continued to answer questions, the operator was asking and, pacing the floor to the front of the apartment, to my surprise, someone is jumping onto my veranda from the left. "Oh, look, as I'm speaking to you, he is coming onto my veranda."

"What does he look like? Do you recognize him?" the operator asks.

As I explain what I am seeing, the person shouts to someone on the other veranda to the right. He jumps over from my veranda to the person on the right as he asks, "Where were you?" He was about five feet with a light complexion wearing a t-shirt and sandals and carrying an arm bag. I got closer to the window and peaked to the right to see if I could see the person he was speaking to, but I could only see a pair of eyes staring back at me as the figure was quite dark. Still, with the phone to my ear, I heard the operator. The cops will be over shortly. "Thank you," I replied and hang up. I continued to pace back and forth, waiting for the buzzer to ring. After about fifteen minutes, I decided to call 9-1-1 once more, worried that someone may be hurt in the apartment.

"Emergency. How can I help you?" asked a male operator this time.

"Good evening, my name is Paula of...." I gave my address and continued to explain the reason for my call. "Yes, madam, you did ten minutes ago. The police officers are on their way. They will be there shortly."

"Okay, I just wanted you, to know what's happening in case something happens to me because the call I made earlier when I checked my phone to redial the last number, 9-1-1, was nowhere to be found on the list."

"Okay, madam, they will be there." I hang up and continued to pace the floor, stopping to look out the window occasionally.

It was about five minutes of pacing the hall that flashing blue lights below the Gardner Express were seen as I looked out the window. Finally, they are here. I wonder why they are so quiet. The absence of the siren indicates something is seriously wrong. I recall one summer; I was asleep when I heard someone saying to another: "Do you want the number?" No response was heard other than PAP, PAP, PAP, *the sound of firecrackers, I thought*, until I felt a strange quietness and got out of bed and looked out the window—cruisers with flashing lights lined the street. They had arrived at the shooting in the park—the scene likens to what I was encountering. I wonder what role that blond woman has in this. What was she put into the big bag she had rested on the park's bench? Where was she going when she walked back to the right, the direction she came from? *Questing thoughts* as I kept looking at the flashing lights and wondering when I would hear the apartment buzzer. A few more minutes passed, and I decided to return to bed, only to have relaxed, my body disturbed by the ringing phone. "Hello?"

"This is officer...." He introduced himself and told me they are in the neighborhood and would be in the lobby shortly.

"Sure, I'll open the lobby door for you, but not my apartment. Check the neighbors beside me and those above to be sure they are okay."

"We'll do that. We'll be there in a few minutes."

I got off the bed and once more started to pace the floor as I listened for the buzzer sound. I got suspicious after five minutes or more had passed and heard no sound of the buzzer; I walked back into my bedroom, locked the door, and got into bed. A minute after, I heard a sound and got off the bed, leaned my ear to the door and heard a knock. "What the hell? Someone is on the veranda," I whisper. The railing that lay on the veranda was heard as being moved. I picked up the phone and keyed in 9-1-1 in preparation to make the call in the event the person or persons tried to enter. Both doors were locked, so if anyone was planning on getting in, there would be time for me to escape or arm myself. Still, with my ear pressed against the door, I listen intently for other sounds. Five minutes had now passed. It was obvious that the person had gone. "I tell, these days the only person to trust is yourself. So long the officer called to say that they were going to be here and up to now there is no one, and the number of the buzzer given on all three occasions I have spoken to them," I spoke out loud. Removing myself from the bedroom door and onto my bed, laying my body to rest, I whisper, "First thing in the morning, I will call to find out what happened." I closed my eyes, breathed a sigh of relief, and drifted off to sleep.

The next day, I called. The phone was picked up by a man. "Hello," he answers.

"Good morning. My name is Paula. I live...." I gave my address and the reason for the call and asked what the outcome was.

"I will put you on to the officer who responded to the call. One moment, please."

I held the phone for a few minutes then a man answered. He sounded young. Perhaps a rooky, I thought.

"Hello, I am officer...." He gave his name; told me he had responded to the call.

"So, what happened?"

"We met someone in the lobby, and when asked if he heard anything, he said no. We then walked your floor and the one above but could not hear or see anything unusual."

"So, that's it?" *With thoughts*, Idiots, someone may have still been in the apartment hurt for all you know. Perhaps waiting for a knock on the door to make his or her move to safety.

"Yes," he replies.

The devil workers, a way to go making me look as if I am a busybody. "Okay, then, I guess that will be all." We both hang up.

§

It would be a week or two after that incident that the strong scent of cleaning chemicals was smelt on entering my unit one day. Strange, *I thought*, never had that smell encountered before. That would be the start of other odors that caused words between me and the tenant right next to my unit one day. I requested him to burn incense or candle to get the scent from the area. I felt embarrassed because other tenants would question me about the smell. Later, it was found that the tenants' actions had some to do with the wicked one's work of a family situation that lacked knowledge.

Years later, in the summer of 2021, the neighbor a crossed from my unit decided to grow a flower garden. Although I complained about the microscopic insects in my unit, my complaints went without a response from management. The time allowed for understanding his reason, perhaps prevention from another incident that had occurred, as earlier explained.

Chapter 14

WHAT WILL BE WILL BE

"A FAITHFUL WITNESS will not lie, but a false witness launches forth mere lies."

Life at the office was becoming unhappy. After all the years of working with the ones I consider family, I notice some with an attitude of avoidance daily. My relationship with some in the office was growing thin, and I could not help but think it was due to my open concept of truths. I thought that a meaningful friendship was developing between me and Shea but found out from one incident that sparked a few emails from her in one day that I responded to truthfully, shows Shea's intolerance discovered beneath the surface. "You were a busy camper this morning Shea. As they say, after a while with certain ones, you tend to develop their attitude; I will say a little prayer for you," I commented as she walked into the office towards her desk.

"I guess your son's attitude is rubbing off on you," said Dan with a chuckle.

If Shea did say something, it was hushed, as I did not hear if she responded to what Dan said.

§

MONTHS LATER...

I was asleep and found myself in a home overlooking two men having a conversation. One said to the other as he entered the room with what seemed a meal for the other and said, "It's time for you to leave."

"Man, give me a break, naa!" the person responded.

As that said, a noise was heard, like a blowout tire or that of a gun, and the cell phone started to ring. "Hello," I answered.

"Hi babe, it's me, Rudolf," the voice responded. After a few seconds of silence in disbelief, since I had not heard from him in such a long time, I asked slowly, "Rudolf," with a chuckle, I continued, "I thought you were deported or something. I told a co-worker during our conversation when your name came up.

"I'm doing fine. I'm working at a chocolate factory."

That said, I could not contain the laughter. From living on Ice Cream Lane to working in a chocolate factory, the man has always been in a sweet house lately. I could only imagine when he said how buff he looked; it must be from the amount of fat he was consuming. His life is comical, and he can care less, laughing right along with those that dominate the lives of others. He certainly has the right attitude.

"See, I always make you laugh, but you know I can't go to school; my head cannot take the studying. You sound so sweet on the phone. Were you sleeping?"

"Yes, I was asleep when I heard a noise and the phone that woke me. It's funny, but I was having a dream as I was overhearing a conversation..."

As I said that, *my thoughts wandered* to perhaps this was his method of trying to control me, especially when the next word out of his mouth; was asking to see me. Immediately, I let it be known I was living a life of celibacy, by saying that I knew it would stop him in his tracks and those that manipulated his life for their enjoyment or pleasure. Still, I also knew that if he saw me now, I was not what he wanted, as outward appearance did matter to him. Further, his vision was going, and *within my thought*, he may see my appearance worse than I really am. Lol. I figured the noise heard just before speaking with him was a threat from someone either to him or to me. My life had limited peace, and I was not about to interrupt the atmosphere; a woman frustrated by situations and people's disappointment will not take it from any fool trying to further confuse my life.

"Two men," I continued. "Were having a conversation, and as one asked the other to give him a break, I heard a loud noise and then the phone. So, what are you up to?"

"I'm living with an Italian girl; babe, she is so controlling. The other day, I told her I would give myself to the police. As I was heading to the station, the woman started following me and almost got hit by a car." Noise is heard in the background. "Yes, I know. I'll be leaving soon," he told someone. "The woman is nuts," he resumes the conversation. "I can't do anything."

"Rudolf, every woman you have, there is a problem. I'm sure you found the same with me."

"No, really, you were the best...." If I was the best, then what happened? my *thought thrown.* "I was just stupid. However, really, I would like to see you. You are always on my mind. I remember those days, especially the sexual ones when you made me feel. When I think of you, I get a hard-on."

It was time to end the conversation, I knew privacy was zero on the phone and in the unit, and I did not want the world to know my private life. "I can't; I plan to visit my sister this weekend, and I'm so busy with work I don't know when it will be." The sentence frustrated him, and he needed to get to his agenda, whether it was with me or someone else. If he had no place to stay for the evening, he would find himself right back into the arms he was running from.

"Okay, I'll keep in touch." With that said, we bid each other goodbye, and the phones hung up.

Chapter 15

THE PSYCHOANALYSIS OF UNCONSCIOUS THOUGHTS

AS THE DAY CONTINUED at work, I was beginning to get to know the group. My spirit had taken to a few, and the others, well, I neither disliked nor hated, just that I preferred not to be with them outside of the office. I was no different from anyone else. Most people have a group, one or three people they prefer to hang out with at work or socially, and nothing is wrong with that. The truth is I battle against negative inculcated thoughts and actions from a few; I preferred having little or no contact. When I got home, a headache that had begun earlier in the day was still with me. I now had to be careful to watch what I ate and took as pain inhibitors and avoid cuts and falls. I always watch what I eat and tried to be careful about what exercises I did, but I felt a bit restricted. To avoid any causes that would send me back to the hospital, I did what I often do at the start of a painful headache, tie a cold, damp cloth around my head and lie still in a quiet surrounding—always works to relieve my headache.

The spiritual definition of Faith is this: Faith is the assured expectation of things hoped for, the evident demonstration of realities though not beheld. My Faith is my confession of having trust in God, not a demand for immediate answers to the problems I was going through. I lay in bed with the damp cloth around my head and, in silence, recalled a pastime.

§

THE NEXT MORNING

I got up, ran through my morning rituals, and went off to work. I logged in and began my day's work. An hour had passed, and ideally, I passed my tongue to the sides of my mouth and sensed a taste of blood. Our senses do not embrace any idea of good or bad but are simply the act of seeing, hearing, smelling, feeling, and tasting. "They may compare to particles of light," says P.P. Quinby. Hmm, this is awkward; my mouth is not bleeding. I once more repeated my action and experienced the same taste. This is bizarre. I wonder about the origin of the taste contemplating whether to reach for the compact mirror in my handbag but feeling a bit shy to do so, sitting between two men who may comment on my vain personality—John and Simon. As I had such thought, a co-worker stopped and told John there was blood on his neck. "Oh, I was just scratching my neck," he told her. I looked up at John seated to my left; that was some itch you had. *I said to myself in thoughts.* And indeed, there was blood on the right side of his neck.

John can be a genuinely nice person when he wants to be. If he dislikes you, you will hear about it. The one thing I noticed about gays—yes, John was gay—they are never timid about expressing themselves. He was married once, and word has it he father one or two children, but he never spoke of that part of his life in detail. He was once a minister, and Lord only knows why he decided to reject the teachings to walk the other way. I had a few suspicions of my own from conversations and felt his unhappiness with the life he chose to live. However, despite his personal problems, he most often made me smile, often from how he dressed, the things he said or the way he put another down and has made me cry once from his accusation of what he assumed my thoughts were of him. This was unfounded, as I liked him. The life some choose to live is not mine to judge. However, I do feel an open mind will help one learn things that enrich one's life. I continued my work thoughtfully, wary of one of two incidents that moved me to pay attention more closely at my body's reaction to my outer world.

Most of us engage in self-talk. Self-talk is a good example of an intuitive way of thinking that influences how we feel and what we do until we stop and stop to do the opposite, which is to listen to our body's response to our thoughts; it is amazing at what is learnt.

For example, one day at the office, Dan, a co-worker, received a call from Nellie, who worked on the other floor. A thought passed my mind as he said, "Wait a moment." He took a few steps away from the phone as if contemplating a thought of his own, then he picked up the phone and responded to the worker. As he did, I unintentionally fluff, a scent so strong I had to pick up an item off my desk to fan while simultaneously giving the message of apology. The question of thought within my mind as I was looking at Shea and paying attention to Dan's actions and whether he also had access to my written work triggered the cause of the incident.

To understand what your body's reaction is alerting or warning you of, one needs knowledge of two things: the totality of subconscious mental activities. Which are thoughts occurring in mind with conscious perception. Within thoughts, as I looked at Shea, I presented a time when her facial expression was directed to Nellie's clothing that smelt funky, and my suspicion of Dan.

Secondly, externalization—in psychoanalysis, a person with a defense mechanism he or she unconsciously attributes inner impulses to the external world. (I am touching a little more in-depth on mind science.) To summarize what I am saying, some of you, like me, have dreams we awake from, and some so disturbing we will dismiss all occurrences. The conscious mind becomes a blank board that was once written on, now erased. The conscious mind's written content is now in your filing cabinet—the subconscious mind. Those thoughts or images in the subconscious are now awaiting extraction by something or someone (for example, Shea's past comment of Nellie, her disrespectful emails and Dan's action, triggered scent) from the outer world. When this happens, those thoughts merge into the conscious mind, causing one to relate past unexplained physical experiences to the external world. The word "unconsciously" used in the explanation of externalization becomes so. As the individual reacts consciously from the subconscious information being seen in the present, the brain impulses move the individual to commit a crime, say things that build or damage relationships, or do things that harm him or herself. These hidden thoughts or suspicions— unaware of them, are causes for our explained personal scent or anxiety attacks.

Chapter 16

WE ARE ALL FAMILY

WHEN THE WORD FAMILY is mentioned, people think of their immediate blood relations. The word family can refer to a group of people who, day after day, month after month and year after year, spend eight hours or more each day. Within the editing department, Our relationship was like such. Within a family where you will find the comical one, the one who displays more understanding, the haughty one, the mischievous one, the talkative one, the quiet one, the cruel one— all whose attitude builds each, for good or bad are within the room.

Innocence is bliss. I will say it is more comical than blissful. A conversation started one evening among the group—the topic was about the uses of lemons and the many applications it is good for, like cooking, cleaning, and medicinal purposes.

"The best to use for washing meats is limes, and they are even better for cases of flu and colds," Alex commented.

"I prefer lemons to limes; they have more juice and a much better flavor."

"Do you know that limes turn into lemons?"

"No, Alex," I replied, looking at him, my forehead knitted as I continued. "They are different; they are two different trees."

"No!" Alex exclaimed. "When the limes turn yellow, they are called lemons." Yes, he is the comical one. Obviously, this seemed logical to Alex. This a comment one might expect from a child, but he is a married man in his late twenties with two children.

"You idiot..." Dan interjects with laughter. "Man, it is two different trees." Dan is the cruel one. He is very outspoken, talks of you behind your back and even exhibits racial dislikes. Do not care who is offended by his comments and could care less if it were his parents sitting in the room—the impression he gave was like the odd couple, him, and Alex. Most nights, they will get into intense arguments, and at the end of the shift, they will walk out of the room together as if nothing had occurred. Barbara and I would look at them, at each other and burst out with laughter. If two individuals have lived up to the saying: do not let the Sun go down with anger in your heart, it would be the opposite with those two; do not let the Sun rise with anger in your heart. Even after Barbara corrected him, Alex insisted it was not two different trees. At that point, no one could contain himself or herself from laughter. Down the hallway we could be heard from within the room.

§

Two days later, Barbara came to work, entering the room with a smile on her face and a can of Lemon/lime drink in her hand before resting it on the desk. With a gesture of cheers, she raised her hand that held the pop can, about to take her seat. "This is lemon and lime pop. I could not get Alex out of my mind; I had to search for this." Remembrance of that night causes those who were there to burst into laughter again. Alex's innocent comments did cause laughter in the room most nights when he would insist on being correct in discussions; he held one, too, longer than they wanted to be in. Throughout the years, I have seen him, like all of us, grow mentally, having gained much knowledge from experiences exposed to situations. For a man with children, a prayer must be said for the family. He did not very much care for John because of his lifestyle, and anyone could see that John's feelings were mutual. On most occasions, when they did have a conversation, John would roll his eyes and comment, not wanting to waste his breath with him. Dan looked up from the computer.

"So, Ho, are you leaving us?"

"Yes, Dan. Is there something I can do for you?"

"I tell ya a long time what you can do fa me," he replied with his Guyanese slang. It was his pet-name for her, but not exceptionally long like copycats; others called her by the same name. I was certain she had not the kind of relationship with them that she and Dan shared to merit such a term of endearment and disliked the fact that she even accepted being called Ho. Calling someone you do not know as such sends and leaves a negative message to those who are strangers in the room. Due to staff turnover, I felt embarrassed for the impression left in the minds of those who left and had mentioned this to Dan. Why did I even care, one may ask. It was not like he was referring to her as a whore, and as true as that may be, I disliked it when disrespect is done to others, even if they deserve it. There is a time and a place for everything. Unfortunately, in his case, there is no place or time when he wants to express himself.

"Dan..." She looks at him, a smile on her face. "You know where you can go for what you want."

He laughs, "See ya."

"Yes, see ya."

"Bye, Ho," said Barbara, laughing. I looked at Barbara, irritated by her lack of respect, as this was not the first time Roxanne was called Ho by her. She, like Dan, had become comfortable within their environment, forgetting who the persons were that they were dealing with. Dan was so explicit at times that Kate-Lyn, the supervisor, had to tell him to cut his conversation as it was much too detailed. Barbara had even taken it upon herself to advise the supervisor; one evening, she left to pick up her husband, who was away for a few days to "work that thing tonight." Kate Lyn smiled, but I saw that she did not take kindly to the comment beneath her facial expression. Each one, including the supervisor, had become the same, so it appeared to them that there was no holding back their words before speaking. On many occasions, I am left to wonder what it is about others that allow them to speak or act a certain way and get away with it, and had it been me in their position, something would have been said or done to put me in my place.

§

During a brief period of employment with an outlet of Midas Muffler on King Street West, I did learn a lesson, the lesson that there is a place for everything. It was a busy day during the week, and not unusual to hear profanity occasionally from the boys. I was the only woman that worked at the shop and was on perfect terms with the boss, at least this I thought until that evening of closing. I had done the paperwork, and my boss came into the office's trailer to check my work. "Very good." I am commended.

Unable to contain my excitement and tongue from knowing my work was complete and correct, I leaned forward with both hands on the desk, looking into his eyes as he stared back at me. "You see, I know what I'm doing," I softly completed. "You don't screw with me." With all paperwork done correctly and money accounted for, the seating area—a large room adjacent to the trailer—was cleaned, cups and mugs washed and returned to the coffee table. The shop closed for the beginning of another day. I bid my boss good night, and we parted for our respective homes.

The next day, I got to work, and my employment was terminated before I could set my belongings down. "What did I do wrong?" I asked with disbelief. According to the night before and all the other evenings, everything seemed to have gone well, so what was this about? He looked at me as he informed, "Because you cursed me last night."

"What?" I swallowed before continuing, "You know that was just a matter of speaking."

"I'm sorry…here is your cheque." I took the cheque and walked away from him without another word. Yes, this was my experience and advice: Do not become too comfortable that you overlook the other's clandestine judging of you.

Regardless of the kind of relationship we had and the fact of where we were, at that point and time, he was my boss and deserved respect. There is a time and place for everything under the Sun, but people's familiarity causes them to overstep their position. I had learnt a hard lesson; one I have never forgotten and one that has been molded into my character into the person I am today.

§

"Yes, bye, Barbara."

Barbara was the editing department's brief backup supervisor. Of African descent, she is of average height, thin with a short-tailored haircut and single with a girl child. From the moment she started with Gilad, my spirit took to her; I assisted her in getting familiar with the campaigns and helped to look over her correspondence to other team leaders when asked. Over the months, we became quite close; I would cook meals for us, as she did. She would occasionally bring back gifts when she went out of town with her date and bring back the details of their meeting, occasionally seeking my advice on what to do with the relationship. I felt any advice would be useless as I could see her mind was made up, focusing on her and her daughter's well-being. An accident caused her to leave Gilad, to never return.

However, I was surprised when she returned to the lunchroom one day to hear that she had announced to the boys that she was a lesbian.

I started laughing. "You did what?"

She also started laughing. "I was just kidding with them."

"I hope you told them so," I immediately responded, as I did not want them to go away with thoughts that I was a lesbian, especially since we were quite friendly.

"Yes, I did, after a few moments," she replied. We then even more started to laugh at the situation.

Chapter 17

UNINTENTIONAL ACTIONS LEND TO LAUGHTER

IT WAS THE END of another day, another dollar, as the saying goes. Earlier during the day. "I don't know why this agent insists on repeating a whole paragraph when she can give an answer in a simple sentence." As Shea spoke, she turned towards me with one hand on her hip as the other rested on the desk. She chuckles when I ask, "Who is it?" And was told the name.

"Oh," I said. "I know her. I had spoken to her about her attitude toward the customers, and her response was, 'It is how you were listening to the call.' That is how she responds to a question. I often shake my head and say the same thing, why not give a simple answer. One thing, though, no one can accuse her of making anything up. Her response is exactly what's on the script."

"I think she's stupid," Shea replies in frustration due to the length of the call.

I continued to smile, thinking of the agent's action, wiser than Shea knows. I do not know the agent but is acquainted with her, and there is one thing I do that my peers and younger ones tend to overlook: being vigilant of others' actions. I could tell that it was obvious that along the woman's journey, she must have learned a forceful lesson in emphasis, *so in my thoughts*, the agent's action justified her personal experiences.

Shea is a divorcee much older than me, who lives with her son. She has been with the department for quite a few years, and since getting acquainted with her, I had developed a fondness for her. If the question asked what Shea's best feature is, it would have to be her smile. She has a beautiful warm smile that lights up her face and makes for beautiful pictures. She has never mentioned her dad but has her mother, who died. She has other siblings who she mentions occasionally.

Roxanne got up to leave. Roxanne is not one to open a conversation, but she will prolong it with her comments. She is born in the same month as me—October, a few days later, and we share similarities. My life experiences have altered my personality. Gone is the interest in hearing stories of others' misfortunes, time spent reading, doing research, writing, playing a few games on the computer or watching television is much more rewarding and peaceable, in my opinion. On the other hand, Roxanne relishes a tell-tale story, whether true or false. She is an only child, and her mother looks like her older sister. She is of average height and build, has a dark brown complexion and shoulder-length black hair, and wears glasses and, at times, contacts. She neither practices nor belongs to any religious organization, although she has some knowledge of the Muslim Faith due to her mother's involvement. According to her, she is still young with raging hormones for the opposite sex. The conclusion is drawn, dedication to any type of religious faith will not go well with her vowing to be celibate before marriage. As she walked towards the door...

Barbara called out, "Goodnight, Ho."

As I continued my work in silence, I wondered at what point she would gain the courage to put her in her place.

"Yes, good night, my bitch," Roxanne responded. As much as her words surprised me, it made me smile to see that she finally got the courage to put her in her place. *Within my thoughts*, I wonder when she will do the same with Dan, as I had told her what to call him when he calls her Ho.

§

A FEW MONTHS LATER...

I got into the office one day to notice Shea wearing an eye patch. Aware of her living situation and how she spoke with such fondness of her son, the thought of being hit by him or any man for that matter, was out of the question. Shea's lifestyle was like mine—work, home, and no male companion to complicate our peaceful lives. What could have happened? I took my seat and began my day's work without wanting to be nosey. Shea got up shortly after that and left the room. This was my opportunity to find out what or who damaged Shea's eye, and the person who would know would be Ada—if not Lilly. Therefore, as soon as the door closed, I made my way over to Ada's desk. "Hey, what happened to Shea?" I whisper.

Ada looked up at me with a chuckle. "She accidentally got her finger in her eye." Ada, also older than me, appears to be much, much older, according to Shea's comment one day that had the whole department laughing when the topic of birthdays came up. Shea said, "I don't know, but according to her celebrated birthday twice yearly, I'll say she is ancient." She is married with children and a bit on the stout side. She chooses her social friends whose character, in her opinion, is flawless. The impression she gives. A good listener, but one is advice; best to keep certain things private or others will know about them. She claims to be of Muslim Faith, kind-hearted and jovial.

"How'd she does that?"

"Pulling the blanket over self."

"Shit!"

Ada laughs at my facial expression as she repeats, "Shit is right. She had to go to the emergency."

"Really." I lowered my body position in a hush of laughter so as not to attract Lilly's attention; I assumed she knew who or what the conversation was about, as there was not much that passed her ear-

240

drums. My ears are sensitive to sound, but sometimes I swear the woman must be wearing some device that picks up sounds faster than I did.

Ada repeats to me, "Really."

I glanced at Lilly, whose fixation on the computer's screen tells me otherwise. "I better get back to my desk."

"Yeah." Ada gestures her head sideways. "Before you know who starts to inquire."

I walk off and back to my desk. For that entire day, I did my work amused by Shea's attire. With the eye patch, she looked like Popeye, the sailor man's wife.

Sometimes, the things we do to ourselves that are painful and exhausting lend to laughter in the lives of others, and only when we look back can we chuckle at ourselves for the humor our misfortune displayed.

§

WEEKS LATER...

I entered the office to see Dan's forehead with a red mark on it and felt a bit fearful as I recalled a dream. The person in the dream looked like him and had the same mark on his forehead. The person seen in a large room with a small container in one hand and with the other, he puts into the container to draw out the liquid that he then sprinkles on the walls as he goes around the room chanting words that I did not hear but could only see as the image's mouth moved. Once seated, the fear subsided.

He was fasting; this I knew. He was likened to the Pharisees when fasting made a big show. I never told him this, but he moved me into researching his religion for more knowledge to better understand some of his practices, which he could not give if your life depended on the—why? He made me smile when Shea asked the question. "But how come you're supposed to be fasting yet eating?" Trying to shed light on his belief was like turning a light switch on which battery or electricity had died; he continued full speed ahead in darkness with his partial explanations. He seemed more impressed by the stories he heard of the religious elders than by obtaining the sacred knowledge of how they become to be who they are. My research led me to understand that Hinduism has its origin in a remote past that cannot be traced to a single individual.

§

Hinduism is the third-largest religion, with over a billion followers. A religious conglomerate of philosophical and cultural ideas and practices originates in India. They believe in truth, honesty, non-violence, celibacy, cleanliness, contentment, prayers, austerity, perseverance, penance, and pious company. Hinduism is a way of life—following the path of righteousness, a law that governs all actions. They believe in one God; however, the gods and goddesses of Hindus represent different aspects of God. There are more than a thousand manifestations of God, but the most fundamental of deities is the trinity. Most Hindus believe that the spirit or soul, the true self of every person, the atman, is eternal. (According to some scriptures, whoever gains insight into the depths of his or her own nature and becomes fully aware of the atman and the innermost care of oneself realizes this identity "with" God and then reaches Marsha.) The Hindu scriptures are referred to as "Shastras." There are two types of scriptures: the "Shriti," which is heard, and the "Smriti," which is memorized and passed on from generation to generation orally for centuries before being written down. Hinduism is simply defined as an individual who accepts and lives by religious guidance of the Vedic scriptures; Learn, Live, and Leave behind your knowledge.

§

"Man, I eat because they say if you are hungry, you should," he replies. I interject because I knew from his earlier comment that the answer was unknown to him.

"It is best for him to eat if he is hungry because he'll be bringing judgment upon himself. The scripture advises that if a person does not discern the body—Christ, and is hungry, let him eat that he may not come together for judgment."

"Ha!" Shea replies as she turns back to her computer screen. Turning back a few minutes, she asks, "Why can't you eat salt?"

"Well...." He seems to be thinking of an answer. "They say salt is the strength or what gives taste to everything, and so we abstain from eating anything that contains salt during this time in the purification of the body."

"True, salt is known for purifying, and it also acts as a cleanser," I added to his comment with a bit more knowledge I did not care to share.

"I see," replies Shea as she once again turns to her computer screen.

I looked at him from across my desk as I smile within. He is still a boy acting like a man with no intention of slowing down. Most of what he knows comes from what he has been told—wrong or right, he accepts and disperses to others, and always with the pronoun— they say. Smart enough not to accept blame for incorrect or partial knowledge. The day was once again at an end.

Chapter 18

WHAT'S IN A NAME?

"MY FIRST CHILD is going to be a boy!" Dan exclaimed. A conversation had started about children and the difficulty of raising them today.

"Oh, really Dan, you know you can't even swim," I responded with a smile as I recalled to mind Rudolf, to see his reaction; knowing that this is a statement most men do not like to hear—the fact that their sperm count is too weak to procreate.

"Don't you know that I'm god? I can make anything happen?"

"Dan, would you stop saying that?" I commanded.

"Why? I am."

Every time he said he was "god," I wanted to tell him what I thought he was suffering from but could never remember the word I had come across in my psychology book. "You are lucky you are among us; some other place, and you'll be placed in a mental institution for claiming to be God," commented John.

"Exactly," I replied.

"Look, there are people with the names Jesus and God. Would they institutionalize them?"

"That is their name by birth, Dan; there is a difference (it was usual to find many people in Jerusalem, even Mexico, with the names Jesus and God). Your name is not God, and to claim that you are, is falsity," I replied in disgust at his attitude. The context of his comments showed he was referring to himself as a "god."

I recalled the conversation me and Zelda had over a guy named Jesus, telling Zelda if He claimed it was his name what was I to do—I got no response—rightfully so, for what could Zelda say in return. The conversation ended with him insisting that he could swim and that he would show me. Therefore, when he informed the group that Mahaila was pregnant in December, I burst into laughter.

"Oh, Dan, you silly boy; you had to show us that you could swim." As the others chuckled, he bowed his head as if in shame with a smile. Dan's hope was for a boy, and his religious belief brought fear to me on behalf of his mental state should his hope of having a boy shatter. He took things of importance for granted, missing the point. Who knows how the spirit turns a thing, or for what purpose, Only Jehovah! He was like some who acknowledge a force at work but do not believe in the power it has to cause an effect. Like Phillip, who left to join the army, he believed that it was okay to continue on the road to destruction, ever so often confessing his sins and all is good as forgotten. Forgetting this scripture that bears on actions, "Do not deceive; God is not mocked: for whatsoever a man sowth, that shall he also reap." –Galatians 6:7.

"You are planning to go to Guyana. Are you leaving her?" Roxanne asked.

"No, she is coming with me. I want my child to be born in Guyana."

"Why?" the question on the minds of most in the room, but I was bold enough to ask when all in unison said, "Yes, why?"

"I want my baby to have dual citizenship."

At least he was thinking ahead, *I thought to myself*. Since they are both immigrants, any children born of them, and their own children would not legally be considered Canadians or citizens. Their status would lose in the legal system. However, the advantages of having his child born in Guyana would cause dual citizenship, and any children born of his child would then be Canadian citizens. That was a good enough answer for me. I stopped all further comments as I continued my work, often listening to him explain how the child's name is chosen and what is done when a newborn enters the world.

Chapter 19

GO TO THE ANT, OBSERVE ITS WAYS

WE ARE ADVISED to go to the ant (animals) and consider their ways. –Proverbs 6:6. By understanding animals, their traits, and their symbolism, we approach life more simplistically and naturally. We are humans with animalistic qualities and likeness; each one's beauty is in the eyes of the Beholder. The word Dog is any of a great variety of domesticated carnivores and a word used as slang. The year 2006 in the Chinese calendar referred to the year of the dog. In the book 10,000 Dreams Explained, a dog symbolizes the guardian of the underworld. In Egyptian mythology depicted by Anubis, the dog-headed God guides the souls of the dead to the underworld—our most secret part. The year 2008 is referred to as the year of the rat. A rat is any of several rodents and is used as slang. The rat signifies a tainted or devious part of our personality or a situation we are in. It can also represent something repulsive in some way.

"Well, this is it!" he exclaimed. "I'm gone tomorrow."

Roxanne rose from her seat as she prepared to leave with him to meet with Mahaila for a farewell drink. I was emotional. I hate saying goodbyes. Lord knows I have said that on too many occasions, and it has always seemed to be a final experience. Life is short and unpredictable, and one never knows if one will have another chance to see that person again. Many things you wanted to say, it just never was the right time or place to say them, and the opportunity may never present itself again…reasons we hang on to Faith, the expectation of our hope.

"Okay, Lilly, take care. I'm going to send you guys' pictures of the baby."

"Have a safe trip and behave yourself."

"All right. Paula, aren't you going to give me a hug?"

I looked at him with tears in my eyes. "No, go ahead," I replied, emotionally choked up. "What are you crying for?" That is an excellent question. What was the real reason I was crying over this rude, obnoxious son of a man? I hadn't a clue other than having to say goodbye. I should be happy that he would be out of my life. His actions and transferred thoughts had caused much emotional hurt in past incidents; one in my childhood, that had occurred with the boy next door.

He was of average height, had a brown complexion, and was good-looking, fingers perfect for playing the guitar or piano. He was the boy that occupied my mind and accompanied Veronica, my nieces, my nephew, and me on fishing trips. One day led to many days of great fishing trips. I knew he liked me, so I flirted with him when I had the opportunity to do so. One Sunday, only four of us were on the fishing trip. On the way home, I took the back seat after helping with putting the equipment and the tropical fishes we caught in the trunk. Not surprised that he would also sit in the back of the car. I was pleased that he did. The car started, and just about a quarter mile down the highway at high speed, the car slightly lifted from the road and landed with a bump, and as it did, I felt a hand touch my thigh. I look over at him as he edges himself closer to me and gently squeezes my thigh, and as he does, he edges them up a bit further. I enjoyed the sensation; the touch of his hand was giving as he rubbed under my knee. I relaxed my leg and body as he slightly squeezed my thigh and began to run a finger slowly up to my vagina. His finger rested on my clit over my panties as he played a tune that caused me to groan.

"Paula…" Veronica shouted from the driver's seat, "Oh, shit.…" In unisons I yelled the same as the car suddenly flew into the air and bumped again, hitting the road. "Is everything okay behind there?".

I grabbed his hand, removing it from between my leg as I responded to Veronica's question.

"Yes, I am. Why are you driving so fast?" a question asked with both guilt and fear in my voice.

"I'm driving at the speed limit. You know this flipping highway; they make it so steep at some points it's like falling off a cliff." Mackenzie Highway its called; it was the only highway in our country at the time. And trips along the highway was one of my delight. It was like being in a different world only one read of.

"I almost fell off one."

"What'd you say?" It was difficult to hear as the wind passed through the windows.

"Nothing, forget it," I loudly yelled back.

I sat back in the car, wishing we would arrive home as soon as possible. Now that I wanted him to touch me, which he did, *within thoughts,* I questioned my next reactions. How far would he go the next time? Do I go all the way with him? I allowed myself to look at him. He had that smirk on his face as if he had just won a conquest of some sort. "I love you," he whispered with a broader smile. My heart beating faster than I wanted it to, I returned the smile and turned my body towards the window as I daydreamed of what the next time would be like. The next time did not occur until after four or five trips because Veronica had insisted, I sat up front a few times, and on a few, I volunteered to sit up front. However, when the second time did happen, he gave me a climax that put a print on my heart. We had never gotten together physically, but he made my fishing trips

pleasurable. Looking back at the memories of him with mixed feelings, I cannot recall whatever did happen to him. All I could remember was that he was seldom seen around the neighborhood.

§

Yes, that was one of the memories his actions with Roxanne triggered. I saw the force at work, battled with the thoughts, and knew
the little flirtatious game she played with Dan and him with her.
People are in our lives for a season for a reason. During that fishing
season, the boy next door taught me how to touch myself to experience pleasure.

When a child, our thoughts and actions are as a child. Once
grown, things done as a child should be done away with. This is possible when understanding is given by knowledge, and wisdom comes
in to guide and protect.

I have been there and done that, but the whispers during the night
and the reality by day forced me to look deeper into the psychic part
of myself. Was the action of others causing my own conscious
thoughts to accuse me? On the other hand, excuse my past actions? I
asked myself. It was obvious, or I would not feel the guilt of a past
action not told to anyone, was the answer to my inner thoughts. I
knew that I was not crazy as some may think, because I claim to hear
voices in the night. I was more alert and aware of myself than many
that walk the face of this earth.

10,000 Dreams Explained further confirms this: a voice that
speaks through, or to us, as in trance work (an altered state of consciousness), has two areas of significance. Through us suggests information for others, whereas to us is more personal. If we believe in
the spirit realm (the world is laying in the power of the wicked one—
Satan), this communication is from a discarnate spirit. When we sup-
press certain parts of our personalities, they may surface in dreams
as disembodied voices. This does not constitute a form of madness.

End of quote. We must rely on God's word for guidance, for it sure is a lamp to my foot that lights my roadway and protection to my soul; God's Word is to me.

"I'm going to be back anyway; take care!"

"Yes, he's going to be back," Roxanne said, looking at me.

"You never know these days, Ro," I responded as I watched them go through the door. "He's probably ecstatic because he saw me crying, but I just hate saying goodbyes."

Lilly looked at me with a smile. "Some people are like that," she replied.

I turned my attention back to work and, as I did, recalled him and Roxanne's actions that had hurt me that past year. They were playing around with each other one day, and Roxanne had put some eye drops into her eyes at one point. "Aren't you going to put some in my eyes, too?" Dan asked.

Roxanne laughs. "I didn't know your eyes were hurting too."

"Yeah, man," he replied.

Silly... *I thought to myself.* Eye drops come in many different formulas for the different effects on one's eye; you do not go around using other people's prescriptions.

"Okay, lean your head back and let me put some into your eyes." I looked with tears at them and thought, now you want to blind me because I speak of what I see and hear. Yes, those two were like a pair of rodents. With all that I observed, I was like a faithful dog—a friend, and to those at the Congregation, I also dealt with.

My shift finally ended. I bid Lilly good night and left the office.

On my way home, I contemplated their action and how they had hurt, but also thought of what their actions were trying to teach. Instead of focusing on the negative part of my inner thoughts, I recalled Bible passages that allowed me to see that the Devil is a man of many designs, and so is Jehovah. Acknowledging the source of our experiences is important, for we never know where life circumstances will lead us. Man, like animals, is awake with a plan each day; the most important is survival. Some will murder you slowly as they manipulate your mind and those associated with you that eventually causes separation. Others will kill immediately to survive; afraid that their dirty secrets will get into the hands of their victim, the situation turned against them—killed. Signs that some of us can see we ignore pass off as life's little coincident. These little coincidences are what confused me and imbued thoughts of fear.

"Finally, home!" I exclaimed as the door key was pushed into the lock. Unlocking the door, I walked in, and immediately took my shoes off, and headed for the bathroom to wash away the stress of the day and get as much rest as I could to start another.

Chapter 20

WE ARE MORE CONNECTED THAN THOUGHT

I WAS ASLEEP when Dan's image appeared. He held the child in his arm as they conversed about the baby's name; he laughed and said, "It's a boy." Then with fingers gesture, he turned the child over, and it was a girl. "You fool," I replied, pushing him as I ask why you don't name her Sangeeta, knowing he wanted to name the baby after the sun. A few days earlier, I had that dream when I entered the office, and they told me he had a baby girl. In addition, as pictures of him and the child circulated in the office, so was the controversy over a picture that showed Dan with a gun to his head. Ada was upset over it, and so were the others.

After listening to their comments and looking at the pictures myself, I comment, "Look, guys, we don't know the reason for that picture. Perhaps he got an acting role, and it was one of the shots." I quickly stated in disbelief at his thoughtless action, "Further, guys, Dan is used to being around guns, and to him, what seems like toys, is dangerous to us. I had a dream, and one of the pictures is exactly what I saw."

"Oh, Paula, you and your dreams," Tim commented.

"But it's true, as I said, he is around guns a lot, and for him, it's like a toy."

"He should not be playing with guns like that," Alex commented.

I could see that he was fearful, as it showed. And wondered as to the feeling felt; very lightheaded that day entering the building. A feeling also felt one evening with Rudolf that caused me to be more alert of self when smoking, and an incident that moved me from then to seldom part take smoking with him.

The memory: I was laughing at a conversation we had when suddenly I felt as if I had reached a point of no return and had to bring my laughter slowly to a stop. Yes, this incident alerted me to a situation ahead of time. At different times, it could be a scent or a pain.

"No, it's true; I did have a dream and saw one of the pictures." I laughed and left further thoughts unsaid as they continued about the picture.

Chapter 21

USE YOUR HANDS TO THE FULL

"IF THE SPIRIT OF THE RULER RISES up against thee, leave not thy place; for yielding pacifieth great offences." – Ecclesiastes 10:4.

They year was 2014, in June it was. During the year, many changes were happening within the company and in the lives of many. I found out that some in management do not really appreciate those who are outspoken. As often repeated, some things are best left unsaid; this statement has advantages as it does disadvantages. It is best to be wary of knowing when to pick your fights. I was stressed from the constant harassment from management about my work, and my relationship with Ada was wearing thin. However, I tried to keep it friendly and respectful, only responding to complaints when necessary. My actions in walking off the job and the changes made by the new CEOs saw my termination from the company. I was out of work, and so were quite a few before and after me. However, as stressful as it was working for the company, retirement was still far off and sticking it out I needed to do so, but the chance was not given.

In June and without notice, the company terminated my service of twelve years, nor did they imply I was about to receive severance pay. I was nobody's fool, knew termination rules and laws, and was aware of the situations around me. Closing my ears and eyes to things heard and seen, looking ahead with faith, confidence, and hope, that those I dealt with, in time, for whatever reason their dislike, their attitude will change. Many of them were not only under the influence of substances, but under a strong force; it was imperative that one knows their truth and stand firm. After a few days, I contacted a lawyer for advice and then started on my case. Time and money were not on my side, so the best option was the Labor Board. I had done all required of me to resolve the issue between me and the company, and it was in the hands of God to guide those involved to making the right and just decision.

Now at home, I had time to think, relax, and contact family and friends I had not spoken to for some time. I learned a few things about my family I never knew, as I did about strangers who would kill to keep a secret from exposure. I was not dead, yet quite a few wanted me buried. Lacking belief and understanding of my work, I was a clown in the eyes of some. It was not over. Time after time, I came home to find my locks open, and time after time, I had the locks changed.

Home again one evening from the Kingdom Hall, the police officers were called, and the Security response unit for the building. "I came home to find the locks open, and I left it locked."

"Are you sure, Mom, you did?" asks the woman officer once inside and the door checked for forced entry. Her question rubbed me the wrong way, accused me of leaving my door unlocked away from home.

"Don't go there. Security is important; I will not leave my home without locking the door." The officers left after many questions and note-taking.

I concluded that the only ones able to enter without forced entry would have to be someone in management or someone with access to a skeleton key without the original keys. I had not given the changes of keys to anyone (before April 2022). Whoever it was, was out to label me as a person forgetful or one who is not quite stable mentally, as now many had evidence of my verbal outburst...from the illegal entry.

A few months passed, and I got a call for an interview and started a new job in November 2014 with a third-party telecommunication company. A job I was curious to check out but not quite willing to accept, about giving up on going out to work, had my mindset of staying home to complete my manuscripts. However, one may conclude that management saw through me and hired me despite my fowl-up on the test. I had nothing to lose and needed the money, so I accepted the job. From above, within my unit, I could hear the recording of phone conversations and felt that my calls would be subject to the same thing. I was no actor, and the situation left me a bit uncomfortable. However, after a few weeks of training and a few weeks into the job, the feeling that this was just a plot to play their game nagged me. The feeling dismissed of their agenda might be—I did not quit but continued my employment, as I was not playing their game.

Life is not a game of sports where spectators watch; eventually, family and friends are involved without their knowledge, which leads to financial loss and pain due to the lack of the player's disclosed intention. I was not an actor and detested being played, playing without verbal communication from the other who intended to use me; I was not about to encourage.

One evening in attempting perhaps to humiliate me, or the others within the room, the Team Leader referring to experiences listed on our résumés, blurted out, "It's what's on your résumés; you should be doing it." I knew I was good at selling; my encounters were with actors, at least some of them, and I was not going to pretend to play with them. Selling the advantages and disadvantages, I did, as I usually will do unto others as I would like done to me. I was now holding two jobs. Occasionally I cleaned for a couple referred to me by one of my hairdressers, and this income supported me in covering a few bills and groceries.

One day after entering the home to clean as I past the library going in the living room while having a conversation, the employer turned to the other and said, "Now, clean your home," followed by laughter. They apparently did not think I heard what had just transpired, but I did, and many negatives passed through my thoughts as to why the words. However, in life, anything you do for another should do, as for yourself. With such an attitude, others cannot but give the credit where it belongs for a "job well done." I, and only I, knew the circumstances I was in, and in no way was I about to let the Devil and those he had in his hold control my life, to death, being the end results. With that income, the part-time job and the Employment Insurance were funds needed to survive, and it would have been foolish to let the negative overpower good judgment.

To conclude, what may have been a negative statement thrown, looking past the words, and knowing my truths allowed me to continue their employment to this day without regrets. We are in this world to grow with each other, but a lack of love destroys our growth as it does our very lives.

Life can be joyous when we look at it this way, here for a time. And, instead of taking defiance at words spoken and actions done by others that may have a negative effect, we should embrace them. I use the word *may* because we all think differently, and actions are done from processing life's circumstances or words of advice—from others perception. Therefore, what will seem negative will be positive to another.

Chapter 22

A SECOND CHANCE

A CALL RECEIVED from Earl. We had talked before, and thoughts of him were strong on my mind when he did call. After a few times speaking with him, he had planned to stop by to visit. We had not talked for a while because he was in a coma from an accident, left with short-term memory, noticed from our conversation.

His visit was overwhelming, and I could not understand his actions. I knew he once loved me, but our lives had changed—he had almost lost him and is now married.

I was fighting not to lose my sanity and keep safe. Until he mentioned Viagra and the purpose for its use, then it made sense his advances. This was not how I wanted to renew our friendship, and I told him straight up. He was like a dog in heat, and this bitch was not about to give it up to satisfy the sexual pornographic fantasy of my enemies—those with eyes on every move I made. Therefore, our visit ended after informing him of my writing goal and the current situation. I walked him to the lobby, where we bid each other goodbye. He later called to inform me that the walk to the subway was easy from the building and that he would stay connected. Staying connected happened a few weeks later; that would be the end of our communication.

Some people are cruel, haughty, demanding, and headstrong, puffed up with pride. Earl had some of these qualities after coming out of the coma. One might think after such an experience, dealings with others and self would be in a calmer state. Still, during a conversation, most of these traits were shown, and his closing sentence really hurt when he said, "Look, girl, I only called you because I came across your number in my phone book." A comment that made the bitch (this she-dog) happy she did not succumb to the evil one's intention.

Chapter 23

SEEKING TRUTH

I SAT ON THE COUCH and contemplated on the past. The days, the months, and the years end so fast that living these days is always a rush; never being able to complete all tasks intended, put off for another day; seldom done. I missed Leila and was very annoyed with some of my congregation. Reflecting on Job's misfortunes gave me some insight into my own circumstances.

Who and why were the questions that bothered me about the person's motive for slandering my character? Not one to talk much on the phone, the only friend and confidant were now out of contact, and so was my sister in a way. They have moved to an area that is a long-distance call. I had to remind myself not to take liberty with the phone because of the cost that could occur, creating financial difficulty. Always a roadblock in my way, I thought to myself; with friendships, I am trying to build, as there is with things I want to accomplish.

Trying to understand the unknown person's motive was only left to conclude that the person or persons had much knowledge of my past and my acquaintances and were exceptionally good at mental manipulation. Seems to have money—an asset that gets them either what they want or need; good at psycho sciences— only not in the way of doing good, but rather the opposites. One needs to be aware of their surroundings, people, and past situations, to combat the inner thoughts that can be subjected to occurrences. Something said or actions of another moving one to react out of character, allowing those present to draw conclusions that may be damaging to oneself. As much as the wicked one's action is difficult to stop, except by their death. Those indulging in malicious slander will stop by the sincerity of truth; as truth is what will set one's conscience (if they have one) free of guilt, and in some cases, even change one's attitude towards others.

Let God be found true, every man be found a liar, proved righteous in words, and win when being judged. Romans 3:3-4.

As much as I looked forward to the New Year, it is often greeted quietly at home with a bottle of wine, watching different musical performers on a televised show with a multitude of people, gathering festively at Nathan Phillips Square to count down the minutes to the New Year. Yes, the end of one year and the beginning of a new year. For some, it really was the end of their lives. And at this final edit before sending to a publisher, the world has lost millions due to COVID-19—a flu-like disease that has plagued the world and has no ending as another new virus known as an Omicron variant is spreading.

John's death is recalled. He was at a club and on his way home when he walked down the stairs that were wet from the rain, slipped, hit his head, and died on his way to the hospital. I was off to church that Sunday when the call came in from Lilly. The last Christmas card reads: "Following the star of Bethlehem… a bunch of wise guys, eh? Have the right to be merry." Brings laughter as it makes tears, instead of sadness, as I contemplate on our many conversations. For many, the loss of a mother, a father, a friend, a job, financial investments, or even their material possessions; despite everything, this is a time of rebuilding all that has been lost to start a new. My personal life career involved construction—a metaphor used, as I am always constructing something and each year never being able to complete my goals or build on friendships. Some would and do give up after a while, but not me. Oh, no, each year passed, sees the same renewed strength and courage. After all, the race is not for the swift but for he that endures to the end. For me, salvation was to fight the fair fight. It was a fight for my freedom. Freedom for my mother, my brother, my sisters, my relatives, and freedom for my friends. I will not be able to give each one their freedom, but by freedom of them mentally, I in turn, frees myself and them. Whatever situation one gets into is by one's desire to have, to hold, or to leave, not done by another. So, it is up to each one to make a change.

Consumed with thoughts of the past, I reflected on my mother. This time of the year ending is mostly a reminder of our relationship—one I miss and will forever cherish. I recall my younger days with her and thinks of a conversation I had with Veronica. "Mommy had lots of men. You don't know; you were small." I did not dare correct her—that was her experience, but little did she know, I was with mother almost everywhere she went, and the only other man I had ever seen my mother with was Mr. Grant. I allowed my sister to vent her inner anger as I listened, the reason I called our aunt Ismay to question her about our mother. A phone call I was avoiding as I knew my conversations were being overheard especially after an incident one evening going home from work.

The phone started to ring while I was in the elevator down to the lobby. As the elevator door opened, so was the phone receiver. "Hello, hello, hello...." I completed the last word slowly; no response came back, so the phone was flipped closed and reopened to redial the received number. When the button was pressed, my phone started ringing. I looked at the phone, "What the hell? Why would my number be ringing?" The phone company was called that weekend, and a service agent was spoken to.

The explanation given: "Anyone with a Blackberry (the name of the other phone forgotten) could have done this. Unfortunately, we cannot trace the call with the time given; it is a bit more technical, something I cannot do for you," said the woman agent.

"Thank you very much for your help. I thought it was bizarre and wanted to know who could have done this. Have a great day."

"You, too," she replied and hung up.

My concerned were the information the eavesdroppers were accessing through my computer and phone that would implicate others' lives, causing a disruption of their lively hood, including mine. The only way to stop such clever ones, including those in authority, is to become informed and educated. I was away from home and did not have much time to investigate my own affairs until many months passed after being terminated from Gelid Communication. Accidently, I discovered many files on my computer in areas I had never looked at before. Like a person gone insane after a brief conversation with a co-worker whose advice was to delete them, this I did and, to my unknown knowledge, interrupted the clever one's intended goal. On putting the pieces together years later, I saw some of the reasons for the obstacles in my way.

Liken to one's home, a computer needs to be cleaned. Getting familiar with what is in your home is to do the same with what Apps and File Folders are on your computer—this is important. Without checking in occasionally, hackers can install programs that eventually steal files and corrupt one's computer.

§

A callback security is a form of Network security in which a remote access server calls a user back at a pre-set number after the user makes an initial connection and is authenticated. The number can be pre-set by an administrator or specified by the user at the time of call, depending on how the admin configures the user's callback options. The callback number should be the number of the phone line to which the user's modem is connected. The remote administrator managing one computer and working at another computer connected to the first across a Network can manipulate communication. Some Network attacks are passive in that information is only monitored. With active attacks, information is altered, with the intent to corrupt or destroy data (a person) or the network itself. Systems use the IP address to identify a computer as valid on a network. An IP address can sometimes be falsely used—known as identity spoofing. An attacker uses special programs to construct IP packets from valid addresses inside an organization's intranet. After gaining access to the network with a valid IP address, the attacker can modify, reroute, or delete data. Thus, conducting other attacks, such as password-based access, gets an attacker right into the computer and network determined by a username and password. After gaining access to a network with a valid account, an attacker can obtain lists of valid users, their computer names and network information, modify server and network configurations, including access controls and routing tables, and modify, reroute, or delete data.

With such danger, I wondered why some companies allow access to information to leave their facilities in view of our times. Daily, one's life is becoming a public spectacle. It never used to be this way. There was a time when one could drive down the streets, walk on the streets, sit on their verandas, talk on the phones, and have much privacy. Gone are those days. Reminding me of a song whose lyrics goes, 'It seems like somebody's watching me,' is a song predictably written for our time. Should those in authority be blamed for the lack of privacy? You bet they should. Clandestinely into the lives of people. They turn those innocents into criminals. Force to make a living, they follow this echoed statement—monkey see, monkey do—they, too, making a play of people's lives.

§

After all the pleasantry, I asks, "Aunt Ismay, I was going to wait until I see you to ask a few questions about Mommy..." I had thought of life, the fact that we are here today and maybe gone tomorrow, that prompted the urgent call. "You know I have never seen Mommy visit Aunt Stella's home, (Ismay's family occupied the back house on the lot that had both homes.) Why is that? Neither did you folks."

"You know us,...." Aunt Ismay began. "We don't like running in and out of people's homes, and your mother was the same. Don't you worry yourself about nothing; your mother was a nice woman."

I had gotten an answer as to why I never saw mom visiting my aunts and vice-a-versa, but not to the many men she had in her life as Veronica claimed, which only left two concluded thoughts of my father's residence at my aunt's home. The fact that he must have seen Mommy with Mr. Grant, or there is some truth to Veronica's claim. On the other hand, Monica claimed it was not so, and I know if I asked Kathleen, she would not have an answer as she had married and left home to move to England. Michael would be the only one to verify Veronica's claim; Daddy left home because Michael had hit him.

Michael, I whispered aloud, still within my thoughts. I wonder how he is and what he may be doing. Thoughts of him covered me with fear of what he could be going through, especially at this time with the difficulties all countries are experiencing. It was difficult for me with a job, much more so for those without an income. And it is much harder for those with a criminal record. Most do not look for the best in people when they have a bit of dirt on them. I got comfort from knowing that he at least had a roof over his head. The fear for him came mostly from the sensation I felt being sexed in the buttocks—a physical experience has never been done. If I had consciously experienced myself spiritually in such an act, I would have jumped out of the dream. Leaving the question, was I fully conscious of being able to jump out of my dream? I know my love for him is extraordinarily strong, and this spiritual connection could be the reason for my psychic experience. This occurrence mentally stressed me, as I worried about my family members and Rudolf, who was in and out of jails like him.

I shook my head, tears filling my eyes as I quietly echoed, how do I tell and make others understand the struggle each day endure, having to fight from losing my sanity? This was embarrassing. Maybe, just maybe, when Hilary said, "I'm not the one who got sexed in the ass," she knew what wicked deeds she or the one she was speaking to participated in. I bowed my head between my legs and looked away from the television with much sadness.

"The way of the wicked is an abomination unto the LORD: but he loveth him that followeth after righteousness." -Proverbs 15:9. And, that I must believe. An end will soon come to the ones who think they are wise in their wicked deeds.

The old year had passed, and this was a new beginning. I got up from the couch, walked to the window, and scanned the surroundings; all was calm in the night sky, and the only star seen was the big dipper. Looking closer, others can be seen, but the beauty cannot compare to being at home when at this time of the morning, the night sky is still illuminated by many stars. I walked away from the window to the refrigerator, put the wine bottle away, then washed the glass and retired to bed.

Chapter 24

WILL NOT GIVE MORE THAN WE CAN HANDLE

ALMOST A YEAR, AND FINALLY, I received a cheque in the mail from Gelid Communication. I was happy that the situation was now behind me. I paid off most of my credit cards, invested some, and was now able to prepare to travel, waiting until my year was up with the new company, so I would not have to reapply if I left before the year. Unfortunately, the forces were again at work, so before the year ended, I was laid off due to the company's financial health. Therefore, instead of being able to take the trip of my lifetime, I was forced to remain in Canada. Throwing all things aside and going ahead with my plans would have created hardship, as monies spent would be money needed. Therefore, I carefully weighed my options and decided this was not the time to travel. As much as I wanted to see my brother and my homeland, if it were in God's plan, I would be alive to be there some other year.

Days passed into months, and one day a call came letting me know that my cousin—Richard, we normally called Brother, who had kept me from falling deep into a depressed state of mind from our many conversations, had died of a heart attack. The news took me by surprise as it did the entire family. I stomped my feet in anger and shouted, getting the anger out of my system as the tears flowed down my cheeks. It seems that the wicked one will stop at nothing to try to have me give up on life, so I had to keep on running.

Now isolated from those in the congregation, friends dear to my heart and my commitment. The Elders failed to accept the truth, hanging onto past reasons to keep me away from those I cared...and whose interest in lain with. People talk about faith, but when one's faith is being tested, that's when excuses are put before wise decisions. When some of us are in positions of power, most tend to look away from the truth to empower their own agenda. However, I kept communications open with family and acquaintances, except the sister I spoke with before the known situation of being disfellowshipped. I knew the secrets of the wicked, and I would not allow them to take my soul like they did of others.

§

MONTHS LATER...

I decided I had to leave the atmosphere I was in, so I spoke with my sister in the States and decided to go for a visit.

§

The telephone invention by Alexander Graham Bell in the 1800s, which became commercially successful in the nineteenth century, was, and still is, the best thing since sliced bread. Used for and as a person's personal logging of information, banking, entertainment unit, social contacts, and networking—the invented phone devise has served us well and has improved with greater technology. However, over the years, it has become a device much used to capture information about others, lure people to their death, and photographs taken, some wished not seen by the public. Hackers have seen fit to use the device to guide the lives of the unexpected, and unless we wake up and become aware of our truths, many of us will be taking actions against our better judgment, pushed by the guides. An incident that confirms the importance of communication leads to better understanding among us, and within my relationships, I relate.

I woke up to a strong scent of being in a hospital. Rudolf was living with me then, and that Saturday, I had a hairdresser's appointment. "Look, I don't want you leaving the house, someone is ill, or something is about to happen." He asked for an explanation, and he was given the reason. I left home for my appointment and thought the day went without incident. On Monday morning, when I got to work, the sad look on their faces, especially the one who was pregnant, told me something was wrong. I thought she had been given sad news about her pregnancy—she had not. The sad faces were news about the child's father. Called out of bed that weekend, he left to meet a friend that ended his life.

It was a Sunday at my sister's. I decided to visit the Kingdom Hall and invited the household to join me—they refused. I got dressed, and my nephew walked me over to the Hall. As we stood talking, Veronica called, all annoyed because she made a trip out of bed by Debra-Ann's request to pick her up due to car problems. When she got to the location, Debra-Ann was not to be found. "Has she called to say where she is at?" I inquire. To confirm my sister's experience. "When Debra-Ann was asked for an explanation, I was told a Jehovah's Witness was passing saw she had car problems and assisted her."

Veronica is told that she had gotten played as the situation is reviewed. The question left with me is, which one is not of their right mind.

Our times are wicked. Be aware of the text messages and the voice on the phone. There is no end to the wicked one's actions.

§

It is funny how we tend to form images of people we have not seen, only to be surprised or disappointed by their appearance. The last image of Veronica was what I had kept with me for over fifteen years; her voice was recognized, the same as it was over the phone.

Chapter 25

HIDDEN LIES AMONG THE TRUTH

THE MONTH OF DECEMBER is a month most celebrate the birth of Jesus; others the end of another year and all the good they have accomplished.

December 25 is the day set aside as Jesus' birth, and many still believe that Christ was born on this day. Still, the Gospels indicate neither the date nor the month of Jesus' birth, nor is December 25 written in any Catholic Encyclopedia. This date is chosen to correspond to pagan festivals that took place around the time of the winter solstice, December 25 in the Julian calendar, and January 6 in the Egyptian calendar, when the day begins to lengthen to celebrate the rebirth of the sun. This is a known fact for us as a guide; if we search for truth, we will find it. Dates are important, and a pivotal date is a calendar date in history that has a sound basis for acceptance and corresponds to a specific event recorded in the Bible.

A key date to determine Jesus' birth is the date Tiberius Caesar succeeded Emperor Augustus. Augustus died on August 17, 14 CE (Gregorian calendar); Tiberius was named Emperor by the Roman Senate on September 15, 14 CE. We read in Luke 3:1- 3 that John the baptizer began his ministry in the fifteenth year of Tiberius's reign, which would be in the year 29 CE. This corresponds with the scripture, and Luke

3:21-23 that shows Jesus was about thirty years old and six months younger than John the baptizer when he was baptized. Which would bring us to the year of 2 BCE in the autumn. Counting backwards, 29 CE minus thirty years equals 1 BCE plus six months equals 2 BCE, which gives us the year and season—Autumn of Jesus's birth. However, the date is unknown since it was unclear if the angels appeared on the actual date of Christ birth to inform the shepherds. Further, their travel to register his birth and timeslot is not documented.

§

Many Carols, written and sung at Christmas time, combine man's creativity from factual passages from the Holy Scriptures, for example, the song, "Oh Holy Night," that talked about the baby born in a manger and the three wise men bearing gifts. However, such songs have lies hidden between the truths. As much as I adore and support the creativity of most kinds, I will reveal the truth where necessary.

As Christians, we not only should speak truthfully, but we should not cover the truth with lies, or hold back the truth (good) when it is in the power of our hand. According to the Holy Scriptures, at Proverbs 3:27 and The Qur'an at The Heifer, Surah 2:42; so, advise.

§

It was our annual pot-luck dinner—to eat whatever is chance to be at hand. There were always all kinds of left-over food, even if everyone did not bring a dish, and our dinner was a success each year. Some from outside the team were also able to part-took with enjoyment, and of course, this delighted the team, especially the ones whose dish they part-take. The editing department was not the only one that had this tradition. Other departments did too. One year did not go well for the inbound department, someone's dish had caused most of them to be sick, and it was a bit hilarious and serious when I was informed that most of the team had called in sick due to food poisoning.

The truth is clearly written and shown. Not all gather to celebrate; they are there with good intentions. Having faith that the one doing wrong will have wrong done to them is also a fact that eventually comes true, and Jehovah is the one doing the judging.

The beginning of a New Year was very soon to start as it came to the end of another.

Chapter 26

LOOK OUT YOU ARE NOT MISLED

FINALLY, THE DAY HAD arrived for me to travel to visit a sister I had not seen for years and did not quite know anymore. People can and will say many things over the phone, but to be in their presence is a completely dissimilar experience. Certain things about someone you know never changes, but life's circumstances can make those familiar things unfamiliar, which brings to the forefront of your mind questions about why they change. However, allowing time and putting oneself in their place helps to understand the change. Changes in a Potter's work, with information, molds a thing...or the individual into what he/she desires the person to become.

I arrived at Pen Station on Christmas eve and had to wait for my sister to arrive. A familiar face is seen as I look at the person trying to recall where I had seen him before. There were no expectations; I was here to be away from the circumstances that surrounded me at home, away from familiar faces and places. This new world contained my family. I had been in it before, embracing the people and their culture and had experience working with them. However, many changes have occurred over the years, the main and most important ones being the 9-11 incident of the US Twin Towers, and the inauguration of Barrack Obama—the first Black President in 2009. These changes brought many changes to the people and country; for some, to a more cautious way of dealing with and handling everything.

A figure is seen approaching with a younger one beside her; the person looks older, frail, and tired like she has been working hard all day. "Paula, is this you?" the voice asks that sounded like the familiar one I had heard and was used to hearing over the phone over the years.

"Yes…" I pause in surprise. "Veronica," I reached out to embrace her and then the younger person; I was informed of before seeing would be my great niece. There was no surprise there as told, the child eats so much, she was getting fat, and she had to enroll her in an exercise class at school.

"I like your hair, auntie, and outfit," complements Sonia.

"Thank you, hon, and I like your shoes," I respond, followed by other compliments and questions. Many things I observed as we walked to catch the returning train back home. Seen were many young army persons, which caused me to wonder why there was so much security, but after a moment's thought, the realization of times change hit my head. Eye contact with a fellow's action sent a negative thought. The train arrived; we boarded and were now on our way home. Over the phone, there was always so much to talk about. Now I felt like a stranger trying to get to know the person sitting before me. I tried to find many questions to ask and kept the conversation going until we got to their area. Once there, my nephew is called to pick us up, and while waiting, informed a bit about the person I was about to meet—a young man's action like that of an older person that caused me to laugh in the night.

The following days were interesting, and the people I left years ago had all changed in appearance and grown. Changes that were not expected, and heartbroken. My last memory of my niece was with her on the bed, reading and making jokes. She is now grown and has two children. My nephews' indifference toward each other caused hurtful feelings and anger as to the advantage the wicked one has over the circumstances. My sister had aged, and with age comes experience and understanding. Still, for many reasons, her understanding was lacking in many areas as she stood on the defense, always looking for reasons to argue. I tried extremely hard to keep the peace and one day's prayer saw to it that the peace was kept until it was time to depart, and so it did.

The day arrived when I had to say goodbye to a family that seemed like strangers. I left with a puzzle, the puzzle of trying to sort out what really went wrong.

§

RETURNED TO CANADA...

My return home in January 2016 was not one that saw me with happy feelings. I was saddened over the situation encountered as I tried to fit the pieces of a world puzzle that would soon unravel and was quite depressed in a home that looked the same as I had left it.

Jesus warned his disciples that when they entered a home in a city or town to say a blessing and if peace dwells there, it would be with them. If it were not, they dust off their feet on leaving. This advice, given thousands of years, applies today. Life is a process of learning; take as an example the astronauts. When they return to earth, they must be quarantined for many reasons, such as adapting to gravity and checking for foreign diseases. For another reason, other than the blessing you give returning to you. In the practice of the latter part, we avoid bringing diseases of all sorts into our homes. Therefore, after a visit from another country, it is wise to wash our shoes and feet before entering our homes or remove shoes before entering our apartments.

There is an advantage to living in a home compared to an apartment. While one may have a vast amount of privacy in a home, in an apartment, one's privacy is limited. Limited, due to illegal entry, the unit is not soundproof, the neighbor above or beside you a hired lookout or look-in to your affairs and hidden devices to catch the unsuspected ones in acts of all sorts.

After a few days, I visited the bank to return and take out a few things from my safety box; I observed an envelope open that was not to be opened until my death. This was a strange occurrence, but like everything in my life, I have learnt the importance of timely patience. After locking the box back into its case and leaving the vault with the agent, the young man who showed a set of new potential employees around on my last visit. When asked how his training went, he mentioned the name of the newly hired employee on board. As I came out of the vault's room, sworn to see the receptionist at the desk, as I looked into my handbag to arrange a few things. I asked, "So, how... ?" then, raising my head noticed no one sitting there, stopped short my intended comment. The young fellow came to the vault's door on hearing my voice, asked what I had just said, and had to let him know, I thought I had seen the receptionist sitting at the desk, but apparently, my eyes played a trick. I walked out of the area with *the thought thrown,* if you did go into my box, it is only a matter of time before your life ends.

A few weeks later, I produced new ideas; one was to ask the superintendent to have the apartment repainted and to pay my second sister a visit. The other was to look out of the area for work. I knew that my efforts where I was, were being stopped by the wicked one's intention, and out of sight is out of mind—one tends to think, but not in my case.

I pondered over my dreams while in the States as I sincerely prayed to Jehovah and ask that he protect and show Veronica the way; I reminded him of her love for him and ask that he shows mercy. He is told of her dreams and asks that she be given an answer.

Chapter 27

TIME REVEALS ALL

A FEW MONTHS LATER, the request to return to the States posed another opportunity to get to know my family, like strangers I had left about a month ago. Regardless of what my family does when they call for my attention or assistance, it will be given, as do my friends. However, whether they will appreciate my actions is to be seen.

It was a bright sunny but cold day on February 11 when I got to the train station and boarded the train, its destination, the United States Pen Train Station. I was about to go back into an area that would take me to a past biblical time. No matter where we go in this world, people are the same; what differs are their beliefs system, and important is to have knowledge to be able to communicate. Knowing a bit about their culture and your awareness is important in survival. Once again, I arrived in the late evening. The area is always busy; I observed those that moved about, some awaiting the arrival of friends, family, and loved ones, as others (the less fortunate) hang around for any given amount. Once again, the person I could not recall is seen; I glanced now and then as eyes meet. I tried not to be so obvious—still, the memory of where seen could not present the place. I turned to see someone embracing the one he was waiting for; and wished for a moment the situation had been in my case. I was on a journey but needed a man's touch to share all the hurt and love built up within my soul. As I stood with thoughts of the couple and how difficult keeping a relationship these days require much willpower and the presents of God within it. As I turned back to where the person stood, he had left. My eyes franticly looked around to see where, but he was gone. Sometimes an opportunity presents itself once, twice in the case of luck and in the case of destiny three times. I wanted to act on an impulse to walk over to where he stood, and a woman not lacking with words to say, "I have been admiring you for some time now and would like to know where we have met each other before." But I was shy to approach, and perhaps he did too. After a disappointing time passed, I focused my attention on my family. I received a call from my great-niece, informing me they had missed the train and are waiting for the next to arrive. This give me more time to observe the area and people passing.

My family arrives, and Veronica's appearance is much different than when last seen; she seems rested. I felt happy for her. We once again embraced each other, and then walked to the area to catch a returning train back home.

The following morning my visit met with someone else talked about before my arrival. We introduced ourselves to each other. I had breakfast with the family and began a day that would turn into days I swear would be a movie I was physically walking through spiritually. A real-life movie that even Gracie (the dog) had a part that was so darn cute, I wished I had a videotape of the whole visit.

§

"In a dream a vision of the night when deep sleep falleth upon man, in slumbering upon the bed; then he openeth the ears of men and sealeth their instruction, that he may withdraw man from his purpose, and hide pride from man." -Job 33:15.

Dreams takes one into a different world, opening a door into other aspects of what is real. A world where the wicked spirits will satisfy our desires by pampering and indulgence, giving knowledge beforehand of things destined to occur, but not without alternative motive that of our total being, as energy drawn from them to us, and we to them, like a wireless circuit. Therefore, dreamers must be on their toes—so speaking, becoming or being aware of their surroundings, and associates.

Awareness must seek movement. Therefore, when awareness of a situation is noted, we must move, or we are caught in the wicked one's trap. Awareness is being conscious. Our consciousness excuses or accuses us, causing growth through strife through life-or-death confrontations. Confrontations do not always have to be verbal or physical but mentally. As you project your inner thoughts of what is right in a situation, your actions demonstrate such mental projection/ or projections.

Once the wicked spirits know of the dreamer's awareness, the fight to eliminate that one is their foremost goal because the dreamer is knowledgeable of their cunning manipulation of individuals to accomplish their goals of life and death situations. It is a fight that dreamers who are not looking for fame or acceptance of friends, family and acquaintances may win if their projection/ or projections and actions are understood.

§

Veronica was still the same defensive person I had left. Conversations never go far since I am not one to prolong an argument with others who close their minds to reasoning.

It is advised: do not give counsel to the wicked (or one who will not listen) as they will only despise you. This is so true. One reason the Elders of the congregation reframe from giving scriptural counsel to disfellowship ones. They make their concerns known and seldom speak or associate with such ones.

My dreams related is what I feared on her behalf, and it was difficult trying to enlighten her already knowledge of some things, as she was not opening the door to accepting counsel.

§

HYPNOTISM occurs with anything that produces sleep.

Trying to educate anyone without knowledge of this will either laugh...or tell you I have been using or doing a certain thing for years that has helped them to fall asleep. However, they fail to realize the activity of the spiritual realm. This said, once in wakefulness, desires are as seeds planted, a seed that will produce either good or bad. Unaware and unconscious, people go about their daily lives falling into the traps set by spiritual beings, or individuals used by those living in an apartment unit that surrounds them. How internally strong an individual is, he or she will be able to master their desires—and will only be able to do so if consciously aware. Unaware, one will respond to the negativity of the outer world that pushes them to compete to lose focus on what is really important to body, mind, and soul. We must be careful of our associations, those that push us beyond the point of losing ourselves. Their agenda may not always be for your good but rather from their desire for riches.

The Bible warns that each one is tried by being drawn out and enticed by his desire. Then the desire, when it has become fertile, gives birth to sin (anything that is over-indulged); in turn, sin (the desire), when it has been accomplished, brings forth the consequences.

I feared that Veronica, like some strangers, was under hypnotic guidance (and a documentary seen of what had occurred in and around the Long Island area many years past may be a correct conclusion.) I know how difficult it is to fight to stay within my truths, as those under Satan's influence try to discredit my efforts and cause conflicts with those I build friendships. Some humans can hypnotize others with their suggestive thoughts. If awareness is lacking, it could be difficult for the individual to get released from their hold, especially in their wake of consciousness. Susceptible to their suggestive thoughts, some then think God is guiding them, and in all truthfulness, they are correct, as Lucifer is a 'god' and is referred to as the 'god' of this system. Here is where accurate knowledge is so important to have, as is communication with each other; due to this fact, we live having spiritual experiences because what may be happening to a person across the seas can be experienced by another physically.

A FEW EXPLANATIONS FOR REFERENCE:

An **aneurysm** develops because of the hardening of the arteries. Persons may develop an aneurysm due to family history, high blood pressure, the risk of subarachnoid hemorrhage and smoking cigarettes may greatly increase the chances of rupture. It could go unnoticed and rupture, releasing blood into the skull and causing a stroke.

The symptoms of an aneurysm are severe headaches, blurred vision, changes in speech, fainting or loss of consciousness, seizures, and neck pain, depending on what areas of the brain are affected and how bad the aneurysm is.

My sister Kathleen lived in England during my constant headaches. As a person who seldom suffers from headaches, I get perturbed when they occur more often than they should, although I know that it is due to my studying situations or dealing with those around me. At the time of these episodes, I had no idea that my sister, in England, was suffering from an aneurysm, a weak bulging area in the wall of an artery that supplies blood to the brain. She on times pass out due to the condition. As some of these symptoms and episodes occurred with Kathleen, I also experienced headaches endured. On nights of dreams, seen is a strange woman, strange as the image was unknown until, within another dream, the woman looked like her with a braided hairstyle; my thoughts of concern became stronger regards, my sister. It was not until Monica—my second sister—told me of her condition did my headaches stopped.

It was Sunday, January 28, 2017, after breakfast. This Sunday morning, I was washing dishes when suddenly I felt a movement in my lower back. Not being the first time, this occurrence almost crippled me because the pain of something moving along my lower back almost caused me to lose my lower strength. With my mind's mental power, I shouted in agony, "Get out of me," while standing with help as I held onto the sink. At the time of the pain, the mental image of a known neighbor who suffered from what I was experiencing—lower back pain, was within my thoughts. As I immediately called Jehovah to assist me, one hand hit my back; in seconds, the pain left. After the dishes, I took a shower and dressed for the Kingdom Hall. After eleven o'clock, I got into the elevator going down and saw no other but the neighbour from the second floor who had crossed my mind during my earlier experience. Standing in one corner as an elderly man stood at the other. The elevator door closed, we looked at and greeted each other and I kept my eyes on the floor (as I tried not to take any negative thoughts with me) until it reached the lobby; bidding her a pleasant day, I left the building.

The conclusion of these incidents is this: no matter what spiritual negatives we experience, we must be strong to exercise love, walk away, and alter our mental thoughts. In addition, whatever negatives we hear, we must be strong to block them out of our minds and express goodness. Finally, what negatives tell us, we must be strong to dismiss from our minds and maintain our goals. A lack of mental, spiritual, and physical strength will make us lash out at another who may or may not have anything to do with the present situation we are experiencing.

This brings me to the practice of some, a practice called black magic or white magic, traditionally referred to as supernatural powers or magic for evil and selfish purposes. Some who are in private practice are without significant chastisement. They hurt and destroy others without regret. I speak from experience as I daily fight the spiritual forces and those they have in their hold, with their concluded idea of healing or playing innocent fun. And this is why I speak out and encourage those who go through similar experiences to do the same. There's no need to feel embarrassed from the concluded assumptions that you are crazy from those who lack knowledge and understanding. Know your truths, make them your own as the true God knows them to be.

§

MY FIRST WEEK...

My nephew came to have breakfast with the family. Gracie was very playful and taken from her parent at a young age; she did not know right from wrong and felt her action was normal. I missed Ace, but Gracie filled the emotional loss, and as the days passed, I fell in love with her. I would compare their pictures and giggle at their differences. The day we were playing around the table caused one of the figurines breaks. She knows she has done something wrong and feels bad that I would be blamed. As I sat on the steps regretting the accident, I could see from her face that she was apologetic. When Veronica's action shows displeasure over the devalued cost of selling the item would be, penetrating my regret deeply over the incident, I turned and whispered to her, "you see, it's your entire fault" Gracie's look is confirmed. My dreams left me a bit confused, and daily I observed my family's actions and could not help thinking my experience, to some degree, affected the household. I tried in my own defense to bring some light to the situation but felt that the words spoken were ignored.

I awoke to a beautiful sunny day, and after my morning ritual of saying my prayers, reading, and meditating on God's word, I ventured out to the kitchen. In a bubble and happy mood, I looked out the window and repeated a verse reminded of the day's beauty sighted in the Psalms. Still, before I could complete what I was saying, Veronica interjects, "There is no calamity happening here...."

"Look, I am in a happy mood and was just repeating a verse I read in Psalms that the day reminded me of. What is wrong with you?" With that said, I walked back into my room. From that day forward, I went on a fast. I would have something to eat early in the morning and nothing else until sundown. Until one day, the yoppá-rattà (drunk) was babbling on within his own world, which raised a question to Sonia, and the given response moved me to drink water.

I had to satisfy the thirst of my enemy. Why would she say something like that to her sister in the form of a joke. Children are impressionable, and words spoken linger for days, months and even years; I *thought to myself.* I turned to Patsy, the caregiver. "Why is it that people don't mind their own business, always looking into the lives of others and exposing their deeds? Who cares whether someone had a taste of someone's private parts? It is his or her business. Dirty minds of some people!" I paused for a moment. "It is not what goes into a person's mouth that defiles them. It is what comes out of it does." I then opened the refrigerator and poured myself a glass of water.

"You are right," echoed Patsy.

"The gall of some people." I shook my head and walked back into my room.

The body is a beautiful and marvelous instrument referred to as a temple of God. Every sport one participates in needs knowledge, and every sport has a technique that, once mastered due to love of it, one not only enjoys self but also brings pleasure to another. Only mature minds understand what love can do.

In life, some people will envy another for what material things they have, their appearance, or intellect, and would do or cause many things to disrupt an individual's life. My nephews' lives are seen from the surface to be okay. However, the youngest one suffers from a mental problem: he cannot control the voices or the entertained collected thoughts. When I found out about one of his sports (boxing) activities, this concerned me even more, and I feared the impact this would certainly have on his mental state. The older one had developed what is known as a tick. This is an uncontrolled motor habit or body movement. Some who suffer from this uncontrolled movement, can cure it by staying focused mentally when the movement begins or by the urge to motor react. One day his action led to laughter. He was about to run an errand when he stopped in front of the car and started to touch his forehead like one does sign the cross. He would go from his forehead to his nose, to his chin, to his lips and to the sides of his cheeks. On seeing him, Veronica spoke, "Look at him, standing there like an idiot, blessing his face." Her facial expression caused me to laugh. Takahashi told to focus when the desire presents itself instead of what he does, is to simply passing his hands over his entire face, as his action makes him look retarded. Like most children, his rebellion is to do as he pleases. That day forward led to many laughable moments, which made some circumstances seen and heard bearable.

Many are gullible when it comes to things of the heart. Therefore, we are cautioned to be aware of the heart, for it is treacherous who is there knowing it. A situation recalled many years that saw the loss of many lives in Guyana influenced by Pastor Jim Joans—gullible, they sure were. Yes, we surely can be deceived innocently by things dear to our hearts. Therefore, caution we should exercise, and Veronica was the same. She would not listen when told to discard religious items sent to her; she insists, "It's a prayer." On the other hand, "It's a medallion."

Holding a return ticket back home, I did not want to leave my family with ill feelings or her angry, so I decided not to insist on the topic but threw some of the medallions out on my opening the mails. I was under the impression that the situation I encountered with the children was not in totality influenced by their own causes but Veronica's actions.

I was in the room; I was busy rewriting my manuscript. Some of my work was lost due to editing it on a portable hard drive that is not usable as using a computer for hours—unknowledgeable of the fact. During an investigation into restoring the information, I found out the cost would be running in the hundreds of dollars I did not intend to spend. Although important, the time and information put into the project were now at a loss. I always holds to this thought: with everything in life, there is an advantage as there is a disadvantage. And nothing happens before it's time. This is true because life is built upon experiences from associations that produce one's growth and wealth. Now, with time, portable hard drives are made to be able to write and edit without notice of time working on devices. On the one hand, I saw the importance of when a purchase is made of anything new; asking questions is important to better use a thing. Further, the rewriting helped me better structure my sentences and position my statements.

The way of life gives us the highs and the lows, the bitter and the sweet, and we must move with both to enjoy living and mature growth.

As I was at my work Veronica entered the room. From a simple statement, Veronica got defensive and started to throw words that caused hurtful feelings. We are both alike in the fact that we will speak our minds. However, Veronica tends to speak without actual proof of a thing. She hears something mentioned. Without full understanding, she will repeat it in a manner to embarrass or degrade you. An example is when a friend told her that all dogs—animals (perhaps)—go to heaven. She repeats this statement without full understanding or meaning, as there is doubt a Pastor believes and teaches such nonsense. I smiled when she repeated the statement and declined to comment as if I should; it would have caused friction, especially since the statement came from a church pastor. I responded, "Did you call me here to embarrass me?" I began to follow her as she walked away. "Look at you; you have everything, and you are still an unhappy person." In a rush, she entered the kitchen, and I walked back to the room. I sat contemplating what had occurred as tears rolled down my cheeks. Not too long after Sonia enters the room, "Auntie," she calls, "why are you crying?"

I shook my head and responded, "It's your grandma; that woman is too much."

"Look, she wants you to take me to the dentist. Mom will have a cab pick us up shortly, so get dressed to come with me." She says and leaves the room.

I was just not in the mood to go anywhere, but I said a little prayer for strength to go through the day what had left of it.

AT THE DENTIST

A few patients sat waiting for their names to call as we were in line. I took out a book, Reasoning from the Scriptures, which is often in my possession. Thanks to technology I am now able to read online, so I have more room in my handbag. I began to read, as I did, thoughts of Veronica entered now and then. Suddenly, I could hear the roll of thunder. I know when I am being spoken to, just from inner thoughts and the outer world occurrences. As the thunder rolls even harder, *in thoughts* I hoped this night Veronica is given a sign. Sonia's name was now called. Within the hour, we were on our way back home.

Chapter 28

WHAT ARE THE CHANCES?

THE DAYS WERE ALWAYS BUSY with one thing or the other to do. This was a good thing as I was taken away from the mental thoughts of my own worries. I wished that situations were much better with the children as I was sincerely hoping to be taken to a few clubs to have a good time, but this I knew was not about to happen after the week of being there. Occasionally a few workers came to the home, and I was introduced to most of them in part.

On his days off, Takahashi will accompany me on walks—this I enjoyed very much, as we got the opportunity to get to know each other better. I insisted he continues his walking exercise after I left, which will benefit his health. He smiles and says he will, but only time will tell if he does. On the other hand, Gracie continued to let us know she is no dog to mess with. I had to laugh one morning after cleaning her area and opening the window to let in the morning's fresh air to cleanse the place of her poop.

During the night, I was in one dream after the other. Seen in my dream a tall-looking fellow who not only had on make-up, but his lady's attire indicated he was an actor of some sort. During a conversation with one who worked at Bissell vacuum reminded me of a company convention. The bosses were dressed in gowns for a fashion-show humor. So, during our conversation when the mention of a call she received from him while he was in the States; it could have been a spiritual connection while I was there. For it is how our dreams alert us of people and places we had visited or will be seeing in the future, by presenting images, symbols, or numbers. In another, I am telling off another person about hygiene, so when Gracie was witnessed washing her paws after urinating, it was not only cute but also laughable. Situations are sighted that bring attention to the connection we all have on this planet.

The day before I was about to leave, Veronica told me she had arranged to have one of the workers give me a ride to the train station. "What you did that for; I told you I would take the train from here. It will be fast and easy than waking someone up so early." The honest truth, I did not want to awake any emotions, especially for someone attracted to, knowing nothing about, and to be sent off before the break of the day into a world I was a stranger to, with a stranger.

"It will be good for me because I don't have to get up early."

I understood my sister's concern about not wanting me to travel by myself so early in the morning and decided to look forward to the day to get to know him a little more.

The day came when I had to leave. I could not sleep and kept thinking everything would be all right with the family and, most of all, my anxious anticipation of meeting the person giving me the ride to the station. I knew all too well that these days people are not always who they show themselves to be. However, my confidence lies in God, and I knew my emotions were perhaps because I had not been with a man in years, which seemed like a decade. Starting any kind of friendship was hesitant due to circumstances, and the other person's endurance calls for mature thinking that may not last. I have had much heartbreak, and could not stand to take another, so I would rather not start any. I knew our thoughts had mentally connected, the one thing that attracted me to him, but I was unsure if it was a good thing. A person's past is their past; some people learn and move on, while others never do. I hoped that his past will not bring any miseries into my crowded world. Further, if I were to have any kind of friendship with him, Veronica would eventually have some negative things to say about it. I was all packed and ready to go. I sat at the kitchen table as I awaited the ride, the opportunity giving me and Takahashi time to chat. A knock at the door told me it was he. He scored a point by being right on time; Takahashi opened the door and greeted him, and he returned the greeting. Veronica rushes down the stairs as he gets the bags to take to the car. He greets her good morning and picks up the bag to head through the door. "I like your hair," he says as he exits.

"Thank you," I replied with a guilty smile as I want to tell him, "I know it is a nice piece." But I knew he was just being friendly as he had seen my own hair and knew all too well what I wore was (a wig), not mine. I embrace Veronica, kisses her, and tells her to take good care of herself. I look at Takahashi with a few last words knowing he, like a shimáuma (Zebra,) will never change, to make sure he looks after himself first and then others.

I get out the door and into the night air that touches my face and give me a refreshed feeling; he walks to the gate, holds it open, and closes it as I walk through the car door, he held open. Comfortable seated, we drove off into the night. I did not know if he was nervous, but he kept talking from one topic to another. Occasionally I would glance over at him, and *in thoughts*, Veronica said you[referring to me] are the only one that talks a lot, but he seemed to be the winner. By the time we reached the train station I was given much information about his life and me of what he needs to know. We stop at a coffee shop to have something as time permits. While we sat talking, I had to focus on not allowing him to see my nervousness as the cup shook in my hand, occasionally holding it with both hands to distract his attention. Why in the world am I so nervous, *I thought*, it is not as if I am about to go into the sack with this man, and if I did, he would be sure to win, as it has been a long time since touched. I kept looking at him as he spoke as I tried to keep my thoughts in check and pay attention to what he was saying and the questions he asked.

Once out of the restaurant and back at the car, he retrieved the luggage, and we walked to the train station. The conversation was informative of our likes and dislikes as we waited in line for the returning train to Canada. The train arrived, the line began to move, and as we got closer, the ticket collector denied his intention to walk me down to board the train. He bends over, kisses me on the cheeks, and wishes me a safe journey back. I informed him that I would keep in touch, and stepped onto the escalator with thoughts of looking back once down on the platform, which I strongly rejected, as I did not want to and did not see him standing there.

Chapter 29

CROSSING THE LINE

FOR THE WAY MAN SEES is not the way God sees, for man looketh on the outward appearance, but the LORD looketh on the heart. First Samuel 16:7.

I loved to travel, see new places, and meet different people. The reason for my lack of material things is not that I could not have afforded to acquire them, but a past dream showed me where my wealth belongs, as explained earlier. I arrived at the train station, where Monica picked me up. On the way, she is informed about my visit, with a few questions asked about her visit during the time spent after the passing of Earl—Veronica's husband.

Was I given an answer regarding my dreams? I think so. When Veronica called to let us know Ace had died, my thoughts immediately returned to one of my dreams. Which brought me to the thought of Jehovah's patience and mercy—not taken for granted and missing its purpose—that only time reveals. Whether Ace's death took the place of another is God's knowledge. The time spent with her seen—is the reaction of an angry person due to the actions of others. A pretentious person who wants others to believe everything is okay. A hard-headed individual who will not change her attitude. An individual who is hard-working and genuinely loves God. However, she will not allow herself to be corrected with accurate knowledge. However, I am thankful that it was not her death, for she loves life and wants to live to see more of it.

During the days at Monica, I searched for work online but would later find it all in vain. The time spent together allowed us to catch up on each other's past life. I found out that Monica, too, had changed a bit, and this was due to her health issues. However, her activities in the Kingdom preaching work kept her physically active outdoors allowing her to keep fit and healthy.

Days before leaving to return home, I am caused to see the wicked one before my very eyes, an encounter that caused hurtful feelings but reveals my strength in paying attention to the word of God. Every morning, I would wait on Monica to have breakfast. Monica insists that since retirement, she will not get out of bed until after ten o'clock. "I have no one's job to do, so why should I be getting out of bed early?" she comments. Surely her comment made a lot of sense; the time was hers to do as she pleased.

One morning, we were at breakfast, and one conversation led to another until it returned to a past incident. My personal experiences do not escape the memory of my mind for any length of time if, for a moment, it will return within the day, a fight I always win. Rather reminds one of the sayings: the race is not for the swift but for he that endures to the end. As memory returns, pride does not take the place of admittance of an apology and correction if I was in the wrong. Something I find difficulty in understanding of those whose memory slips. For it is a fact that each one's memory will slip, but it returns—this is known as temporary amnesia—on the other hand, for those who suffer from memory loss—known as Alzheimer's disease, now that is another case. Earlier in this book, the different types of amnesia one can suffer from are mentioned.

§

Reference of this I reveal: Once again, I will say my anger towards my sister holding me back from the expression of words caused the figurine held in my hand to shatter to pieces, as I told her not to dare raise her hands at me. My sister, however, insisted on bringing forward two figurines from the cabinet; she claimed to be the ones on the shelf of the home she once occupied. "Monica," I now called, a bit angry with her. "Those are not the figurines." I said with an affirmative cuss word.

"You are a liar, a liar, those are the figurines," she shouts...

"Are you calling Jehovah a liar?" I shout back, taking my physical self from the situation.

"You are a liar. You should wash your mouth with soap. I could just imagine what goes on where you live. That is how you probably curse those people. How do you expect to go out in service?" With that said, she walks up the stairs to her room.

"I could have cursed you," I yelled after her. I could have, but seeing ahead of the situation, I allowed God to be found true while being tested.

In all truthfulness, it may have been, as there are many figurines in her home. But for sure, one was missing, the one that broke in my hand. Or she glued the pieces together, forgetting she did when brought forward as evidence. Or fearful to admit the truth of what did happen that surprised us both. I did not expect my anger so forceful to cause the damage. Nevertheless, the truth is the truth, and that cannot and will not change in the eyes of the one who sees, and judges each one, in all things.

I return to the couch with a book entitled, The Physiology of Consciousness by Robert Keith Wallace, Ph.D.—Introduction by John S. Hagelin, Ph.D. As I tried to read the book, my thoughts of why Monica's recollection of what occurred was not correct, and the look in her eyes was not like someone angry or hurt, but someone who had hate within their soul; did produce many disturbing conclusions. I chuckled over the mention of washing my mouth out with soap and did hold back from commenting, as this would have caused deeper friction. Further, when she came back down the stairs, she closed the blinds and then attempted to work on a piece of material with a knife, that did cause some fear to surface. My life's truth were with Jehovah, and I let go and let God at that moment. After about ten minutes, Monica returns up the stairs to her room, and moments pass before she returns.

"I have to get some groceries," she implies.

"I will come with you; just give me a moment." Yes, I had to leave the house, and wanting to further understand my sister's action, I needed to go. I got dressed, and we drove to the grocery store. The shopping experience was a pleasant one. I was reminded of how to make bread. I am told a bit about the neighborhood and the people, and the accident by someone running into the back of the car that saw the investment of the new one she now drives. The accident re-called a past one we did have on the way to the Kingdom Hall one evening. As I explained, she did recall exactly what had occurred. We arrived back at her home safely.

At times when looking back at life's situations and are given a clearer understanding of knowledge, we are left with laughter as we see the actions of people, to what they selectively remember; and given hurtful feelings from the lies told that almost or did destroy (our) a person's life or career. Looking back, the hate in my sister's eyes was the pain she was experiencing then. Chemo is not a pleasant situation to go through, coupled with other emotional issues. As a clock gives us the time each day it goes forward, so should we; however, Jehovah sees to it when time stops for each of us. As all things are revealed with time.

§

ON THE WAY HOME

After having a Mother's Day breakfast on Valentine's Day with her and my nieces, A call to Veronica is placed to wish her all the best on the day. As we drove mostly talking about my life's struggle tears started to flow, tears I had to control. Suddenly ahead, a blanket of fog appeared; we drove into and out in about three minutes to a clearer view. We were surprised at what covered only a section of the road. We arrived at the apartment complex; I embraced her with a kiss and thanked her for the ride. I wanted to invite her but knew she wanted to return home, so I declined. Once at my apartment door, keys inserted, I found the lower key-knob unlock. I entered the apartment and immediately called to leave a message on the superintendent's answering machine; as to my thoughts on seeing a note requesting entry into the apartment while I was away, date and time, along with the request to see her left. Monica was not told of the incident, as I did not want to add any stress to her circumstances, and did not want to hear any negatives.

After unpacking, I cleaned up the house and sat down to have a cup of tea while I opened my mails. One mail from the housing complex requested information. This request moved me to retrieve the information from my files. However, back, and forth through the files could not locate the information. At this point, I was upset and decided that perhaps my eyes were playing tricks, so I left the task of looking for another day. It is advised never to make decisions when upset; so, it is in putting things off for another day, is to be true.

The next day the superintendent calls to say she will be at the door shortly if this is okay. She is given a yes, and within minutes, a knock on the door brings me down the stairs. The door is open, and she is greeted and requested to enter the apartment; her action is observed. But I cared less if she had any device to record what was about to be stated as I stood true to myself. I related what I encountered on arriving home, but that was not all. I could not find information in my files that were missing. Whoever it was that entered the home had many opportunities, given the time I was away from the apartment, to search my home. Why trouble my personal belonging is questionable. The superintendent reminded me that when we are angry, we tend not to notice things and advised me to search again and call the police department to make a report. After the superintendent left, I returned to searching my files and placing a call to the police department. However, I had problems getting through to the department and could only do so after speaking to the Housing Complex security officer, who gave me a direct contact number. On receiving an answer, I am told someone will be at my apartment shortly; I hangs up. The officer finally arrives and is taken to my room, where my files are kept. I proceeded to open the luggage and to show him in order how my files were and what was missing. The officer took notes and informed me that fingerprints would be difficult to obtain from one of the bags due to the material, but he would let head office know about the incident, and someone else will be in contact. After he left, I continued my search only to find that the first page of a complaint letter was missing. Why take the first page? I formed the question *within thoughts*. These people are presumptuous. Are they trying to say it is I, and there is nothing you can do as there is no evidence? Oh, boy, they are so clever that they are no good. Perhaps they thought with the games they played that I would not remember the persons name on the first page, but I do. I quietly spoke to myself as I know they probably have had the opportunity to put all kinds of listening devices around my unit, as I had discovered, once by accident, hidden behind my entertainment unit. How long the device was hooked up to my radio and television, I do not know. Monica informed of the incident and advised me to throw it in the garbage. Actions are taken after taking a picture of the gadget.

Yes, the way of the wicked ones is clever. If you are unaware of the circumstances, they will have the world of fools thinking all sorts of negatives about you through their clandestine manipulation of your life. After given time had passed, and no one called or showed up to investigate further, I took it upon myself to visit the Police Department, where I laid a complaint and left, leaving the situation with its concluded results in the hands of the Lord.

The actual days past was approximately four. While going through my files, I discovered the missing tax information in exactly where it should be, in exactly the place showed the police officer as I went through the years consecutively filed. However, still missing is the first part of the complaint letter. The current year's tax information had already been completed and was missing when the years looked over only showed up to 2014. Wanting to call to let all parties know found the information claimed missing, I listened to the inner voice that told me not to take any action to do so. The past year's tax information was returned but was dispersed, knowing that personal information only required to be kept for five (to ten for business) years.

This incident reminds me of the fragility of the mind. The physical power to do, the sight to see, the ear to hear, and the ability to speak can easily be taken from us. Reason for thanks and appreciation be given to God each day of our waking to embrace a new day.

§

Memory loss has a general term known as **dementia**, called dementia of the Alzheimer's type. Dementia is not a normal part of aging. Still, as we age, the risk factor increases due to plaque buildup—protein deposits between the nerve cells, blocking communication among nerve cells needed to service other cells. Plaque builds are also caused by habitual smoking. Scientists are not sure when a problem begins, which prevents part of the cells from running well but contributes to Alzheimer, plaque buildup, neurofibrillary tangles, and other brain pathology, leading to death within four to twenty years after the onset of the disease.

The brain has one hundred billion nerve cells (neurons). Each nerve cell connects with others to form a communication network. Some nerve cells have certain jobs, such as thinking, learning, and remembering; others help to hear, see, and smell. Such as the Parasympathetic nervous system located towards the front of the brain responsible for the accelerating pulse rate. Dilating the pupil of the eye, the function of the sweat glands, secreting urine and retaining and inhibiting the muscles diverting blood from the skin and intestines. Activating the adrenal gland located just above each kidney to secrete adrenalin. While the Sympathetic nervous system, one of two major subdivisions of the auto-nervous system, supplies muscles and glands and is concerned with general activation and mobilizing the body's fight or flight reaction to stress or perceived danger.

The brain likens to electrical hardware when not used. Over time if equipment keeps failing, bolts and wires maybe rust or need tightening. If not fixed or oil can prevent proper function. The brain works similarly and needs assistance in its maintenance of cells. We do this by recording important information (as we do on computers, we back-up information). Although the information is stored in our subconscious and evolves to outer stimuli, assistance given to our brains by writing down important information needs, will play an important role in day-to-day survival done according to our activities. We need to assist those cells to function, also by foods consumed for the health function of our brain such as Nuts, Salmon, Blueberries to mention some.

§

We live in a world where computers are not the only thing that controls our daily-acquired means of living. But living among people who seek an opportunity to destroy our ability to function mentally by their actions which leads to stress, mental fatigue, to debilitating muscle function that causes diseases of all sorts. As hackers' interference into a computer destroys a person's file, so it is with one holding a vendetta that pushes one's brain capability and capacity that, over time, some cells weaken, causing (memory loss) dementia. Further pushed by an individual's destructive actions (an example of destructive action mentioned earlier about leaving my unit door locked, to coming back and finding the door unlocked, papers and items missing) is actions that could lead to dementia. Mistakes do happen, but when a person knows what is of importance, mistakes just do not keep happening. When the destructive actions continue, it becomes a constant hitting at the brain. The brain's cells weaken, bringing forth difficulty remembering newly learned information, confusion about events, time and places, unfounded suspicions about family, friends, co-workers, and professional caregivers, to a more serious effect such as speaking, walking, and swallowing.

Memory loss eventually develops into an irreversible state known as Alzheimer, and one becomes susceptible to transferred thoughts. Some in society who have this disease deny or find it hard to recognize Alzheimer's. This irreversible, progressive brain disorder slowly destroys behaviour and is the sixth leading cause of death.

Family members with a member who suffers from memory loss recognize the problem more as dementia. However, it is important not to diagnose a family member as having dementia, as the individual's brain maintenance is dependent on themselves and chooses not to recall information that is not relevant to them as it is to the one seeking confirmation. The best thing to do if a family member keeps forgetting pertinent information is to have them see a doctor.

Chapter 30

RECOGNIZED STEPS TO HEALING

"THIS I SAY THEN, Walk in the Spirit, and ye shall not fulfil the lust of the flesh." Galatians 5:16

This scripture calls for an in-depth understanding of the spirit's presence; only when understood will one be able to control the desires incidental to one's happiness and good health.

The works of the flesh are fornication, uncleanness, loose conduct, idolatry, the practice of separatism, enmities, strife, jealousy, fits of anger, contentions, divisions, sects, envies, drunken bouts, and revelries. All of which God shows patience towards us, as he knows our ignorance of being curious. Misery and death to our souls we incur due to a desire for a partner to fulfill our sexual needs, an impatient attitude toward others due to envying them for what we don't have or due to underline racist resentment of their nationality, and political disunity (practice of separatism) will have its reward in full. All these things without mature thinking, will lead to our death of our spirituality.

On the other hand, the spirit's fruitage is love, joy, peace, long-suffering, kindness, and self-control. With these foremost in our lives, tendency to overlook certain actions sometimes we are able to do.

People drive us to fits of anger—a work of the flesh—a state of emotion many today find hard to control. Exercising self-control—a fruitage of the spirit—is pushed aside when faced with some whose ignorance is ridiculously hard to tolerate and tempered when underlining racist attitudes exists. We are not perfect, and will make mistakes. Looking for perfection in words and deeds from others without judgement we should all practice.

Most of us like things explained to us. The more information gathered, the more we tend not only to be biased toward a person's artistry but also feel a sense of comfort. With the thought that the information will protect us. Equipped to help ourselves—to some degree, this is true. But with all things, what works for one may not work for another. However, the truth is all the information one gathers will assist **in understanding** a life's situation. Experience allows one to feel physical and express heartfelt emotions, and moves one to action to the healing of self.

When we read about allowing the spirit to guide us, do we understand the words' meaning and, with the knowledge attained, how to stand. We must stand firm against the opposite of what the *spirit of this world* may be moving us to do, that is, out of character (moral goodness) and that of Christian love. Actions that push us from negative situations of our lives towards their goals.

This brings me to share this advice as I did at the opening of the Second Part of Until My Dying Day, and once read; you hopefully will get my point: Before we do anything, **think**...or you will act in rage, where you should act calmly; or you will write of yourself where you should write of your characters.

A scripture in the Qur'an states, "On the earth are Signs for those of assured Faith. As also in yourself: Will you not then see?" –The Scatter Winds, Surah 51, 20-21.

Yes, today, more than in the past, Signs of mental confusion around the world amongst a vast majority not having information logically process is seen even from those as intelligent humans within society.

A situation that made a news headline has to do with a young businesswoman who stabbed another young woman in our financial district. Concluded statements of her action are that she is being controlled by something in her body. A person having much sense to know that she is being guided led to committing an act of cruelty towards another who has done her no wrong. Even dismissing her lawyer and having enough sense to accuse the quote-unquote (professional) psychiatrist of asking stupid questions. This is a person so intelligent her knowledge lacks understanding and self-control; thus, within her experience, she failed to apply logical application and the strength to alter the mental thoughts that were moving her to perform the act. Not fully knowing what Ms. Dibasari's experience/ or experiences are, another experience will clear up or shed some light on mental distress.

One sunny afternoon on the way to catch a bus from either direction to my destination, I stood at the stop that had a shelter. Standing looking both ways to see which bus would arrive first, from a distance, a woman approached. However, attention was not on her but focused ahead of her to see if a bus was approaching the street from the circular turn of the road which would move me to cross to the other side of the street. As the woman got to where I stood, she burst out loudly, "Why are you looking at me? You think I can't see you through those glasses" referring to the sunglasses.

"Look," I responded, "I am looking for the bus. Don't you be picking on me, for I mind my own business?"

I became annoyed with her boisterousness, maintaining a firm stand and awareness was important to avoid further escalation or perhaps a mental issue the woman may have experienced at that moment. Comments did not quiet the lady; she continued with her accusation. It was not until a neighbor who lives in the building, who is acquainted with me, came forward to ask, what was the matter, and then ask the woman why she was picking on me, to leave me alone, that she quieted down.

The question remains, did I have reasons to lash out at her? I have been living in the building with many mental and physical situations. If it was not security personnel knocking at my door with claims of disturbances from other tenants, it was coming home to the locks on my unit door open or lights left off. And lately, having to deal with tiny micro insects trying to get into my head due to new renovation of doors and windows that, if were overseen by management, future hassle now presented may have, been avoided. Patience with self and others is as important as eating to survive. Forced to stand on my own from lack of having others to relate my stressful situations to, who would understand and be of some assistance, to avoid a point of mentally breaking down, I had to learn **how to read**—read the actions of those around me, to understand how best to react. An often-noted fact, people aware of secrets, with good ideas and intentions, are the ones most often in society given difficulties. Which brings me to this point of explanation, it is good not to tell people every little details of your life, especially your dreams. For those without understanding who are resentful of you will use your circumstances against you.

This we need to remember, life is a series of lifting ourselves up, not dependent on others doing it for us. It is difficult to always be positive, but we must be if we need to lift and have others' assistance.

No one, I repeat no one, can live another's life; only play (or act) the person's life. All persons have an influence—to some degree, over others. How a person dress influences another, and in their occupation, they influence another. With that in mind, Jesus brought to our attention the differences between people and drew attention to a tree. He asks, do people gather grapes from thorns or figs from thistles? By their fruits, you will recognize them. So, the force that moves you, try to be strong enough to do that which is kind to self, as the good we do to self, in turn, is doing good to another.

You may ask, in what way? In the way that in time by God's grace, the wicked one will learn the reason for his existence through you. The victim's actions are to see intentions of the heart as God's to see to guide. Believe, if not note this, for what bad one does to another—in time, is done to self. It may not be of the same depth, but nevertheless, at a level one does not want to experience. Here is a statement many have heard before: "God told me to do it." Is the person wrong in saying such words? Those who know the truth will say—no, and they will be right, but in the person's sense of truth, he is not wrong, for the God and ruler of this system is Satan—Revelation 12:9-12. He is not only wicked; HE is psychotic and influences the actions of the unbelievers and innocent ones to doing as he desires.

However, this scripture states, "Let no man say when he is tempted, I am tempted of God: for God cannot be tempted with evil, neither tempteth he any man." – James 1:13.

Mental stress robs one of many good things in life if not strong to fight back. A foolish, thoughtless action of others puts in the way walls difficult to overcome. To the point of living in poverty. Although poverty has an upside, it pushes us to be creative about our situation and calls for mental balance. The difficulty comes when those allowing the victim lack understanding of their situation and fails their every attempt to achieve—this may be promotions to a higher position within a company. And at this point of writing, it is with pleasure that some business owners have seen that those with autism have much to offer once trained properly. More companies now, with such ones employed. However, the foolish ones cannot see, wrapped up in their own survival, fairness is not a strong suit of theirs; they kill the survivor's intentions; remains the victim.

The weapon of hypocrites is the tongue, the deadliest of truths. Their voice can be that of an angel while sapping the lifeblood out of a victim. Are you an actor? Embrace the job of an actor. Are you a civil servant? Embrace the job of a civil servant. Are you a community volunteer? Embrace the job of a community volunteer. Are you a medical professional? Embrace the job of a medical professional. Pretending to be other than you are in your practice can damage your association with others. I am often told to worry about myself; this is something not done. One may conclude that love moves me to be concerned about the welfare of others.

Months later, another trip is made due to a death in the family; another reason, another chance to get to know him and my family.

Chapter 31

DEATH, FINALIZES OUR CROSSOVER

THE YEAR WAS 2016. I arrived home from the Kingdom Hall, changed into my house clothing, and began to clean the unit. Suddenly, I fluffed as though the corpse plant had bloomed. On Monday morning, the phone begins to ring. Recently, a sense of fear comes over me when it does. Not only is it that most of my immediate family members are aged, but life in this chaotic world is short-lived for many.

"Hi Paula," Veronica's voice was heard at the other end. "Petal passed away this morning."

"No, she passed yesterday. As I was cleaning...." I explained, and whether Veronica believed or not, my experience warned me of something about to occur.

This the month of June, the morning started a bit on the cool side when I got into the taxi heading to Union station. After about half an hour of waiting for the train it arrives, I boarded and got a comfortable seat by the window; ten minutes later, it was on its way to New York. An hour into the journey, Veronica is called to inform her that I am on my way and the time the train is scheduled to arrive. With much time on hand to think of what and how to present God's word of the resurrection hope, the book of Numbers and Deuteronomy came back forcefully to review. Deuteronomy 28 stood out consciously concerning the questions directed to my Heavenly Father. The Bible was open, and scriptures sighted; once done, this gave me the words I would say, and so a notepad taken out of my bag, I began to write my thoughts with acknowledgement of all in attendance.

Once again, traffic moved back and forth at the station, people coming and going as others like myself stood awaiting our pick-up companion. I waited for quite some time before the man of interest would arrive and could not help to think whether the woman who also stood across from me waited for the same individual I was. A few phone calls were made back and forth to each other as to why the delay; I was informed that traffic outside was chaotic. I found this the case when I got outside the station. He waited for parking. Another call was made to my sister, letting her know of the situation. Finally, parked adjacent to the station, he ran over and embraced me with a kiss on the cheeks. Attention is noted how tall he is. Somehow, he seems to have grown a few inches, although it is said that growth in height stops after one past thirty years. Even with the heels worn, I felt uncomfortable. It was not a love connection, as faults are overlooked. He picked up my bags and led the way to the car.

New York, New York, is truly a city that never sleeps. Getting on the right road back to my destination was difficult as cars and people made it difficult. It was early in the morning, a few hours away from the break of dawn and the city looked as if people were on their way to a nine-to-five job. Now on the right track toward our destination, the conversation picked up where it left off before I travelled back to Canada. He was a bit hungry, and I wanted to have a Long Island Iced Tea, so we stopped at one of his favorite restaurants, and I was quite pleased with the drink served, so pleased I ordered another Long Island Iced Tea, which got me into a mental state I wanted to be—relaxed. We talked for a while, and then the decision to leave was agreed on. On the way home, the conversation geared off track of mentally stimulated interest. Under the circumstances, he tried to make the meeting a pleasant one, to that it was.

During their occasional meeting when he came to the home, I could not quite understand the relationship between Veronica and him. From what was observed, it seems his indebtedness would cost him should he make the mistake of disrespecting their program—whatever that is, and I did not want to be caught in the middle.

Jobs are hard to get, this I know from my own circumstances, but there is so much a person can do when they have other resources than the average person. So, when some are constantly with an excuse, such as in his case, "If I don't sell, I don't get paid." I wonder why not seek another that would pay when you work. Not doing so is just another excuse to sit around for a handout. In addition, anyone who cannot control and maintain their responsibility is assured would be leaning more on his or her partner to carry a load. I have been carrying my load for as long as I have been on my own and has helped a few along the way in my life. Not even taking advantage of the year-end Income Tax—dependences potion to recoup some funds. And has not even received an award for the care given to some. During one of our conversations, he is informed of the knowledge I had of my sister's situation with him and do not want to be caught in the middle.

After pondering upon the information given, Veronica's explanation made no sense. The funds received—enough to take him to court—whether she recoup past payments or not, at least, she will be given a time when he must leave the premises, occupied by another that would help her to reach her financial debt comes the end of each month. Some do believe in calmer—what goes around comes around. This said, in time, it does. My last conversation months after returning to Canada ended with me hanging up after his comment, meant for my ears or directed to someone in the office. However, the call not returned spoke volumes; I never did call again, and neither did he.

§

Finally, the day of the funeral embraced us, sunny and hot. With directions from Alice, we all got into the car to make it to the church on time. However, delayed a bit due to Veronica's nervousness, we were finally on our way. Once within the neighborhood and with much driving done, "Are you sure you got the address, correct?" asks Veronica.

"Yes, exactly as she said," I respond, looking out the car window.

"We are here, but that is not the church's name. I know the church; I have been here before."

"Then, if you did, how come you can't find it?" I ask.

"I don't know. Leave it up to that Alice to give man the wrong direction," she responds.

The decision was now made to drive further down the street, located the church and a parking spot.

A moment of surprise and excitement stirred the room as family members noticed each other. We embraced and kissed. It was not difficult to notice most eyes were focused on the far corner where the noise came from as we joined the line heading towards the coffin. The service was over when we arrived, so I was left holding the paper of the thoughts I wanted to give, all because of the delay in finding the church's location.

Everything says happen for a reason; sometimes, words are best left unsaid. After reading it, according to Monica and Veronica's opinion, "It is her day, and what you have written seems to be focusing on you." This was not my intention; I figure they missed the point. However, I was happy that at least I got a chance to see her once more before they laid her to rest. Veronica declined to go to the burial site as the distance was quite far, so instead, we drove home after picking up some West Indian food from her favorite restaurant.

DEATH...

Afraid? Of whom am I afraid? Not Death, for who is he? The porter of my father's lodge. For I will one day say, Death, where is your sting? No more will I hear their cry. As much abashed me. –Time and Eternity. –B. M. Lustol

The New Jerusalem is spoken of in Revelations 21:5, where HE says: Look, I am making all things new, and in verse seven, he says: **Anyone** conquering will inherit these things.

I know there's a belief that the dead continues to live. This is not so. Whether you live in both worlds, that of the physical and spiritual, at death, our lives end as we know it. As we are laid to rest until HE resurrects us from the dead, as stated in Revelations 20:5,6. When we die, our breath goes out and all thoughts perish (Psalms 145:4). Therefore, with all our energy, we must pursue our dreams (Ecclesiastes 9). As each one live doing unto others as they would like done to them. And for the believers, live the ten commandments as you express yourself in the areas calling to exercise justice.

As stated in Chapter six, the end of this world has another eight hundred and ninety-three years left as of 2021. Time to live, learn and leave behind. However, God can end it as he wishes, as he did in the past [the account of our history in Genesis 7:11-24]. A God known to be a spirit of His word [performance at Genesis 9:11-17] logic leads us to conclude that we can fix the mess we have created on this planet or allow the planet to destroy us from its toxicity and gases.

Without you and me, we doing the right things toward each other, and with our environment, it can be assured that we are working toward the death of our lives.

So, I say this my dear friends....
When I am dead, my dearest, Sing no sad songs for me;
Plant thou no roses at my head or shady cypress tree:
Be the green grass above me with showers and dewdrops wet;
And if thou wilt, remember, and if thou wilt, forget.
—Christina Rossetti, Song.

The weeks were going fast, and the time was soon approaching for me to head back home to Canada; Monica had to leave the week before. Soon I will have to say so long until we meet again to my family; I have come to have a bit more understanding than my last visit.

Monica's presence did not make much difference in Veronica's defensive attitude. She always finds an argument of something within one's words express. This is what I mean…some of us have what they call a fetish—any inanimate object having no intrinsic significance of sex but arousing erotic feelings. One day on our way out of the home, a conversation erupted with aroused feelings. The conversation center on a television show where the brother's feeling for his sister overtook him into committing a sexual act. Moved me to comment on feelings I had experienced, as I concluded that nothing is wrong with someone having such feelings once they do not act upon them.

For further understanding, this was a day of shopping, and the decision was made with Monica to send some food items and clothing home to my brother. This was my first-time shopping for a man. I enjoyed my shopping experience at Winners and Marks & Spencer clothing stores. As I examined and picked out some clothing, I felt sexually aroused. This was my first experience, and I did not know what to make of it. I deeply love my brother like I have for a cousin—Courtney, who passed away during a basketball game. And is familiar with the feelings of jealousy, but sexually aroused—this is the first, and only found out that the feelings felt is known as a fetish, any inanimate object arousing erotic feelings.

"You are crazy," she responded.

"You lack knowledge and should shut your mouth," I respond

"How could you have sexual feelings for your brother? Don't you see that you are crazy?" she continues.

Shutting out all other words Veronica would say, I stopped the argument after my last comment, "I will never find someone; not with the way you carry on."

It is difficult to explain certain things to give some a clear understanding when their minds are closed. An open mind gathers much useful information, but with a closed mind, one will cut themself off from acquirement. Some people will continue to be, without making changes that enrich their life, and will try to stop those who try to. The goal is to remember that learning requires an open mind to take in information, validate and adapt; with such an attitude, it is difficult for others to put a blinder over one's eyes.

That incident has caused me to know what brotherly love is; it is the type of love Jesus has for his followers known as Agapic love. A secondary type of brotherly love that is altruistic and selfless, and is a combination of erotic love; a primary type of love that is passionate and erotic and rooted in sexual attraction. A love that will destroy a presumptuous wicked one or give one's life on behalf of the other. And this is the type of love I feel for some who are related to me in the Lord.

§

Finally, the week I must leave, an opportunity is presented for my niece and great-niece to get together. It was a beautiful sunny day. We decided to go to the movie, and since we had time before the start of it, the decision was to go for a drink, and we could catch up on what had been occurring in our lives. After the movies, I was dropped off, and Debra Ann and my great-niece were wished a safe and fulfilling life.

It was surprising to hear what had been occurring in my niece's life, and I was annoyed that the situation between her and my sister had deteriorated to the point it had, but I understood her anger. On the other hand, I wished that instead of turning to strangers for help, she had turned to me or God's word. But due to the type of work she did, to release the mental stress and guilt over her actions towards Veronica; a psychologist was needed. That would be our last meeting; she died on June 12, 2019. I wished time would have allowed us more to be said and done.

The next week, I had to leave, so I started to pack and tried to arrange for a taxi, as I did not want her to call Jack to do so. However, when I went up the stairs to speak with Sonia, who stood with Veronica, immediately after hearing my voice, she started an argument. An argument, perhaps due to her forgetfulness that she was informed of my departure date or did so to get off her chest a few things confusing her mind; whatever it was. I prolonged the argument by responding instead of reinforcing the point that she was told and had asked me to postpone the date; I could not. Unable to sleep, partly due to the argument, I tossed and turned right into the early morning when it was time for me to get ready to leave.

A taxi called is seen leaving as I got to the door and had to make a second call. The driver refused to go to the required destination as the dispatcher needed to be first informed; what to do? I turn to the voice of Veronica, who happens to be outside close enough to hear the conversation, speaking out that she would take me to the train station.

The drive on the way was very silent; comments hoping to get a response from someone, did not. I am one not to hold a grudge after responding to a situation despite the results. Truth is, not something many people can do, and others are shown how well I am adaptable. Once we got to the train station, Veronica explained what I needed to do. I lifted my luggage out of the car and thanked Patsy—the caregiver, for all the delicious meals she had prepared and my sister for her hospitality.

Now the car door closed, I walked off into the train station to purchase a ticket and board the train back to Canada.

Chapter 32

HAVING NOTHING YET POSSESSING ALL THINGS

HAPPINESS IS A JOURNEY with winding roads that leads you to it. At times, you question why a different path was chosen when looking back to see a path that could have caused less misery; wisdom steps in to show the reason—for growth, it was needed.

What I mean by holding nothing yet possessing all things is this: When you, as I am living spiritually, can detect the demonic forces in your life, you will not succumb to the intended actions that push you into confrontation with (family members or close friends) them or others (strangers). Instead, you will act in the manner of one wise: A person who is aware of the intended action of the wicked and flee or indulge them in finding out the truths you seek. In doing so, you live to fight another day with your truths as it corrects intended wicked thoughts or deeds.

As a people who look for proof giving examples that may fall at the waste side as has God's counsel and the prophets' experiences. I will say that you need to have Faith in your own circumstances that what wicked deeds are being done will soon be over. Recall your childhood, or as a parent, your own child, who enters this world with the same expectation as you did—to be protected and loved. Although your life may have been rough, you are not alone. Each family member has different strengths, try to lean on those that uplifts yours. And so, it is with those who have been through life having to handle difficult circumstances. Our shared difficulties overcome teach others how to live.

Whether someone is open to learning is not your business. For every wicked action/ or reaction, there is a paid consequence. They, you, and I, as we, are in this world to learn from the successes and failures of others. Therefore, put your trust in Him, who has your best interest at heart and a place prepared for you out of Satan's system.

§

It was November 2019 during my elder sister's Kathy's visit—three months before the news hit that a virus known as COVID-19, which originated from Wuhan, China, was spreading worldwide. What started like the flu, usually during the winter, felt different, with a persistent cough that brought up thick mucus.

"Paula, you know you always get the flu during the winter months," my sister said when I called with my concern.

"Monica, this is different. When I cough, I bring up very thick mucus and, with it, headaches. I don't know if it's something I caught from the restaurant."

On the other hand, Veronica told me to visit the doctor to see if I have walking pneumonia. Overly concerned, I visited my doctor, who sent me for a chest- x-ray. A few weeks forced me to see the doctor again in December, who had recommended taking the flu shot; eventually, I took it with a prescription for puffers and tablets. However, in January, the symptoms worsened, with persistent coughing and headaches forcing me to the emergency.

After the seen exam of my chest x-ray, the doctor came into the room with a nurse, asked a few questions, and stated: "We are unable to help you, but we will give you something that will assist you." He prescribed an inhaler that brought down and out the mucus, giving me some ease to breathe, and the headaches were not so bad. Seen was my family doctor, another recommended by my dentist at the time, and another at St Michael's Hospital—with three different types of puffers, an inhaler, and some pills, I conquer.

To look back is to appreciate with tears of joy my brother's help—guided by Jehovah on knowing how to do what he did— resulted in my life. To experience what it must have been like fighting to survive during my childhood—too young to comprehend the effect of an epidemic H2 N2 flu virus that almost killed me.

The world has seen and counted thus far four million deaths due to the COVID-19 virus. A New Year that has not only seen the catastrophe of a virus, but with-it financial hardship, isolation, and greater mental problems. That the sense of touch so important allowing us to feel, knowing we are alive—from the standpoint of the giver of life and loved from the standpoint of human appreciation. We have seen since the past few years become a thing of the past.

Isolation is terrible. It can lead to psychological problems, like hallucination, self-mutilation, and craziness—craziness, contributed by those living around us, to mental illness, due to their clandestine actions; failing to see the damage afflicted, and so the victim's outburst is perceived as an illness—but is it? I have often spoken out loud about the mentally manipulated thoughts and actions of those around me. The reason for speaking out is to bring them and others around me to the consciousness of actions that could cause mental damage to the inexperienced ones, but they can care less.

Some lived to laugh at others—those who fall victim to their mental games. Had I not been strong—thanks to my heavenly father's gift of his word, that gives me the ability to see as I understand the one knowledgeable and the one wise in their wicked deeds, I would have fallen victim years ago, like the Shoppers Drug Mart incident of 2015.

We need to listen and pay attention to those we hold dear and become aware of those around our environment. Not because something seems unbelievable does not mean it is not real or true.

The year 2020 began the year of creativity in advance technology. Technology, which aided some from their isolation, has done more damage than good by those who saw man's advancement as a tool to further their goals, whether the spread of hatred or mind manipulation of developed circumstances in one's life. Therefore, becoming awake and aware is crucial to our survival at this time of our lives. For to the wicked ones' end, unawareness gives achievement for their intended goals. Careful observance of what the media shows and informs us of, awareness will protect us from falling victim to their clever designs. Not everything seen or heard should be taken as facts. The world today is filled with actors/actresses and manipulators of technology. Verbal communication as does human contact must be done. The upside to our current isolation situation is to appreciate what we do not have—contentions.

Isolated but not confined, using time wisely becomes important to our mental health. Isolation will further contribute to mental problems if we, who are awake consciously, do not reach out to family members, friends, and acquaintances. In doing so, we inadvertently maintain our own health. We, as a people, cannot prevent mental illness; however, we who are mentally balanced can collectively assist in the care of those mentally ill by how we interact and treat them. Communication is a key factor. We need to listen, and we need to express our concern about their perception of matters mildly. When words fail or we lack understanding; first, we must acknowledge the personal thoughts and feelings being expressed without condemning them. As each takes care of themselves, become informed of mental illnesses to recognize symptoms; encourage the sufferer to seek help, consider their needs and mental illness; be kind, gentle, patient, loving, and forgiving. I know this may be hard, for I am living among a tormentor.

Do not condone some whose actions continue to evade justice, like Satan; they are clever manipulators of lies that blind the truth from the hearts and minds of innocent ones—they have no clue. Therefore, how we use our time in isolation has a lot to do with our mental health as it will for our financial well-being.

The years since COVID-19 have been difficult, but none compared to 2022, in seeing my dear sister Veronica's passing on April 1. Many questions still remain from dreams I have had and regards her attitude; words spoken that were confusing to some towards the final days of her passing with those who were present in her life. The "one" trying to get rid of the root my fight remains. However, my confidence remains in our Lord Jesus, that if I continue to do my part, the Lord will do his. My experience gives words to this written song yet to be published, the lyrics: 'To give thanks and praise with these lips of mine my Lord.'

Shalom...Peace!

THE END

Afterword

UNTIL MY DYING DAY was created from many encounters, especially one that started off, I thought, on the right path. We met accidentally over the phone—he had dialed the wrong number. We planned to meet, and from there, our relationship developed to the point of me moving in with him. Life was good for a few years until one night at a club called These Eyes, owned by his friend, I worked part-time after my other job. A conversation developed with another friend of his, visiting the club that night; he was informed of the next day. The discussion involved getting his photography hobby rolling into a paying profession. Little did I know it would strike a nerve days later. I got a beating so bad; it was something never to do again—try to help in his career. That day led to another and another; I eventually left his home with the vow not Until My Dying Day would I allow myself to be in an abusive relationship.

Years passed, and reflecting on our relationship, I saw a man who was jealous and had no self-control when it came to his anger. Only he knows his reasons, as I never ask about his past relationships. He could have never asked for a better person than me, for in me, he had an, independent person, a worker of nothing to be ashamed of, a good cook, keeps a clean home and some excellent times. Life is what it is—experiences; we learn, accept, forgive, and move on.

Many are the plans of man, but God is the one who directs our steps. And I am happy to say thanks to His word, it is truly a light to my path and protection to my soul; I lived to tell my truths.

Bibliography

Works consulted for the body of this book are from:
10,000 Dreams Explained by Pamela J. Ball
The King James Bible
The Qur'an

A Look Into Ms. Lustol's Up Coming Novel,

Never Be 4 On New Years Day.

THEME

IT HAD NEVER SNOWED in this world since all knew themselves from Adam. However, this New Year, the Gods had something planned for everyone.

Despite the hardships most were experiencing, Bernadette's only concern was finding a way to keep the town's Mall—Paradise Quest, open for as long as possible. This was the town's main shopping center, where most worked and shopped. All knew that the recession was imminent, but some could care less, so when the economic conditions and nature's wrath cared not whether you were rich or poor got worse, all hell broke loose—it was swim or sink, or in this case, the fittest of the fittest were the ones that would survive. Thieves were breaking in, one house after another, and showed no mercy for life, as homeowners were killed if they got in their way. Businesses were being hacked, and sensitive information was taken at demand ransom for data retrieval. Businesses were closing as the recession worsened, and the homeless were showing their lives matter.

Security at the Mall was tight, and guards were most vigilant as the last thing Bernadette wanted was the owners to be in debt without funds to recoup losses, as this would cause them to close shop and leave.

It was strange that the day started on the chilly side, and this was the topic of the town's people. Some were inattentive to what was happening, while others prepared themselves and went about their busy day left at the end of a new year in ah as they witnessed the gods' power.

Chapter 47

WAY ACROSS TOWN

CONSUMED WITH HIS PLANS for the evening, he did not know what was about to occur around him. The snowstorm had started on his way back to the city, and the temperature was biting cold. For some with underlining physical problems, the temperature causes debilitating joint pain; it affects a productive day with the children who saw the sight and embrace the chill as gifts from Santa Claus—others, from God. For all, this was not a welcoming New Year expected.

He wished he had an extra layer on his head as he approached the Clinic. With a scarf tightly wrapped around his neck and the hat shallow onto his face, he notices the street calm of traffic and pedestrians and wishes he had also worn a boot.

He reaches the door as if someone belonged; he fishes out the keys from his pant pocket with a paper that had the combination. He opens the door and steps in, noticing a dimmed light in the hallway. He closed the door and switched on the pen torch.

It gave enough light that he could see what he wanted to see. He walks to the back of a cabinet where he used to keep essential documents and uses the combination he had, but unfortunately, it does not work. He breathes in and exhales, not surprised to encounter a block to his plan. In the position of Philomena, he walks out of the room and to her desk. "She has to have the information I need somewhere here, but where?" He pulls on the desk drawer; it is closed. His eyes moved to the top of the desk in search of a paperclip and noticed her Rolodex—something of interest he needed, but not now. He grabs the paperclip and undoes its design; once straight, he bends it, so it gives two points, pushes it into the keyhole, and twists it a few times while pulling on the draw handle. Finally. It opens, and he looks for the folder that reads—receptionist. The folder is open, and he searches for the information he needs.

Philomena always kept backups on paper.

"Boss," she would say. "You never know when the system will go down or stop working altogether. So, I prefer to keep a paper trail. And I know we could lose it, but think of my action as covering all ends." She was right. Unforeseen circumstances require preparation. So that when they occur, situations can be managed with some success.

The combinations he found but did not say what belonged to what, this, he was sure she kept in memory, presenting a puzzle he had to solve. He wrote the numbers on a sticky pad, put the folder back, pushed the draw closed, and walked back to the room as he tried the combinations.

* * *

MEANWHILE

In Papadopoulos's private office, Peppa gave her boss his holiday gift.

She was one he trusted and often treated as his wife, and he received her womanly dues granted. In the heat of passion, an alert is sounding.

"Doll," he said, releasing himself and telling her to get to the showers. She left the room, and he looked at the alert that indicated it was the Clinic. He is aware of break-ins, so he calls one of his boys.

"Clive here."

"Clive, I need you to go to the Clinic; we have a situation."

"On it, Boss. I will call later."

He hangs up, and without a care in the world, he heads to the shower to join Peppa.

* * *

BACK AT THE CLINIC

One of the combinations worked; he puts a mark beside it and wonders what the other belonged. With the torch pen in his mouth, he flips paper after paper, taking snapshots of the ones he looked for; a set of keys and cash were in the vault. What he had gone through to this point tempted him to take the seen cash—deserving, he ponders looking at it. He closes the door, walks back to the reception desk, and begins looking through the Rolodex. He found Peppa's name with all the information he needed and a few other acquaintances, and just about to grab Shyann's data, he heard someone at the door. He made a run for it, removing and fixing the scarf around him so that it covered his facial features.

The door opens, and Clive enters.

He looks at the alarm, pushes a number, waits a few minutes, and pushes a few more. He looks at the desk and notices the order in which it was, was not by Philomena. With her, everything had its place at the end of the day. He closes the door and begins to inspect the property—he inside, the other outside. A whiff of cologne moved him to do a thorough search. "Where that smell is coming from," he whispers to himself. Moving briskly from room to room as lights are switched on, he bumps into the culprit and swings a right hook that catches Patrick in the jaw; he moans. Suddenly, the lights went out— what timing, what luck. Eyes used to the dark, Patrick saw the figure and threw a punch; a fight started. Clive threw two punches to his ribs, and he bent down in pain; he took advantage and threw a few upper punches to his head and more at the site as he went down.

Patrick saw another coming holding the foot and threw him off balance, causing him to fall to the ground. He gets up with excruciating pain and runs for the door, but Clive is quick on his feet; he runs after him, grabbing him by the coat and throwing another punch to his side. "Ow," he shouts, the pain almost paralyzing him, sending madness to his brain, he sees the only weapon before him in its holding bin, pulls it out, and as Clive calls a name, he went down unconscious from a hit to his head with the umbrella. Patrick limps to the door, and as he is about to grip its handle, the door comes flying into his face sending him back into the wall. Jack goes to throw a punch as he surfaced with the umbrella missed and got whacked on the head. With both out of service, he walks out in pain, closes the door behind him, and briskly walks back to his car. He opens the door, gets in, reclines the seat, and lays back as he soothes his pain. Pressing his fingers to his nose, the pain sends a message that it is broken; he feels a warm liquid and notices its blood. He reaches for the glove compartment and realizes it's not his car, so he wipes his nose in the scarf. The situation put a hurdle in his plans for the evening. And as he lays there thinking that his visit to Mr. Papadopoulos would have to be another day, a bright light engulfed the neighborhood, and his car shook.

* * *

MERCY MEED HOSPITAL

Patrick walked into the hospital, and the sight increased his physical state feeling more of his pain. He hurried over to the receptionist's desk and explained his situation to the woman, who informed him that the wait would be a maximum of three hours. "Would you like me to continue," she asks, looking at him. He thought for a moment as he glanced at his watch, then toward her with the okay to continue. Minutes later, he found the waiting room crowded with patients. He located a seat and called Philomena, who picked up after four rings.

From his distance, Edna is seen being wheeled into the room by two paralegals.

"Are you okay?" She immediately asks worriedly.

"The truth...I am in pain."

"Were you in a fight?"

"Yes. Just a broken..." he is interrupted for a moment. "Just a broken bone to fix," he laughs.

"Oh Patrick, what mischief have you gotten yourself into.?"

The question went unanswered as one woman shouted, "That was the reason for the earthquake." All eyes turned towards the television screen as the announcement of a meteorite the size of three delivery trucks touched down, destroying a town and most of its people, as camera shots of the chaos in the village are shown. "No one expected this catastrophe," says the announcer. Stay tuned while we get more information from NASA, as we get..." a picture flashed on the screen. "To our local news, if anyone saw these four individuals, you are asked to report to your local police station; they are suspects in a robbery at Max All You Need Convenient Store."

Patrick squinted to see who they were, but facial recognition was impossible with their disguises.

"What's going on, Patrick?" she asks.

"Turn on the TV on the news channel."

She gets up from the bed and walks over to the entertainment room, and as she is about to turn on the TV, he asks, "Did you feel the building shook earlier?"

"A little trimmer—yes, but I experience this a lot in this building."

"I had no idea but knew something odd was about to occur when a flash of light engulfed the area I was at, and my car shook to the point that it was almost on its side. Well, I am getting the answer."

With disbelief, while the phone kept silent to her ear, he called "Philomena."

"Yes, I am here looking at the news. Oh...so sad, life is so unpredictable these days. One minute you are here, and the next, you are gone."

"I know. Okay then, I have to go; I just noticed a patient of mine. It would be another three hours before I get home. I will call you before getting there."

"Okay, see you in three hours, just you be safe getting here, bye," she says with a smile as they both hang up.